Dr. B.R. Ambedkar and Social Justice

Dr. B.R. Ambedkar and Social Justice
Towards a Egalitarian Social Order

Meena Book Publications
New Delhi

Dr. B.R. Ambedkar and Social Justice: Towards a Egalitarian Social Order

2016

ISBN : 978-81-9303-551-1

Rs.495/-

Published by : **Meena Book Publications**
140, Street No. 9 C, Prem Nagar,
Karawal Nagar, Delhi - 110094
Tel : 9868280998
Email : meenabookpublications@gmail.com

Sales Office : 21/4648, Ansari Road,
Daryaganj, New Delhi
Ph: 011-23277141

Printed at : Milan Enterprises, New Delhi

This book is dedicated to the people who have sacrificed their lives to spread Dr. B.R. Ambedkar's Ideology

Contents

III. Constitution, Social Justice and Equality

Acknowledgements

I am thankful to Ex. Supreme Court Judge, Hon'ble Justice K. Ramaswamy for delivering the inaugural address at Dr.Ambedkar Social Justice Conference, 2014 and this book would not have been possible without the encouragement and support ofProf.MohanGopal,I shall ever be grateful to him and also many thanks to Hon'ble Justice Suresh Kait for attending the conference and sharing his vast knowledge on the issues of Social Empowerment. I would like to extend my sincere thanks to Dr.Meena Dhanda and Dr.Annapurana Waughray who have travelled all the way from United Kingdom to share their expert knowledge on the issues of caste system in the international sphere, I also extend my sincere thanks to Prof.SukhadeoThorat for his support and guidance, I also thank Prof. Chalam for his speech on the topic of Higher Education and Dalits, Senior Journalist MallepaliLaxmaiah, Prof. Krishna Reddy,Prof.Mallesh for their support and encouragement ,special thanks to Md.Ismail Khan for his support and sincere thanks to the teaching and non teaching staff at NALSAR for extending cooperation and finally to the members of Ambedkar Forum who are optimistic to bring a change in the society by professing Dr.Ambedkar's Philosophy.

Introduction

Scholars have defined social justice as one division of the concept of justice while others were of an opinion that it is concerned with distribution of benefits as rights and deserts.Social justice could also be understood as equal share in political power by all the groups in the society.Roscoe Pound equates social justice with social engineering to explain the satisfaction of the human wants, and he believes that Law plays an important role in transforming the society by meeting the overall interests of the society. John Rawls argues *"that social justice is concerned with rules and practises (social system) that structure a social system and govern the relations among the human agents within it.Johnrawls focused on this topic when he found that the distribution of human life prospects is strongly affected by a social basic rules and practises by its social institutions or basic structre. Which would therefore become an object of moral attention and possibly reform".*[1]

By analysing the provisions of the constitution of India we could come to a conclusion that the primary agenda for it is to secure social justice to its citizens. It contains many provisions to uplift the powerless and the weak. Glanville Austin commenting on the Indian constitution in his book *"Working of Democratic Constitution* "says" no other constitution in the world offers so many rights for social upliftment as the Indian constitution does". It was also held by the Supreme Court in *S.P. Gupta case* that constitution is a document for social reform, therefore there is an obligation on the legislature, judiciary and the executive to ensure the provisions of the constitution are duly followed and implemented to ensure justice and also to remove suffering of the millions of the people in the country.

The principle of Equality of opportunity which is embedded in the concept of social justice would pave the way for accessing the opportunities by the groups which were historically denied the basic social rights such as employment, education, dignity

1.Thomas pogge on Rawls concept of justice.

and positions of power in the society. Dr.Ambedkar, father of the Indian Constitution worked tirelessly for securing justice to the historically disempowered sections and he ensured their rights through the fundamental rights and directive principles of state policy. The constitution of India is one such document which is armed to put an end to social injustice and can pave the way for society to be established on the lines of liberty,equality and fraternity

Exploitation and The Means to End

The Indian society is fragmented and stratified into various social groups .The marginalised sections of the society such asScheduled Castes, Scheduled Tribes, other Backward Classes, Minorities continued to be exploited today in various forms. According to the report of Ravi. S. Srivatsava to NHRC, the Scheduled Castes and Scheduled Tribes and Most Backward Castes[2] are the main workers in bondage and forced labour in India. As per the NCRL report of 1991,Eighty nine percent of the employers of bonded labourers were agriculturists.[3] The wages paid to the bonded labourer is very less and it is not sufficient to sustain in the present times .It can be easily inferred that places where incidence of inequality is high, there is acute poverty, which forces people into bonded labour.

Dr. Ambedkar in Constituent Assembly stated

"On the 26th January, 1950, we are going to enter upon into a life of contradictions. In politics we will have equality and in social and economic life we will have inequality. In politics we will be recognizing the principle of one man one vote and one vote one value. In our social and economic life, we shall by reason of our social and economic structure, continue to deny the principle of one man one value. How long shall we continue to deny equality in our social and economic life? If we continue to deny it for long,we will do so only by putting our political democracy in peril. We must remove this contradiction at the earliest possible moment else those who suffer

---

2. Ravis.srivastava, January 06 ,2005 ,Bonded Labour in India: Its incidence And Pattern Accessed November 1st 4,Http://Www.Ilo.Org/Sapfl/mationresources/Ilopublications/Wcms_081967/Lang--En/Index.Htm
3. ArjunSen Gupta, Report on Conditions of Work and Promotion of Livelihoods in the Unorganised Sector, August 2007, Pg129http://nceuis.nic.in/condition_of_workers_sep_2007.pdf

from inequality will blow up the structure of democracy which this Constituent Assembly has so laboriously built up."[4]

The Right against Exploitation, contained in Articles 23-24,[5] lays down certain provisions to prevent exploitation of the weaker sections of the society by individuals or the State. Article 23 provides prohibits human trafficking, making it an offence punishable by law and also prohibits forced labour or any act of compelling a person to work without wages where he was legally entitled not to work or to receive remuneration for it.[6] However, it permits the State to impose compulsory service for public purposes, including conscription and community service. The Bonded Labour system (Abolition) Act, 1976, has been enacted by Parliament to give effect to this Article.

Agriculture employs close to seventy five percent of the population. The scheduled castes, other backwards castes and scheduled tribes are widely represented as landless labourers and share croppers, but with failing agriculture there is an exodus of these communities from villages to the urban areas where they are mainly employed in construction as laborers and other menial jobs without any social security measures. National Crime Records Bureau statistics say close to 200,000 farmers have committed suicide in India since 1997.[7] The non-availability of credit, higher cost of production and fall in prices are few of the factors that are pushing farmers to indebtedness. The incidence of farmers' suicide is considerably more among the Other Backward Castes (OBCs)[8] and indebtedness and its attendant economic distress is the main reason behind suicide by farmers.[9] The fundamental malady behind the farmers' indebtedness and distress is the uneconomical state of farming.[10] Dr.Ambedkarrecognised the issues faced by the landless scheduled castes and backward classes in his book titled "States

4. VOLUME XI,CONSTITUENT ASSEMBLY OF INDIA,Friday, the 25th November, 1949
5. Constitution of India
6. M.P.SINGH,V.N.ShuklaPg no 201 ,Ninth Edition
7. SuvojitBagchi, Punjab suicides cast shadow on polls available at http://news.bbc.co.uk/2/hi/south_asia/7992327.stm
8. Dr.NarendarJadhav, ,Farmers, Suicide And Debt Waiver An Action Plan For Agricultural Development Of Maharashtra, Government Of Maharashtra July2008
9. Id.
10. Id.

and Minorities" and suggested protectivemeasures to end exploitation in the following :

"Agriculturalindustry shall be organized on the following basis:

(i) *The State shall divide the land acquired into farms of standard size and let out the farms for cultivation to residents of the village as tenants (made up of group of families) to cultivate on the following conditions:*

(a) *(a)The farm shall be cultivated as a collective farm ;*

(b) *(b)The farm shall be cultivated in accordance with rules and directions issued by Government;*

(c) *The tenants shall share among themselves in the manner prescribed the produce of the farm left after the payment of charges properly leviable on the farm;*

(ii) *The land shall be let out to villagers without distinction of caste or creed and in such manner that there will be no landlord, no tenant and no landless labourer ;*

(iii) *It shall be the obligation of the State to finance the cultivation of the collective farms by the supply of water, draft animals, implements, manure, seeds, etc.;*

(iv) *The State shall be entitled to-*

(a) *(a) to levy the following charges on the produce of the farm: (i) a portion for land revenue; (ii) a portion to pay the debenture-holders ; and (iii) a portion to pay for the use of capital goods supplied; and*

(b) *(b) to prescribe penalties against tenants who break the conditions of tenancy or wilfully neglect to make the best use of the means of cultivation offered by the State or otherwise act prejudicially to the scheme of collective farming*"[11]

Empowerment of Women

Dr.Ambedkar codified scattered Hindu laws into the Hindu code bill. The Bill proposed to make four changes. First was that the widow, the daughter, the widow of a pre-deceased son, all be given the same rank as the son in the matter of inheritance. In addition to that, the daughter also be given a share in her father's property, her share is prescribed as half of that of the son.[12] The

---

11. Dr.B.R.Ambedkar, STATES AND MINORITIES ,What are Their Rights and How to Secure them in the Constitution of Free India ,Memorandum on the Safeguards for the Scheduled Castes submitted to the Constituent Assembly an behalf of the All India Scheduled Castes Federation,Published: 1947
12. Hindu Code Bill ,Available at http://www.ambedkar.org/ambcd/64A1.%20On%20The%20Hindu%20Code%20Bill.htm#a01, accessed on 5 April,2014

other female heirs had already been recognised by the Hindu Women's Right to Property Act of 1937. The rights of maintenance and succession of women, which was conferment of proprietary rights to women was not accepted by the parliament.[13] Dr. Ambedkar argued that the concept of divorce, mainitance and property rights for women existed among the shudras, untouchables and the tribals. If Hindu code bill recognises these groups as Hindus, customary practises of groups also must be accepted. He argued the imposition of the customary practises of small minority among Hindus would be disadvantageous for the large social groups. His bill was defeated on the floor of the parliament despite being an official bill. It was a very progressive bill which would have empowered women. However some of the provisions of the bill were incorporated into the Hindu succession and Hindu marriage and guardianship act. He resigned from the ministerial post from the cabinet in 1951.

Reconstruction of The Society

The primary objective of Dr.Ambedkar's idea was to establish a just society or a society that is based on the principle of justice. In his own words "ideal would be a society based on liberty, equality and fraternity".[14] Castes are the building bricks of Hindu social structure. It is this process of division. Groups called castes have been permanently assigned high or low ranks simply on the basis of birth, the social ranks and their respective duties ordained by god for humanity. They were intended to remain fixed and unmovable like the limbs of the body. They cannot properly exchange either their place or function.[15]

He wanted individual to be centre of the society. He recognized the two essential principles. *"the first is that the individual is an end in himself and that aim and object of the society is the growth of the individual and the development of his personality,society is not above the individual and if the individual has to subordinate himself*

---

13. Dhanvijay,Vaishali , Dr.BabasahebAmbedkar's Efforts For Women Empowerment And Present Status Of Women In Society, Electronic International Interdisciplinary Research Journal (EIIRJ), { Bi-Monthly}, Volume-I, Issue II, April 2012, ISSN 2277 - 8721, p. 113, accessed on 5 April,2014
14. Dr.B.R.AmbedkarAnnihilation of caste system
15. Report of The Backward Classes Commission Report ,1980,Available at available at http://www.ncbc.nic.in/

to society in the caste based society an individual has no place , in a caste based society a person relationship with the member of his or her class or with members his her or her class or with members of other class are already fixed",

In the ideal society, relations have to be based on liberty, equality and fraternity. Hence, the objective of the society shall be to protect the individual's right. He said that any good social order or society has to go through the two tests namely "the test of justice and the test of utility." Besides the two tests,one of the most important components is justice or the principle of justice according to him, the norm or the criterion for judging right or wrong in the modern society is justice[16] and justice is simply another name for liberty, equality and fraternity.[17]

He observes that the new doctrinal basis is the first step to formulate the new doctrinal basis of the religion. According to him,religion has to be in consonance with liberty, equality and fraternity. It mean to reformulate the Hindu religion from scriptures such as Upanishads, which carries the philosophical basis of Hindu religion. He also recommended to remove the principles which are against the spirit of fraternity and associated mode of living. The doctrinal basis of Hindu religion prohibits the principles of liberty and equality to the masses of this country. The masses are denied right to education, military training and political power. His concern was to make these rights available to the majority who were denied these since time immemorial.He suggested that first step should be to organise a new social setup on the basis of justice and the way one views life must be changed in order to give the masses their rights. He also suggests that they must adopt a new way of life or values which is conversion. Conversion, the leading to a new life actually means going through a death experience which means rejecting completely the old life before entering into new. He remarked "you must take the stand that Buddha took, you must take the stand which Guru Nanak took, you must not only discard the shastras, you must deny their authority, as did Buddha and Nanak"[18]

---

16. Dr.Ambedkar, Philosophy of Hinduism,Writings and Speeches, vol. 3 published by Government of Maharashtra
17. Id.pg 25.
18. Id.

1

Reconstruction Through Annihilation: Caste and Modern Society

- Deepti Somani & Ashwin Varghese***

1.1 Introduction

That caste is a problem modern society in India will have to thoroughly deal with in the reconstruction of an old, archaic, fixed and more importantly a pre-eminent exploitative social order, had been firmly established in the Indian struggle for independence and the nation building project. Dr. Bhimrao Ramji Ambedkar's thorough analysis of the caste system in India attempted to fundamentally establish that the mechanism of caste is inconsistent with the new social order that India was striving for.

The strength and character of Dr. Ambedkar's analysis lies in its utter simplicity and astounding genius. His analysis is not only deeply informed and reflective of the existing social structures and ideologies, but also takes into account key general principles and lays bare the underlying structure which is self-sustaining and more importantly has withstood the test of time. It is in his ability to lay bare the essential mechanism of the caste system, that he has been able to very radically articulate the means of annihilation of the caste system. Ambedkar's genius lies in the fact that he has been able to extract the essential structure of the exploitative system that can be used as a benchmark to analyze caste for posterity.

*Deepti Somani, B.S.L., LL.B., ILS Law College, University of Pune; currently practicing as an Advocate at Calcutta High Court.

**Ashwin Varghese, M.A. (English), University of Delhi; presently working as an independent researcher based out of Delhi.

The purpose of this paper is to revisit Ambedkar's analysis of caste as it appears in his two fundamental texts; *Castes In India and Annihilation of Caste* and attempts to show how the key features of his analysis, subsequent advocacies and method have been distorted and confused, despite constitutional provisions, with policy which has resulted in a quasi-democratic social order today.

For the scope of this paper, we will attempt to do a nuanced reading of Ambedkar's analysis and methods, see how they have been enshrined in the Constitution of India.

The paper begins by placing caste in context and examining the essential mechanism of caste; that of maintaining endogamy; and notes the persistence of this mechanism despite certain superficial changes in the system itself. It then moves on to a more nuanced analysis of the caste system, its mechanism and source of power, and takes note of how the means of imitation and excommunication along with the means of maintaining endogamy creates the institution of caste. Along with this, the paper also looks at how religion plays the role of fortification and perpetuation but does not form the essential function of the caste system, while analyzing the nature of Hinduism through the distinction between the ideas of Rule and Principle.

Having outlined this, the paperattempts to understand Ambedkar's ideals of reconstruction of society in the context of nationalism and the need for social reform before an imminent political revolution, also touching upon Ambedkar's conception of Democracy.

Following this, we will show how the Constitution of India, taking cognizance of the aforementioned analysis and concerns, was envisioned as a tool for social reconstruction, in which was enshrined the principles for social revolution to pave the way for a democracy founded on liberty, equality, fraternity and justice.

1.2 Castes in India

Dr. Ambedkar argued that there were two qualitatively different groups which had not only been historically crucial, but continue to be fundamental, to both social organization and social dynamics. These two groups were caste and class. Historically, the Vedic Varna system, which was a class order, had been subsequently transformed into a caste order, and in modern India the nascent class order was continually and complexly distorted and defeated by caste order[1]. Caste and class are tied together in a very complex relationship with each other, which will be dealt with more extensively in a later section. This relationship between caste and class became the point of his challenge to Marxists and the socialist factions in the political atmosphere of India, when he asked them whether the Indian proletariat, caste-fragmented, can ever become a class in itself, let alone a class for itself[2]. Ambedkar argues that the formation of caste based society, coupled with gender inequity was to safeguard the interests of the Brahminical groups in relation to other groups, maintain their moral and mental control over them, and preserve their position of power, prestige and privilege[3].

Ambedkar's arguments cannot be understood without taking into account India's socio-political atmosphere, namely the struggle for independence, the nation building project and the imaginings of a new social order. In this backdrop, the principle argument that Ambedkar's analysis puts forth is that the institution of caste and the social system that perpetuates it, is inconsistent with nationalism. According to Ambedkar, caste destroyed the concept of ethics and morality. To quote him:

"The effect of caste on the ethics of the Hindus is simply deplorable. Caste has killed public spirit. Caste has destroyed the sense of public charity. Caste has made public opinion impossible. A Hindu's public is his caste. His responsibility is to his caste. His loyalty is restricted only to his caste. Virtue has become caste-ridden, and morality has become caste-bound.[4]"

He gave a strikingly simplistic analysis of caste that can still, in spite of the changes in the caste system, be used as a

1. P.D. Satya Paul, Dr. B.R. Ambedkar and his Vision for Reconstruction of Indian Society, 1 International Journal of Multidisciplinary Education and Research 4 (2012).
2. Id.
3. Id.
4. B. R. AMBEDKAR, THE ANNIHILATION OF CASTE, § 13.1 (1936) [hereinafter "AMBEDKAR"].

benchmark to judge its prevalence. He proposed that the only thing essential to the nature of caste is the practice of endogamy. He noted that *"Caste in India means an artificial chopping off the population into fixed and definite units, each one prevented from fusing into another through the custom of endogamy.*[5]*"* Endogamy as a feature is not peculiar to caste system in India alone; globally many endogamous groups exist without the problem of caste; however most such groups exist in mutually exclusive units, by means of an illustration Ambedkar notes that the African Americans, the indigenous tribal population-the American Indians-and the dominant white population of the United States of America are an appropriate illustration for this. Why this system of endogamy poses a peculiarly difficult problem in India, is because of the subcontinent's cultural homogeneity. It is this cultural homogeneity that binds each endogamous group in a mutually exploitative relationship.

While noting that all people are ethnically heterogeneous, Ambedkar noted that it is the unity of culture that is the basis for homogeneity, and in this cultural homogeneity no country rivals the Indian peninsula. This homogeneity is what makes the issue of caste more daunting, what is peculiar to castes in India is the relationship between endogamy and exogamy. Ambedkar argues that *"endogamy is foreign to the people of India...with the people of India exogamy is a creed and none dare infringe it, so much so that, inspite of the endogamy of the Castes within them exogamy is strictly observed and that there are more rigorous penalties for violating exogamy than are for violating endogamy*[6]*";* this is especially true when we consider the punishments meted out by caste panchayats like the khap that are still dominant. Moreover "with exogamy the rule there could be no Caste, for exogamy means fusion. But we

---

5. available at http://ccnmtl.columbia.edu/projects/mmt/ambedkar/web/readings/aoc_print_2004.pdf

6. B,R. AMBEDKAR, CASTES IN INDIA: THEIR MECHANISM, GENESIS AND DEVELOPMENT 7 (1916).

have castes... creation of castes, so far as India is concerned, means the superposition of endogamy on exogamy.[7]" The analysis of this essential function, i.e. the means utilized for the preservation of endogamy against exogamy[8], holds the key to annihilation of castes and the advent of a new social order.

1.2.a Caste Today

That a single caste hierarchy is universally acknowledged and accepted by everyone within the caste system is a gross misreading of the ground realities has been effectively established by many contemporary sociological accounts on the subject. The eminent sociologist M.N. Srinivas, in his works has observed that "The rural scene in most parts of India is characterized by the existence of dominant castes, which own a substantial amount of local, arable land, enjoy strength of numbers, have a high status in the local pecking order, and wield considerable power over the other castes.[9]"

It is undeniable that the caste system, as existed in the ancient times- with its rigid hierarchy - does not exist in the same form today. The power and influence once held by the upper caste has now been shifted to the dominant caste. This evolution in the caste system has been waylaid by the colonial British administration and the subsequent nationalist struggle and the imaginings of a new social order. Srinivas observed that *"caste system traditionally permitted a certain amount of mobility. With the establishment of British rule, however, while certain routes to upward status were closed, many others were opened up. The development of communications, the integration of the regional economies into a national economy and the latter's being linked to the British imperial economy, the building of new towns and cities, the rise of new occupations, and last but not least, the slow but sure British moves towards the introduction of the principle of equality of opportunity, and the popularity of democratic and libertarian ideas among the Indian elite, provided the leaven for later massive changes in the system. As a result of the forces released by*

---

7. Id. at 8.
8. Id.
9. M.N. SRINIVAS, THE EVOLUTION OF CASTE IN INDIA 163 (2002).

British rule, the radical measures introduced during the last fifty years of independence, caste is undergoing systematic change.[10]"

This is not to say that the problem of caste has vanished or that exploitative hierarchies have been done away with. Those at the lower rungs of the caste system are still subject to humiliating and inhuman treatments. That India, even now, has not been able to eradicate the scourge of manual scavenging is testament to the fact that caste is still an exploitative social structure.

These subsequent, but superficial changes, do not affect the veracity of Ambedkar's analysis, and this is where his genius lies. What Ambedkar outlines, is the underlying mechanism of an exploitative social structure which is based on the principles of caste. This mechanism is not affected by either the hierarchy in which it manifests itself at any point in time, or by a change in the philosophy that sanctifies the institution of caste. The mechanism itself is persistent enough to adapt to superficial changes.

1.3 Caste System : Mechanisms and Power

For Ambedkar, the religious fervor of the caste system is not its essential feature. He noted that *"It is true that Caste relies on belief, but before belief comes to be the foundation of an institution, the institution itself needs to be perpetuated and fortified.*[11]" In other words, the religious philosophy that perpetuates and sanctifies caste is separate from the institution of caste itself, for Ambedkar the belief in the institution that perpetuates and fortifies the system comes after the mechanisms have been firmly established. Confusing the religious foundation of caste as its essential feature is the bane of caste analysis. "The 'idea of pollution' has been attached to the institution of Caste, only because the Caste that enjoys the highest rank is the priestly Caste... [Therefore]... the "idea of pollution" is a characteristic of Caste only in so far as Caste has a religious flavour.[12]" The religious foundation of the caste system is only a superficial layer, while the kernel is the

10. Id. at 164.
11. Supra note 5, at 31.
12. Id. at 7.

means of utilizing endogamy over exogamy.

InCastes in India, his 1916 essay, Ambedkar theorizes caste as a source of power and argues that women were used as gateways of the caste system and that control over them through child marriages, enforced widowhood and sati (being burnt on a dead husband's pyre) were methods employed to keep a check on women's sexuality and more importantly to "maintain the numerical equality between the marriageable units of the two sexes within the group desirous of making itself into a caste.[13]"This is essential to provide conjugal rights to the members of a group from within, which in turn is fundamentally important to preserve the principle of endogamy.

1.3a Brahmansim, Imitation and excommunication

Brahminism was the term that the anti-caste movement preferred over "Hinduism." By Brahminism, they didn't mean Brahmins as a caste or a community. What it refers to is the domino effect, what Ambedkar called the 'infection of imitation', that the caste that first "enclosed" itself-the Brahmins- set off [14].

One of the key contributions of his analysis of the mechanism of caste was this aspect of imitation. In Castes in India, he observed that "classes have become Castes through imitation and excommunication.[15]"He describes that at some time in the history of the Hindus, the priestly class, or the Brahmins socially detached itself from the rest of the body and through a closed-door policy became a caste. "Endogamy...was a fashion in the Hindu society, and as it had originated from the Brahman caste it as whole heartedly imitated by all the non Brahman sub-divisions or classes.[16]"This, he argues is the infection of imitation.

Moreover, he observed that the status function of caste was directly associated with this aspect of imitation, "*The status of a Caste in the Hindu Society varies directly with the extent of the observance*

13. Id. at 10.
14. ARUNDHATI ROY, THE DOCTOR AND THE SAINT (2014)..
15. Id. at 31.
16. Id. at 24.

of the custom of Sati, enforced widowhood and girl marriage. But observance of these customs varies directly with the DISTANCE ... those castes that are nearest to the Brahmans have imitated all the customs and insist on the strict observance thereof.[17]" This imitation is the key that perpetuated the mechanism of endogamy over exogamy, coupled with this is the aspect of excommunication, where any class or community that has the courage to violate the norms codified by imitation, is penalized by excommunication and the result is a new caste. This mechanism of imitation and excommunication along with the means of maintaining endogamy over exogamy is what, for Ambedkar, creates the institution of Caste.

The 'infection of imitation,' like the half-life of a radioactive atom, decays exponentially as it moves down the caste ladder, but never quite disappears[18]. It has created what Ambedkar describes as a system of "graded inequality" in which "there is no such class as a completely unprivileged class except the one which is at the base of the social pyramid. The privileges of the rest are graded. Even the low is privileged as compared with lower. Each class being privileged, every class is interested in maintaining the system.[19]" Brahminism, Ambedkar writes, "is the very negation of the spirit of Liberty, Equality and Fraternity.[20]"

1.3b Fortification through Religion

The religious foundation of the caste system is a source of considerable power, he observed that *"religion is the source of power is illustrated by the history of India where the priest holds a sway over the common man often greater than the magistrate and where everything, even such things as strikes and elections, so easily take a religious turn*

17. *Id.* at 27.
18. Supra note 13.
19. B.R. AMBEDKAR, DR. BABASAHEB AMBEDKAR: WRITINGS AND SPEECHES 102 (2003).
20. BHAGWAN DAS, THUS SPOKE AMBEDKAR: A STAKE IN THE NATION 51 (2010).

and can so easily be given a religious twist.[21]" This is why Ambedkar professed applying the dynamite to the Vedas and Shastras, not because undermining the religious sanctity of caste would lead to the annihilation of caste, but because by breaking the fortifications altering the underlying institution becomes much more plausible. He makes a much more nuanced analysis of Hinduism as a religion by pitting it against the ideas of 'rule' and 'principle', which will be elaborated in another section in the paper.

To judge that caste is on the decline because the hierarchies have changed or because the religious foundation upholding the sanctity of caste has toned down is a particularly fallacious argument. Indeed the only true benchmark of judging the existence and prevalence of caste is by analyzing the mechanism that perpetuates endogamy.

Eminent sociologist André Béteille gives a very comprehensive overview of how the Indian intelligentsia dealt with the issue of caste at the time of independence. "*Caste had become a subject of debate and discussion before Independence, and more than one view was formed regarding its pervasiveness and strength... There was the view of the colonial government...that caste was not only the pre-eminent institution of India, but that it permeated every area of life, and the idea that caste could be dispensed with was wishful thinking. As against this was what I may call the nationalist view, to which Indian intellectuals by and large then subscribed, that the importance of caste had been greatly exaggerated by the colonial administration, that it was clearly on its way out, and that its decline would be greatly hastened once India became independent.*[22]" *He notes that,* "*[T]he Indian perception of caste at the time of independence had been shaped, at least to some extent, by the dialectic between the colonial and the nationalist views regarding its place in the present and future society of India.*[23]"

The Indian intelligentsia at this stage was characterized by a peculiar misperception; of perceiving the religious foundation

---

21. AMBEDKAR, supra note 4, at § 3.2
22. ANDRÉ BÉTEILLE, CASTE IN CONTEMPORARY INDIA 162 (2005).
23. Id. at 163.

of caste as the essential feature of the system. This *"misperception of caste common among the Indian intelligentsia at the time of independence was due partly to the misplaced emphasis on ritual in accounts of it by civil servants and others in the preceding decades... whatever place religion may have had in it in the past, the future of caste lay not with religion but with politics... immediately after Independence, the Indian intelligentsia failed by and large to dwell on the future role of caste in politics... They knew that it was there but hoped that it could be made to wither away – through rapid economic development, through the spread of education, and through science and technology.*[24]*"*

What Béteille succinctly notes here is that the source of power and fortification for the caste system, in the post independence era, shifted from the religious sanctity of caste to the nature of politics in modern India. It is worth noting here that the essential feature of superposition of endogamy on exogamy remained largely unaffected.

1.3c Nature of Hinduism: Law, Rule and Principle

Noting that the religious foundation was a source of considerable power and sanctity for the caste system, Ambedkar did a striking analysis of Hinduism in an attempt to dissociate the religious principle from the institution of caste. In Annihilation of Caste, Ambedkar writes,

"The only question that remains to be considered is – How to bring about reform of the Hindu social order? How to abolish caste? This is a question of supreme importance.[25]*"*

His analysis concentrates on the Hindu religion as contained in the Vedas and Smritis. Describing the religious scriptures as 'multitude of commands and prohibitions[26]', he writes:

"What the Hindus call Religion is really Law, or at best legalized class-ethics. Frankly, I refuse to call this code of ordinances as Religion. The objectionable part is that this code has been

24. Id. at 166.

25. AMBEDKAR, supra note 4, at §20.2.

26. Id. at §23.3.

invested with the character of finality and fixity... how can humanity endure this code of eternal laws, without being cramped and without being crippled? I have, therefore, no hesitation in saying that such a religion must be destroyed.[27]" At the heart of this injunction is a fundamental distinction that Ambedkar makes between 'rule' and 'principle.' He observes:

"Rules are practical; they are habitual ways of doing things according to prescription. But principles are intellectual; they are useful methods of judging things. Rules seek to tell an agent just what course of action to pursue... A principle, such as that of justice, supplies a main head by reference to which he is to consider the bearing of his desires and purposes, it guides him in his thinking by suggesting to him the important consideration which he should bear in mind.[28]"

...Doing what is said to be good by virtue of a rule and doing well in the light of a principle are two different things. The principle may be wrong but the act is conscious and responsible. The rule may be right but the act is mechanical. A religious act may not be a correct act but must at least be a responsible act. To permit of this responsibility, Religion must mainly be a matter of principles only. It cannot be a matter of rules. The moment it degenerates into rules it ceases to be Religion, as it kills responsibility, which is the essence of a truly religious act...Now the Hindu Religion, as contained in the Vedas and the Smritis, is nothing but a mass of sacrificial, social, political and sanitary rules and regulations, all mixed up. What the Hindus call Religion is nothing but a multitude of commands and prohibitions.[29]

...Once you clear the minds of the people of this misconception and enable them to realise that what they are told is religion is not religion, but that it is really law, you will be in a position to urge its amendment or abolition...So long as people look upon it

27. Id. at §23.5.
28. Id. at §23.1.
29. Id. at §23.2.

as religion they will not be ready for a change, because the idea of religion is generally speaking not associated with the idea of change. But the idea of law is associated with the idea of change, and when people come to know that what is called religion is really law, old and archaic, they will be ready for a change, for people know and accept that law can be changed.[30]"

1.4 Reconstruction of society

It is important to give emphasis here on his analysis of caste as an old, archaic and fixed structure. India at this point in time, was on the verge of a creating a new social order, an order that was founded on the grounds of Democracy and based on the trinity principles of liberty, equality and fraternity.That Ambedkar actively advocated for this new idea only added to the zeitgeist. What Ambedkar essentially tries to do in his analysis is first to lay bare the structure of the underlying institution, and then to show that this pre-eminent institution is inconsistent with the ideals that the country was actively striving for and that achieving the ideals of democracy without annihilating caste is wishful thinking.

He argued that "the first and foremost thing that must be recognized is that Hindu Society is a myth…In every Hindu the consciousness that exists is the consciousness of caste. That is the reason why the Hindus cannot be said to form a society or a nation.[31]" He believed that the Indian society based on caste system clamps social oppression, economic exploitation and political suppression and further explains the ethnocentric belief that the Hindu social system, perfected for all times, has prevented the reconstruction of the Hindu Society and stood in the way of a revision of vested rights for the common good.

At the core of reconstruction of society lies the need for change in social order for, "nothing can be built on the foundation of caste. No nation, no morality.[32]" While the Jatpat Todak Mandal

30. Id. at §23.6.

31. Id. at §6.2.

32. B.R. AMBEDKAR: WRITINGS AND SPEECHES 304 (2003).

aspired to 'Remodel Hindu Society', Ambedkar stressed on 'Reconstitution of the society' by annihilating caste and its ideological notions[33].

InAnnihilation of Caste, Ambedkar articulates the irrationality of the category of caste and argues, *"Reason and morality are the two most powerful weapons in the armoury of a reformer. To deprive [a person] of the use of these weapons is to disable him for action. How are you going to break up Caste, if people are not free to consider whether it accords with reason? How are you going to break up Caste if people are not free to consider whether it accords with morality? This wall built around Caste is impregnable, and the material of which it is built contains none of the combustible stuff of reason and morality.*[34]"

1.4a New social order : Nationalism, Social Reform, Political Revolution

Ambedkar deeply reflected on the issues of nationalism and what constitutes a society and how caste system in India is antithetical to a society based on common humanity. He noted that *"Men constitute a society because they have things, which they possess in common...the only way by which men can come to possess things in common with one another is by being in communication with one another. This is merely another way of saying that Society continues to exist by communication indeed in communication.*[35]" *He further argues, "For that purpose what is necessary is for a man to share and participate in a common activity so that the same emotions are aroused in him that animate the others. Making the individual a sharer or partner in the associated activity so that he feels its success as his success, its failure as his failure, is the real thing that binds men and makes a society of them. The Caste System prevents common activity and by preventing common activity it has prevented the Hindus from becoming a society with a unified life and a consciousness of its own being.*[36]"

---

33. Supra note 1, at 6.
34. AMBEDKAR, supra note 4, at §22.25.
35. Id. at §6.6.
36. Id.at §6.7.

He emphatically observed that "so long as caste remains, there will be no Sanghatan and so long as there is no Sanghatan the Hindu will remain weak and meek.[37]" These arguments have to be understood in the context of the independence struggle and the nation building project. It is this context that draws power to his analysis. A country on the verge of independence needs to organize itself, at this point an analysis that reveals that caste is inconsistent with Sangathanalso establishes that caste effectively opposes the nation building project.

At this juncture Ambedkar proposed a new social order, which was not only antithetical to caste, but also conducive to nationalization. He noted that, *"my ideal would be a society based on Liberty, Equality and Fraternity... An ideal society should be mobile, should be full of channels for conveying a change-taking place in one part to other parts. In an ideal society there should be many interests consciously communicated and shared. There should be varied and free points of contact with other modes of associations. In other words there must be social endosmosis. This is fraternity, which is only another name for democracy. Democracy is not merely a form of Government. It is primarily a mode of associated living, of conjoint communicated experience. It is essentially an attitude of respect and reverence towards fellowmen."*[38]

To make this transition to a new social order, social reform is of crucial importance. The essential question Ambedkar explores in Annihilation of Caste relates to the relationship between social reform and political change. While Ambedkar's contemporaries including the Congress argued that political reform must precede social reform; differing with them, he argued for social reform preceding political and economic revolution. While the Congress insisted on delaying social reform to usher in political revolution, Ambedkar found primary contradiction in this argument and writes:

---

37. Id. at §10.3.
38. Id. at §14.1-2.

"Every Congressman, who repeats the dogma of Mill that one country is not fit to rule another country, must admit that one class is not fit to rule another class. How is it then the 'social reform party' lost the battle... That political reform cannot with impunity take precedence over social reform in the sense of the reconstruction of society, is a thesis which I am sure cannot be controverted.[39]"

Ambedkar in this context made a further analysis of the kind of social reform that was essential to this project and noted that "it is necessary to make a distinction between social reforms in the sense of the reform of the Hindu family and social reform in the sense of the reorganization and reconstruction of the Hindu Society. The former has relation to widow remarriage, child marriage etc., while the latter relates to the abolition of the Caste System.[40]"

Not only did Ambedkar assert that "Political Constitution must take note of social organisation[41]" but he also made a strikingly similar argument with regard to the precedence of social reform over economic reform. He questions, "Can you have economic reform without first bringing about a reform of the social order?[42]" For Ambedkar, the thrust of 'reconstruction of society' was based on social reform for he believed that substantial political and economic change would follow only when there was sincere engagement with social change.

Ambedkar also understood that the concerns of social reform and political revolution were inseparable and writes: "...they will find that in the making of a Constitution, they cannot ignore the problem arising out of the prevailing social order....the emancipation of the mind and the soul is a necessary preliminary for the political expansion of the people.[43]"

Grappling with the questions of a new social order, he also proposed some benchmarks, according to which an ideal society

39. Id. at §2.14-16.
40. Id. at §2.14.
41. Id. at §2.18.
42. Id. at §3.8.
43. Id. at §2.20.

should be constructed, he noted, "The questions to be asked in determining what is an ideal society are: How numerous and varied are the interests which are consciously shared by the groups? How full and free is the interplay with other forms of associations? Are the forces that separate groups and classes more numerous than the forces that unite? What social significance is attached to this group life? Is its exclusiveness a matter of custom and convenience or is it a matter of religion?[44]

In the Constituent Assembly of 1946, he discussed the framework of the Constitution and spoke, "Our difficulty is how to make the heterogeneous mass that we have today take a decision in common and march on the way which leads us to unity. Our difficulty is not with regard to the ultimate; our difficulty is with regard to the beginning[45]".

1.4b Democracy

In order to establish an inclusive society, Ambedkar looks at democracy, not as a political arrangement, but as "a mode of associated living. The roots of democracy are to be searched in social relationship, in terms of the associated life between the people who form the society.[46]" He defined democracy as a "form and method of government where by revolutionary changes in the economic and social life of the people are brought about without bloodshed."[47]

In the Conversion Conference of 1936, Ambedkar expounded the philosophy of human beings and the ideology of democratic revolution comprehending not only social, legal and civic equality but also religious equality. These qualities were to be achieved in the trinity of 'liberty, equality and fraternity' by Constitutional rights and guarantees and much more significantly by the reconstruction of society based on this trinity principle.

---

44. Id. at §19.3.

45 DHANANJAY KEER, DR. AMBEDKAR: LIFE AND MISSION 480 (1990) [hereinafter "KEER"].

46. Id. at 480.

47. Id. at 61.

1.5 Constitution - Blueprint for Reconstruction of Society

The Constitution served as the blueprint for a society based on national reconstruction. The Constitution of India, in order to reconstitute the society on the democratic foundations of equality, liberty, fraternity and justice, incorporated legislations for equality and equal opportunity in all spheres of life. Fundamental Rights and Directive Principles of State Policy lay down the roadmap for a democratic and inclusive society.

In order to create social polarization among the victims of the Brahmanical social system, Ambedkar engineered the category 'Backward classes' which would cover three principal components, the Scheduled Castes, the Scheduled Tribes and the Other Backward classes. Under the mandate of the Constitution, provisions relating to Fundamental Rights and Directive Policies were aimed at securing social justice for all the socially and educationally Backward Classes in the country[48]. Granville Austin, leading Constitutional authority writes, "The majority of India's Constitutional provisions are either directly arrived at furthering the aim of social revolution or attempt to foster this revolution by establishing conditions necessary for its achievement.[49]"

Ambedkar's main concern was to privilege and legalize "constitutional morality" over the traditional, social morality of the caste system[50]. Speaking in the Constituent Assembly on 4 November 1948, he said, "Constitutional morality is not a natural sentiment. It has to be cultivated. We must realise that our people have yet to learn it. Democracy in India is only a top-dressing on an Indian soil which is essentially undemocratic.[51]"

Though Ambedkar is regarded as the founding father of Indian Constitution, a look at the Constituent Assembly debates reveal how disappointed he was with the final draft of the constitution. Arundhati Roy points out "Still, he did succeed in putting in place certain rights and safeguards that would, as far

48. Supra note 1, at 9.
49. Addresses on the 50th Anniversary of the Republic of India (2000), available at http://parliamentofindia.nic.in/jpi/MARCH2000/CHAP1.htm.
50. Supra note 13.
51. DAS, supra note 19, at 175.

as the subordinated castes were concerned, make it a document that was more enlightened than the society it was drafted for.[52]

1.5a Trinity principle

Ambedkar argues that caste is nothing more than "this anti-social spirit, this spirit of protecting its own interests.[53]" The Constitution as an instrument of reconstruction strives to build a nationconstructed on the promise of annihilation of caste and all other forms of discrimination, in order *"to secure to all its citizens: JUSTICE, social, economic and political; LIBERTY of thought, expression, belief, faith and worship; EQUALITY of status and of opportunity; and to promote among them all FRATERNITY assuring the dignity of the individual.[54]"*

Ambedkar writes, "The question for him is whether he minds one class ill-treating and suppressing another class as a matter of system, as a matter of principle–and thus allowing tyranny and oppression to continue to divide one class from another.[55]" He argues that it is impossible to categorize and classify people and therefore, all such attempts are inherently arbitrary and irrational and, therefore, inherently unjust.

This notion finds a fundamental place in India's Constitution; where the primary objective of its provisions against discrimination is to reverse such arbitrary classifications. In order to check inherent caste based discrimination, Ambedkar asserts the need to find methods to check default discrimination and revealed one such mechanism in his treatment of equality, caste and discrimination under the Constitution.

Ambedkar argued for fraternity and conceived individual liberty as the foundation of reform and social progress, but understood equality as inevitable but not beyond correction. He writes, *"...it can be urged that if it is good for the social body to get the*

52. Supra note 13.
53. AMBEDKAR, supra note 4, at §7.3.
54. Preamble to the Constitution of India.
55. AMBEDKAR, supra note 4, at §3.9.

most out of its members, it can get the most out of them only by making them equal as far as possible at the very start of the race.[56]" *He further states, "Equality may be a fiction, but nonetheless one must accept it as the governing principle. A man's power is dependent upon (1) physical heredity, (2) social inheritance or endowment in the form of parental care, education, accumulation of scientific knowledge, everything, which enables him to be more efficient than the savage; and finally (3) on his own efforts. In all these three respects, men are undoubtedly unequal. But the question is, shall we treat them as unequal because they are unequal? This is a question which the opponents of equality must answer.*[57]"

1.5b Constitution and Annihilation of caste

Annihilation of Caste serves as the fundamental key to interpreting the Indian Constitution. Ambedkar argues that caste is nothing more than "this anti-social spirit, this spirit of protecting its own interests.[58]" It is this definition of caste that finds its place in the Constitution. While the Indian Constitution does not explicitly define 'caste', there are nearly 100 references to the term in the Constitution. It employs the term in two ways: Firstly, caste is employed in the phrase "Scheduled Caste," most often in association with 'Scheduled Tribes' and 'weaker sections,' but also with the phrase 'backward classes.' Secondly, caste is also used in the provisions prohibiting "discrimination on grounds of religion, race, caste, sex" and 'class,' 'place of birth,' 'language, 'descent,' and 'residence[59].'

In the first sense, caste denotes various groups and tribes of populations. These are groups for whom certain political provisions of representation were made (Scheduled caste, Scheduled Tribes) and also include those who suffered historical discrimination at

---

56. Id. at §14.7.
57. Id. at §14.5.
58. Id. at §7.3.
59. Laksmi Gopal, Ambedkar and Annihilation of Caste, 2 The Bangalore Review (2014).

the socio-economic level. In the case of the former, caste is a remedial measure to reverse irregularities in the distribution of power that occurred under the British and Hindu rule. In the case of the latter, caste is a matter of historical suppression. Legal provisions are made for these groups to correct historical political and socio-economic inequalities, respectively[60]. Thus, in both cases, it functions, as Ambedkar concisely described, as an "anti-social self-protecting spirit."

Further, while analyzing the various grounds for discrimination that accompany caste, one finds that each has a significant history of discrimination. Under the British, race was a legal ground for discrimination. Under caste- Hindu rule, caste was a ground for discrimination. Sex was a ground of discrimination under the course of many patriarchal systems and rulers. The Zamindari system and various other economic institutions practiced discrimination on the grounds of class and its associated category 'residence.' Under the Mughals, 'religion' and 'place of birth were actively used as grounds for discrimination.

Remarkably, the Constitution does not equate the various grounds. The phrase 'any of them,' is purposefully employed and signals that there is no claim of equality between the various possible grounds for illegal discrimination. Rather, the term caste in the Constitution has been used to suggest that the rationale for all grounds derives from the objective to counter previous histories of discrimination. Considering that the first objective of the Constitution is to secure, in the first instance, justice and, in the third, equality, it seems necessary that the Constitution would make provisions to ensure the reversal of historic incidents of discrimination leading to inequality and injustice. The lack of such provisions would hamper the potential for liberty and fraternity (the two other objectives set out in the preamble). Thus, a study of the aims and ends of the Constitution demonstrate that one possible legal definition of caste is as a system of social organization that results in practices that have been prohibited variously, but

60. Id.

in particular by Part III, Article 15, 16 and 17 of the Indian Constitution[61]. Furthermore, it continues as a system of categorization and classification that aims to reverse historic instances of discrimination.

With several references to the term 'caste', the definition of caste in the Constitution is not static but fluid. Article 366, clause 24 of the Indian Constitution defines 'Scheduled Castes' as 'such castes, races, or tribes or parts of or groups within such castes, races or tribes as are deemed under article 341 to be scheduled Castes for the purposes of this Constitution.'Clause 25 restates the same with regard to 'tribe or tribal communities,' and refers to article 342 of the Constitution. Article 341, defines Scheduled Castes as any 'castes, races or tribes or parts of groups within castes races or tribes, which shall for the purposes of this Constitution be deemed' by the President after consultation with the Governor, to be Scheduled Castes in relation to the State." Article 342, once again, makes a similar statement with regard to tribe.

Thus, the meaning of 'caste' is always evolving. It is the recognition of the ever-changing texture of discrimination in the Indian society. It is also a provision for a definition broad enough to ensure that no population will be trapped in poverty and subjugation and thereby denied, justice, liberty, equality and fraternity because of this antisocial spirit, this spirit of protecting its own interests, which Ambedkar recognizes in certain groups and social structures.

Ambedkar provides a broad, adaptable and ever evolving definition for caste. He acknowledges that constant change is fundamental to the world and society and understands that the shape of discrimination will constantly be altered. Therefore, in the Constitution, he transforms the category of caste and liberates it from its immediate location within the structures of religion and politics. Ambedkar's usage of the word 'caste' ensures that the Indian Constitution will be able to make provisions against

61. Id.

all or at least more potential instances of discrimination to ensure justice, liberty, equality and fraternity. Ambedkar through this usage of the term 'caste,' under the Indian Constitution has legally annihilated caste as we knew it and re-caste the concept in a new form–as a weapon for emancipation.

1.6 Conclusion

Despite legally annihilating caste, Ambedkar's aspirations of an inclusive society have not been realized fully and biographer Dhananjay Keer explains this paradox as the incompatibility of ideologies. He states, "Indians today are governed by two different ideologies. Their political ideal set out in the preamble of the Constitution affirms a life of liberty, equality and fraternity. Their social ideal embodied in their religion denies them.[62]"

Ambedkar had warned that 'political democracy cannot succeed where there is no social and economic democracy[63]" and it is this failure that has resulted in establishment of present day quasi- democratic social order. Scholars have cited several reasons why despite existence of several legal provisions, Ambedkar's articulate transformation and annihilation of caste remains far beyond the grasp of the consciousness of a majority of citizens in power and close to power. Political revolution has brought about representation from these groups in the political spectrum but what is required is a real social change in the relative strength of the forces operating in society. Many believe that there exists little, if any, debate on caste in India. Post independence, while reservations and merit are frequently debated, there is remarkably little debate about caste and the importance of common humanity.

There exist several legislations and schemes for socially and educationally backward classes, however, most of them focus solely on reservation in education and employment and granting scholarships to them while totally ignoring engaging with these groups in their fiscal and social development.

---

62. KEER, supra note 45, at 459.
63. BHAGWAN DAS, THUS SPOKE AMBEDKAR 30 (1979).

Ambedkar in his grand scheme of reconstruction of Indian society, fought for rights of representation as democratic rights. Branding the Brahmanical society is based on Culture of Reservations- keeping education, rule and economy reserved 100% for the Brahmanical castes and relegating the Bahujans to service, he wanted to usher in democratic society based on the Culture of Representations[64]. He engineered the idea of the category of 'Backward Classes' covering three principal components: Scheduled Caste, Scheduled Tribes and Other Backward Classes to secure social, economic and political justice for all the socially and the educationally Backward Classes in the country, under the mandate of a new Constitution. With a view to foster a culture of representation, Ambedkar sought to break the monopoly by proportional representations and create a policy to bring SC, ST, OBC on one platform in order to break caste system. With a view to establishing a new social order, the Constitution provided for reservation in politics, education and employment for people belonging to backward classes. However, many scholars believe that the underlying problem is that method of reservation has been confused with the policy. Providing representations or fair access or equal opportunity being the policy, the quota mechanism is a method to secure fairness. Over the last decade and so, the government has extended and introduced reservation across spheres but has failed to create an environment where the society has changed the way it looks at lower castes.

In his resignation speech as a law minister of independent India, Ambedkar said: "To leave inequality between class and class, between sex and sex, which is the soul of Hindu society, and to go on passing legislation relating to economic problems is to make a farce of our Constitution and to build a palace on a dung heap.[65]" This quote aptly captures the present day situation.

---

64. Supra note 1, at 7.

65. KEER, supra note 45, at 499.

On 2 September 1953, Ambedkar declared in the Rajya Sabha, "Sir, my friends tell me that I made the Constitution. But I am quite prepared to say that I shall be the first person to burn it out. I do not want it. It does not suit anybody. But whatever that may be, if our people want to carry on, they must remember that there are majorities and there are minorities; and they simply cannot ignore the minorities by saying: 'Oh, no, to recognize you is to harm democracy'".

The focus of policy and political interventions is still myopic, political factions, civil society and the state functionaries still seem to believe that rapid economic development would break the systems of inequality. On the contrary, the need for social reform is as important as ever, while India is witnessing rapid economic development, the underlying structures of inequality are restricting large sections of the populace to benefit from this economic development.

Without the much needed social reform and reconstruction, archaic and persistent structures of inequality will always exist, and continue to propagate a quasi-democratic social order.

2

Ambedkar's Pragmatic Society, Myriad of Empty Dreams or Reality

- Sanskruti Samal. & Sughosh Subramanyam Neergundha***

2.1 Introduction

In modern times science has been viewed by the east and west in different ways. Science is a mental enlightenment for the west. This view has not been accepted by the east, which sees science as a tool to dominate and suppress. This topic has received a critical appreciation with modern and postmodern scholars. Very few men in the east used western scientific approach for the benefit of mankind. One amongst the few was Baba Saheb Ambedkar. He believed that men from time to time revisit questions about inherent belief and ideas with changing times and circumstances so as to reconcile their past with the present in light of scientific developments so as to gain confidence and hope for a better future.

He emphasized on eradicating untouchability in order to institute a new social order based on the principle of equality. His entire life has been a saga of unremitting war for social justice. As the undisputed spearhead of the dejected groups and the foremost draftsman of the Indian Constitution, the name of Dr. Bhimrao Ramjee Ambedkar will always be reminisced in the pages of history. Dr. B.R. Ambedkar frolicked as a vivacious character in whittling the modern society. He muscularly deplored the contemptible defiance of the Brahmanical Hinduism towards the dalits and sought deliverance from the persecution of double born. The

---

*Sanskruti Samal,Second Year ,B.A.LLB (Hons) National Law University, Odisha.

**Sughosh Subramanyam Neergundha,Third year ,B.A.LLB (Hons) National Law University, Odisha.

caste system that relegated more than one fifth of the population to levels worse than animals for more than two thousand years of inequality became the prime target of his life.

He believed that, at the present day, religion, as a subject of critical or scientific inquiry, of both practical and theoretical significance has attracted increasing attention, this can be ascribed to:

a. the rapid progress of scientific knowledge and thought ;

b. the deeper intellectual interest in the subject ;

c. the widespread tendencies in all parts of the world to reform or reconstruct religion, or even to replace it by some body of thought, more ' rational 'and' scientific 'or less' superstitious'; and

d. the effect of social, political, and international events of a sort which, in the past, have both influenced and been influenced by religion.

Whenever the ethical or moral value of activities or conditions is questioned, the value of religion is involved ; and all deep-stirring experiences invariably compel a reconsideration of the most fundamental ideas, whether they are explicitly religious or not. Ultimately problems of justice, human destiny, God, and the universe arise ; and these in turn involve problems of the relation between ' religious ' and other ideas, the validity of ordinary knowledge, and practicable conceptions of 'experience' and 'reality'. From time to time men find themselves forced to reconsider current and inherited beliefs and ideas, to gain some harmony between present and past experience, and to reach a position which shall satisfy the demands of feeling and reflection that gives confidence for facing the future.

According to Dr. Ambedkar 'Caste does not result in economic efficiency, caste cannot and has not improved the race, caste has however done one thing, it has completely disorganized and demoralized the Hindu, He said, the Hindu often complain of the isolation and exclusiveness of a gang or a clique and blame them for anti-social spirit. But they conveniently forget that this anti-social spirit is the worst feature of their own caste system.[1] His approach to any aspect of life was scientific which means observation and experimentation; he used existing knowledge available to prove that the Indian caste system is an anomaly because it did not achieve any efficiency economically or otherwise in the society.

Politics has always been for power and Ambedkar knew that the high caste politics would ensure that the downtrodden will not be able to penetrate in the political system unless the whole conception of caste is wiped out from India. Though he framed the law that every person was equal before the law but he always maintained that the equality cannot be achieved unless every person could attain equality and equal status in the society. He believed that 'Equality before law' is not a solution at all because in the modern world of privatization and globalization the equality before law is of very little consequence. He dedicated his life to achieve social equality, which he could not imbibe in the constitution.

2.2 Ambedkar's View on Social, Economic& Political Reform.

The road leading to the destination of social reform is not a smooth ride rather it is filled with numerous hurdles. Social reform in India has less admirers and many critics, essentially falling in to two categories one being the political reformers and the other being the socialists. Ambedkar believed that without social efficiency no permanent progress in any other activity was possible. If one observes the Hindu society its state of affairs is saddening because caught between the shackles of evil customs and differences based upon caste, it is not in a state of efficiency and Ambedkar believed that relentless efforts must be taken to eradicate such evils and differences and to bring about a revolution in the society.

Eminent personalities like the Congress President W.C Bonnerji believed that political reforms do not have any bearing

1. ANNIHILATION OF CASTE, DR. AMBEDKAR REPRINTED BABA SAHEB AMBEDKAR WRITING AND SPEECHES, published by government of Maharashtra (1979).

upon the social reforms, quoting his speech from the Allahabad Conference of 1892:

"I for one have no patience with those who shall not be fit for the political reform until we reform our social system. I fail to see any connection between the two...Are we not fit (for political reform) because our widows remain unmarried and our girls are given in marriage earlier than in other countries? Because our wives and daughters do not drive with us visiting our friends?Because we do not send our daughters to Oxford and Cambridge?"[2]

But does this conclusively prove that social reform has no bearing on the political reforms? Ambedkar cited several incidents from the past to draw upon the treatment of untouchables to counter the arguments presented by the Congress President. The instances of the traumatizing past still loom in the present times. Citing the events of the past told by Ambedkar himself, where the untouchables during the Peshwas rule were not allowed to use the public streets if a Hindu was coming along, lest he would pollute the Hindu by his shadow. The scenes are not much different now, even after decades the difference still exists, though it's heartbreaking but the truth can be seen even in the elite educational institutions where modern education also failed to eliminate such boundaries.

Questioning the majoritarian rule by the upper class Hindus' Ambedkar said that how can they be fit for the exercise of political power when they do not allow a large class of their own countrymen like the untouchables to use the public places like wells and schools, and for how long shall these differences exist? Ambedkar strongly believed that let the political reformers drift to any direction they wish to, they will find that in the making of a constitution, they cannot ignore the problem arising out the existing social order. However one should not suppose that political reform and social reform have limited bearing upon each other. History stands as evidence to the proposition that political revolutions have always

2. B. R AMBEDKAR, ANNIHILATION OF CASTE, Critical Quest Publication (2007 ed.)

been preceded by social and religious revolutions. Ambedkar supported this argument by retelling the histories of various nations around the globe. The religious reform started by Luther was the precursor of the political upliftment of the European people. In England Puritarianism led to the establishment of political liberty, which further helped in the foundation of the New World. Considering the Arab example, where Prophet Mohammad underwent series of thorough religious movements before the Arabs could proclaim themselves as one of the biggest political powers. Even the Indian Scenario supports the conclusion drawn by Ambedkar, Chandragupta Mauryas' rule was preceded by religious and political revolution brought about by the emergence of Buddhism. Guru Nanak brought about religious and social revolutions within the Sikh community which then lead to the political emancipation of the Sikhs. Recounting history anymore would be a futile exercise because these examples are enough to suffice that political emancipation the people is not possible to attain without the liberation of the mind and soul of the individuals.

2.3 Fallacy of the Socialists :

According to Ambedkar, Socialists in India walk upon the footsteps of their fellow counterparts in Europe and they seek to interpret Indian factual history by using tools of economics and hence resulting in economic interpretation of the Indian factual history. The socialists preach that property is the only source of power by the virtue of man being an economic animal hence his activities and aspirations are bound by economic facts. Therefore the socialists propound that political and social reforms are nothing but mere illusions and real reformation lies in economic emancipation of the masses by equalization of property which will prevail over any other kind of reformation. However one may contend that economic motive is not the only motive which activates the human society. If such had been the case then why do millionaires find their shelters under the guidance of some penniless Sadhu? Why the rich escape to places like Benaras or Himalayas to find their solace under the charm of a half -naked

Fakir? This proves that social status of an individual by itself is a source of power which might be devoid of economic soundness of the individual.

The fallacy of the socialists lies in drawing a parallel between the European Society where property as a source of power is predominant and the Indian Society. What they fail to understand is that it's not only the property which brings about power but religion and social status too are sources of power and authority, where essentially a man has control over the liberty of another. One might be predominant in one stage and the other is predominant in another stage. If liberty is the goal that we dream to achieve, liberty which essentially means when one man will break the domination of the other, then indeed it cannot be concluded that economic reform is the only means to achieve the end of liberty. If the social status and religion are essential attributes of power then social and economic reforms should come to the forefront, thus the doctrine of economic interpretation of the history adopted by the socialists can be countered in this manner. But the essential question which Ambedkar posed to the socialists was that: Can economic reform be obtained without bringing about reforms in the social structures? Is it enough to believe in perfect equality in the treatment of the various classes. The crux lies in the facts whether he minds one class succumbing to the tyranny and oppression by the other which will continue to divide one class from another. Well it can be concluded that the socialist ideal of economic reform cannot be obtained unless there is a social revolution resulting in a seizure of certain powers. It's obvious here that the seizure of power should come from the proletariat, but will the proletariats ever come together to achieve the socialistic goal of economic equality? Can it be said that the proletariat of India, recognizes no differences other than the differences based on economic standards? Can it be said that the poor themselves do not stand divided against the lines of caste or creed, high or low? When there are lines of differences everywhere, then on what front will the poor stand united against the rich? Even if by fortune's grace the socialist goal is achieved, will they then not have to deal with problems posed to them by the existing social order and structure, is what was questioned by Ambedkar back then against the propounders of Socialism. Ambedkar countered socialists by arguing that how a socialist state in India can function without having to struggle against the prejudices observed by the Indian people in maintaining their distinctions about high and low, clean and unclean etc. Ambedkar said that in order to make socialism a definite reality the socialists must first deal with problems of caste and social order. Quoting Ambedkar himself:

"The socialists will be compelled to take the account of caste after revolution if they do not take account of it before revolution. This is the only way of saying that, turn in any direction you like, caste is the monster that crosses your path. You cannot have political reform, you cannot have economic reform, you cannot have economic reform, unless you kill the monster."[3]

2.3a Ambedkars' View on Caste and Economic Efficiency :

It's a matter of deep shame that even after hundreds of years, even when we have entered into the age of modernity the caste system is still being followed in the rigid sense. It is a pity that, it is being defended in the name of "Division of labor" and it is well-known social principle that such a division is essential for an efficient society. But what we fail to realize is that caste is not only a division of labor but also is the "division of laborers'" themselves. It's rather unique to the Indian society where division of labor is accompanied by the gradation of the laborers'. Generally the division of labour is based on natural aptitudes but the Indian scenario differs hugely. This principle is essentially violated in the caste system, when the tasks are allocated on the basis on social status of the parents, which is positively pernicious.

It is natural for an industry to undergo changes, with such changes the individual must have the liberty to change his profession, without such liberty to adjust him to the changing circumstances the person will be left without any livelihood. The rigid caste

3. Supra note 7.

system of the Hindu society doesn't provide for the same. One cannot practice an occupation unless he belongs to it hereditarily. Ambedkar blames the rigid caste system as one of the root causes of large scale problem of unemployment, where a Hindu can better starve to death rather than be allowed to change his profession. Here the division of labour is not based on choice or preference rather it is pre destined. Hence it is one of the biggest social evils prevalent in the times of industrialization.

Another characteristic of the Hindu society is that, there are many professions which are degraded by the society itself. Such is the condition that, those practicing it wish to escape it. Here quoting Ambedkar again:

"What efficiency can there be in a system under which neither men's hearts nor their minds are in their work? As an economic organization caste is therefore a harmful institution, in as much as, it involves the subordination of man's natural powers and inclinations to the exigencies of social rules."[4]

2.4 Ideals of a Caste-less Society

For Ambedkar an ideal society was one which was based on 'Liberty, Equality and Fraternity'. Ambedkar associates the idea of fraternity with that of democracy. By democracy Ambedkar doesn't mean a form of state but a form of associated living, an attitude of respect and reverence towards your fellow beings. Ambedkar held that the followers of the caste system, would not believe in the ideals of liberty because it would also mean liberty in choosing ones profession. But such an objection is a clear indication about the perpetuation of slavery; which essentially represents a form of society wherein a group of men would exercise the control over the conduct of their fellow beings. Ambedkar held the view that equitable treatment of humans is desirable that is true, but this also should not be forgotten that humans themselves are not equipped enough to classify or assort amongst their fellow beings. Quoting Ambedkar:

"The statesman must follow some rough and ready rule is to treat all men alike not because they are alike but because classification

4. Supra note 7.

and assortment is impossible. The doctrine of equality is glaringly fallacious but taking all in all it is the only way a statesman can proceed in politics which is a severely practical affair and which demands a severely practical test."[5]

2.5 Ambedkar's Deweyan Buddha

The life and works of Ambedkar is nothing but a reflection of the influence of the teachings of his professor of philosophy at Columbia University, one of the nation's best- known public intellectuals, a positive pragmatist by nature. As one scholar says, "Unless we understand something of John Dewey...it would be impossible to understand Dr. Ambedkar."[6] This influence ran through his writings as well as the strategies and tactics he formulated.[7] There is plenty in Dewey's writings to suggest that he would have seen such valorization of experience as an 'immunizing strategy by which the rationales of oppression in other culture can be protected from criticism.'[8] Dewey considered oppression as an experience, a means of enriching oneself with various subjective experiences loaded with not just controlled inference but also intelligence. For Dewey the proper contrast is 'not between experience and reason, but between experience that is funded by the procedures and results of intelligent activity, and experience that is not.[9]

Dewey was a positive pragmatist, he believed science cannot be adjudicated by questioning its origin or antecedents rather by reasoning the consequences, success in predictions and controlling the track of nature. According to him human are imbibed with rationality and it is what continued to form modern science. Quoting Dewey:

---

5. B. R AMBEDKAR, ANNIHILATION OF CASTE, Critical Quest Publication (2007 ed.).
6. K N KADAM, "DRAMBEDKAR'S PHILOSOPHY OF EMANCIPATION AND THE IMPACT OF JOHN DEWEY" IN THE MEANING OF AMBEDKARITE CONVERSION TO BUDDHISM AND OTHER ESSAYS (Mumbai: Popular Prakashaned., 1997).
7. ARUN P MUKHERJEE, B R AMBEDKAR, JOHN DEWEY AND THE MEANING OF DEMOCRACY, New Literary History 345-70 (2009 ed.).
8. Id.
9. Id.

"Science had institutionalized doubt by converting it into a positive ethic of inquiry- what is called "scientific attitude' or 'scientific temper' defined as 'the will to inquire, to examine, to discriminate, to draw conclusions only on the basis of evidence after taking pains to collect all available evidence."

In order to understand Dewey conceptualization of science lets re quote him:-

"The data of science are not 'the given' but rather 'the taken' that is, they are selected from the totality of experiences by socially embedded human beings, with the express purpose of finding clues to the solution o the problem at hand."

But what is important for the purpose of this essay is to understand the pertinence of the questions about scientific temper and place of science while dealing with a casteless society and religious conversions. The relation between the two is quite deep, because it was scientific reasoning which made Ambedkar's Buddha a sacred figure for the oppressed masses. And it was John Dewey who gave Ambedkar a mould of scientific reasoning into which he cast the image of Buddha.[10] In order to understand and appreciate the intricacies involved in the principles behind Amedkars' Buddha its' important to understand its root causes which lie in the delusions in various folds of Hinduism. As we have discussed above the upper class hindus' discriminate the other classes on the basis of the occupation practiced by them, because these occupation are seen with aversion andsuch classes are banned from participating in activities of everyday life. Such an attitude is seen amongst the upper class not because they are inhuman and take pleasure in oppressing their fellow beings, but because they have a strong religious temperament. The root cause of this caste based discrimination lies in our Shasthras, it is true that the society will not change its conduct unless the masses cease to believe in the sanctity of the Shasthras. The fault is not of the people who follow it but of the Shasthras which preach this.

---

10. MEERA NANDA, PROPHET FACING FORWARD, Critical Quest (2006 ed.).

The turn towards Buddha and ancient non- Brahmin philosophies was in part an attempt to find a cultural homologue for materialist and skeptical traditions in India's minority non-Vedic traditions.[11] Ambedkar recognized that the experience of oppression has also left them deformed and in need of repair: 'tolerance of insults and tyranny... has killed the sense of retort and revolt. Vigor and ambition have completely vanished , the people have become helpless, unenergetic and pale and everywhere there is an atmosphere of defeatism and pessimism...'[12] After being subjected to years of oppression, the realization was drawn upon the untouchables that the greater interests lie in annihilating caste than modernizing it. The roots of the caste system had strong grasp over the Hindu society; it is why Ambedkar felt socialism in India would turn out to be just a dream, unless social reforms are carried out.

Ambedkar's Buddha teaches how to bridge the gap between facts and values, between how we know the world we live in and how we treat our fellow beings.[13] In a changing society, there must be a constant revolution of old values and Hindus must realize that if there must be standards to measure the acts and men, there must also be readiness to revise those standards.[14]

Undoubtedly the conversion into Buddhism gave the untouchables a new identity combined with self-confidence, purified from old superstitions and rigid rituals and gave rise to a new culture. Many autobiographical accounts and sociological studies attest to the changes: replacing old idols, fasts, and ceremonies with readings from The Buddha and His Dharma, an explosion of creative expression of new rationalist and with a growing sense of self-worth and pride.[15] Buddhists have achieved a new identity, symbolized by their change of name. The new optimism is strongly

11. Id.
12. AHIR, SELECTED SPEECHES OF AMBEDKAR, Bluemoon books (1997 ed.).
13. MEERA NANDA, PROPHET FACING FORWARD, Critical Quest (2006 ed.).
14. Supra note 8..
15. MOON VASANTH, GROWING UP UNTOUCHABLE IN INDIA, New York, Rowmen and Littlefield (2007 ed.).

connected to ideas about self- reliance, rejection of the old Hindu values and a rational approach to their own self development.[16] Fitzgerald finds that the educated, politically mobilized minority among neo Buddhists take the scientific temper of the Buddhist teachings into their lives.

2.6 Ambedkar on Minorities of the Indian Society.

The highest aim of a society, Ambedkar believed, was the "growth of personality".[17] A liberal society is duty bound to give enough liberty to each individual to assume any socially desirable role that he finds suitable for himself. For Ambedkar, democracy was the political form best suited to bringing about the kind of just society he envisioned. But governments required people to take on different social roles, he argued, which tended "to develop the personality of the few at the cost of the many", something that was antithetical to democracy.[18] Ambedkar understood Indian society wasn't one which was made for individuals but rather one for the communities. Though our colonial masters believe unity as one nation would be a dream, as we were divided on many fronts such as caste, creed, religion, language etc. But our nationalists believe that inspite of all dividing lines, the one thread which bound us together was the cultural and geographical togetherness.

But Ambedkar was not swayed away by his fellow nationalists, he strongly believed that social divisions in our society are deep rooted and cannot be done away with so easily. Democracy was not just a principle which was to be followed, but it was a necessary social condition for the people to reside together in a single community. However, he said, "men live in a community by virtue of the things they have in common ...aims, beliefs, aspirations, knowledge, a common understanding".[19] This common understanding or the like-mindedness was essential for the people

16. TIMOTHY FITZGERALD, 1994, BUDDHISM IN MAHARASHTRA: A TRIPARTITE ANALYSIS, B R Publishing Co., (2001 ed.).
17. B. R AMBEDKAR, DR BABA SAHEBAMBEDKAR WRITINGS AND SPEECHES, Bombay: Education Department, Government of Maharashtra.
18. Id.
19. Id.

to live in a community. People did not become like-minded simply by living in proximity, nor did they lose this shared sensibility through distance.[20] But what is essential to understand here is that, through participation in a group the people develop shared values, sentiments and qualities. Communication and participation between groups, Ambedkar believed, was "essential for a harmonious life, social or political", but in India there was no such participation. Hindus, Muslims, Christians, Parsis, and Jews, each had their own like-mindedness, isolating them from the others, and it was this isolation that was "the chief evil".[21] Moreover, the Hindus were further divided by caste, castes had their own like-mindedness and were so divided from each other as to make the term "Hindu" practically meaningless.[22] But the deepest lines of divide was between that of the 'touchable' and that of 'untouchables'. It was because of this social disparity that Ambedkar had asked for a separate electorate for the so called, 'untouchables' during the 1919 reforms committee.

And where, there existed divisions and disparities in the social order, how can democracy sustain in such a society? For where a democracy had a formula of one person, one vote, with the majority opinion carrying the day, in India, people's political sympathies were determined by their community rather than by secular concerns.[23] Thus, he asked, how could one know if an elected candidate would represent the interests of all the members of his territorial constituency rather than simply those of his community?; moreover, in an election, if two candidates belonging to different groups claimed to represent the same issue, a voter would mark the ballot of the person belonging to his community rather than any other.[24] But if a situation arises where in larger body of voter, will belong to a particular community, then they

20. ShabnumTejani, The Necessary Conditions for Democracy, XLVIII, Economic &Political Weekly (2013).
21. Supra note18.
22. Supra note 19.
23. Supra note 18.
24. Supra note 25.

would ensure that the candidate of their community comes into power. The polarization and the communalization of the society will make the minority community a vulnerable one. The democratic formula left minorities "without any chance of personal representation".[25] For a government to be "popular", it had to be not only for the people, but by the people. Thus, separate electorates for untouchables were necessary to ensure their personal representation.[26] He believed that although electorates should be structured to reflect the communal divisions in India, their effect would not perpetuate these divisions, but, in bringing people who would not normally meet into public service, it would foster a new like-mindedness - "if the Hindus become resocialised with regard to their attitude towards Mohammedans, Christians, etc, and the Mohammedans, Christians, etc, become resocialised with regard to their attitudes towards the Hindus, or the touchable Hindus with regard to the untouchables, caste and divisions will vanish".[27] We can essentially infer that these separate electorates were formed with the intent of protecting the minorities institutionally.

For Ambedkar no democracy can survive without the protection of the minority interests. Minority safeguards were required, he wrote, because unlike in the British system of government where the majority was constituted by political opinion, "in India the majority is a communal majority"[28] India would be ruled by an exclusive class that could run the administration according to its own ideas, violating every principle of just government - "Such a state of affairs could not be called democracy. It will have to be called imperialism".[29] On the point that reservations undermined national unity, Ambedkar was scathing he retorted back electorates had "nothing to do with the religious or communal nexus", they were "but a mechanism to enable a minority to return its true representative to the Legislature"[30] Minorities demanded reservation

25. Supra note 18.
26. Id.
27. Supra note 25.
28. Id.
29. Id.
30. Id.

in order to safeguard their interests, their voices were left unheard for ages as the majority(belonging to the Hindu upper castes) had monopolized both the public as well as the political sphere, and they chose to ignore the tormented voices of the oppressed lower caste minorities. Reservation will bring about new hopes amongst these oppressed classes by ensuring a legitimate political participation hence inculcating the values of national unity. Quoting Ambedkar:

"Unfortunately for the minorities in India, Indian Nationalism has developed a new doctrine which may be called the Divine Right of the Majority to rule the minorities according to the wishes of the majority. Any claim for the sharing of power by the minority is called communalism while the monopolising of the whole power by the majority is called Nationalism. Guided by such a political philosophy the majority is not prepared to allow the minorities to share political power nor is it willing to respect any convention made in that behalf as is evident from their repudiation of the obligation (to include representatives of the minorities in the cabinet) contained in the ... Government of India Act of 1935. [31]"

2.7 Ambedkar on Women Empowerment

Caste and gender are linked together by intrinsic lines, Ambedkar was the first one to understand this. According to Ambedkar there exists a vicious cycle between women being oppressed and caste being perpetuated; with the underlying fears of miscegenation and being carried forward with the strict rules of endogamy. Though restrictions on the liberty of women is not something just unique to the Indian Society, but Hinduism itself perpetuates this vicious cycle by placing stringent restrictions on women and their sexuality in order claim the purity of caste. Controlling their sexuality was just a means to achieve the end of caste purity by making the women of higher caste un-accessible to the men of lower caste. The evils of child marriage, confinement within four walls and restrictions in work sphere, compulsory

31. Supra note 25.

ascetic widowhood, veiling and even sati are results of the rigid caste system and meeting the goal to protect endogamy.

Ambedkar revealed these intrinsic ties between these social evils and caste practices during his days in the Columbia University. Later in his days as the country's first law minister he advocated for the reformation of the personal laws with special emphasis on the marriage laws like ensuring right of divorce for women, declaring polygamy as illegal, legalizing of inter-caste marriages etc. He being a progressive pragmatist, he understood without special provisions for the emancipation of the women in the private sphere, the constitutional procedure of caste equality will only remain as a theoretical goal.

It must be mentioned that dalit movements have shown sufficient solidarity with the women movements seeking for greater autonomy. These can be seen in the movements of Pandita Ramabai, Phule and Periyar. Only Phule and his anti-caste movement defended Ramabai, Phule like Ambedkar was able to connect Ramabai's critique of the religious ideas and ideals that justified women's oppression to the scriptural justifications for the caste hierarchy.[32] The uniqueness of these protests lie in their approach towards reasoning, rationality and science, like the Weberian plowshares of mind or much essentially like that of Deweyan-Buddhist. The scientific and rational approach of these movements made these revolutionaries question the unreasonable rituals, taboos, myths etc. They propounded the principles of secularizations of the imagination. To the extent these dalit modernists do privilege the 'proto-scientific' aspects of it, which are rooted in manipulation and control of nature in the process of production, which was the province of the laboring castes. [33]

The constitutional goal of achieving equality by eliminating all kinds of disparity on the basis of caste, creed &gender remains

32. UMA CHAKRAVARTHI, REWRITING HISTORY: THE LIFE AND TIMES OF PANDITARAMABAI, New Delhi, Penguin Books (1997 ed.).

33. KANCHAILAIAH, TOWARD THE DALITIZATION OF THE NATION, IN WAGES OF FREEDOM: FIFTY YEARS OF THE NATION, OUP (1998 ed.).

like an unachievable dream. But undoubtedly the democratic structure, right to vote, modern economy has largely affected the socio-political basis of the caste based social order. With the secularization of the imaginations of the masses, there was a secularization of the ideologies. Hence with the spreading of such secular ideas only a handful of die hard followers justified the karma-dharma based caste system.

The rules of exogamy are so rigid that any infringement or violation invites rigorous penalties; over this exogamous society is overlaid the principle of endogamy.[34] There is a difference between racial or tribal endogamy where the universe is large and coterminous with cultural homogeneity, and caste endogamy where a homogeneous population is split into mutually exclusive units within which both the principles of exogamy and endogamy operate in all their rigidity this "superimposition of endogamy on exogamy means the creation of caste".[35] But clearly it is far from easy to reconcile the principle of endogamy with the principle of exogamy. For this to be possible, there must be in place complex rules of marriage that take account of the difficulties in maintaining an even sex ratio among persons of marriageable age from marriageable groups within a caste: "the problem of caste, then ultimately resolves itself into one of repairing the disparity between the marriageable units of the two sexes within it".[36] Imbalances in the sex ratio arising from the death of a spouse within a caste-"surplus women" and "surplus men"-then are dealt with in one of three ways: a surplus woman may be burnt on her husband's funeral pyre.[37] She may then be subjected to enforced widowhood but this is not easy either because she may still be attractive enough to threaten the morals of the group.[38] The second solution then lay in enforced widow hood with the

34. KALPANAKANNABIRAN, SOCIOLOGY OF CASTE AND THE CROOKED MIRROR: RECOVERING B R AMBEDKAR'S LEGACY, Economic &Politica lWeekly (2009 ed.).

35. AMBEDKAR B R,CASTES IN INDIA IN VALERIAN RODRIGUES, OUP (2009 ed.).

36. Id.

37. Id.

38. Id.

widow being stripped bare of anything that might be construed as a source of allurement.[39] Quoting Ambedkar;

"A surplus man could not be burnt on the funeral pyre of his wife "simply because he is a man" and a person who wields authority "as a maker of injunctions...".Nor could he be condemned to celibacy, because he is an asset to the group. The only way balance can be maintained with reference to a surplus man is to find him a wife from girls below marriageable age, so that the balance in the marriageable cohort is not disturbed. Sati, enforced widowhood, and girl marriage are the three mechanisms through which endogamy, and by extension caste is preserved and perpetuated."[40]

The fulcrum of Ambedkar's argument is that castes are born and thrive through the use of gendered violence, patriarchal relations within castes and exclusionary processes between castes.[41] Membership within the caste is controlled and regulated through the use of sati, enforced widowhood and girl marriage and in a radical departure from the reform position, Ambedkar's articulation of these issues ties the question of the annihilation of caste to the rejection of women's subjugation within caste.[42] The anti-social spirit, in Ambedkar's view, which pushes a group to protect its own interests by shutting out other castes, "is as much a feature of the different castes in their isolation from one another as it is of nations".[43]

2.8 Ambedkar on Nationalism:

Ambedkar believed that the ideology of nationalism propounded by Gandhi, Congress and other political parties like Hindu Mahasabha was nothing but propagation of communalism at the hands of the majority. Before plunging deeper into the issue, one must understand Ambedkarian perspective of what is a nation? "Nationality is a social feeling. It is a feeling of corporate sentiment of oneness which makes those who are charged with it feel that they are kith and kin".[44] It is a feeling simultaneously

39. Id.
40. Supra note 45.
41. Supra note 42.
42. Id.
43 Supra note 42.
44. Supra at 25.

of inclusion, "a feeling of fellowship", and exclusion, "anti-fellowship".[45] Its ties are so strong that they supersede class differences and separate "those who are not of their kind". Nationality, for Ambedkar, also involved a deep emotional tie, "a longing not to belong to any other group".[46] One must wonder that what can foster such sentiments, a common culture, values, language, past etc were very essentially in invoking the feeling of patriotism.

However, even after this debate one question remains unanswered -did the Hindus and Muslims compose one nation? Had a shared race, language and culture "fostered in them a feeling that they long to belong to each other?"[47] According to Ambedkar, it was not so. Quoting from Ernest Renan's essay on nationality, he wrote that race should not be confused with nation - "human history is essentially different from zoology", in which race tended to lose its importance.[48] Rather, Renan pointed to the importance of "a common possession of a rich heritage of memories" and "actual consent, the desire to live together, the will to preserve ... the undivided inheritance which has been handed down".[49] But then again a question arises, whether the Hindus and Muslims share any common historical past/memory where they shared a sense of joy? Any matter of pride? Any matter of sorrow? Ambedkar again denied to this, as there was no common achievements. There was no common historical memory, according to Ambedkar, thus "the things that divide are far more vital than the things which unite".[50] Equally, "forgetfulness" of past divisions was as important as remembering what was common to forge a national identity.[51] Yet Ambedkar believed that this would be impossible for the two communities as their pasts were tied to their religion and to hope that either would give up their religion

45. Supra at 28.
46. Supra at 25.
47. Id.
48. Id.
49. Id.
50. Id.
51. Supra note 25.

was "to hope in vain".[52] For nationality to exist there needed to be more than a common race, language or culture. There needed to be a "spiritual essence", a tie of kinship. Above all, it required "the will to live as a nation".[53] However, Ambedkar's support for the reorganisation of states along linguistic lines came from the belief that they would create "social homogeneity" and thus "make democracy work better".[54] A heterogeneous society would be divided from within.[55] In a democratic framework this would surely lead to inequities, "cases of discrimination, neglect, partiality, suppression of the interests of one group at the hands of another group which happens to capture political power".[56] A homogeneous society was better suited to democracy for there would be no social hostilities to encourage an abuse of power by a single group.[57]

India's communal character meant that there would always be one group that became a dominant class and sought to subordinate those weaker in number and social position. The only way around this was to move people out of one region into another where there was a closer social congruence.[58]

Ambedkar's solution was to have "one state, one language", each state should be a linguistic unit, but to avoid the pitfalls of creating further nationalisms, the regional language could not be the official language of the state, which had to be Hindi.[59] Thus the administrative unit should be the linguistic state but the administrative language should be shared across the nation.[60]

Ambedkar's argument to transfer populations between states to engineer ethnic and linguistic homogeneity is at odds with any formulation of liberal government.[61] That linguistic states,

52. Id.
53. Supra note 25.
54. Id.
55. Id.
56. Id.
57. Id.
58. Id.
59. Id.
60. AMBEDKAR, THOUGHTS ON LINGUISTIC STATESIN BAWS, Vol 1, Bombay: Education Department, Government of Maharashtra.
61. Supra note 25.

even after population transfers, would contain minorities was to be expected-"in every area there will always be one community which by its numbers happens to be a dominant community" and which, by virtue of this "becomes a sole heir to all political power which the area gets".[62]

2.9 Conclusion

Messiah or emancipator for many, Bhimrao Ramji Ambedkar being a progressive pragmatist, he advocated thought process to be channelized towards solutions. Like Buddha he wanted each individual to be enlightened and awakened by his own forte. He was of firm belief that political upliftment of Indian society is not possible without liberation of Indian mind-set. He was very critical of Indian socialists who concentrated merely on the economic emancipation for political and social reforms. Contrary to their ideas Ambedkar believed in reformation in caste and social structures for such emancipation. His idea was to create a modern Indian society based on principles of liberty and equality. His views on rigid caste system as a basis of economic decline in India have been proved beyond doubts.

He also believed that for social emancipation of India women empowerment is essential. He reasoned that caste system in India has been built on the facets of discrimination, patriarchal relations and gender bias. Caste has used tolls like sati, widowhood and child marriage to fire its needs. His idea ties social emancipation of India invariably with that of women empowerment.

On the front of nationality he advocated that for nationality to exist there needed to be more than a common race, language or culture. He advocated for spiritual ties and will to live as a nation as essential requirements of nationalism. Ambedkar's solution for a unified India was one state one language policy. He believed that this would result in unifying states under one language that is Hindi. After going through all his life works we have to decide what we will take from his life, We must strive to understand core value of Dr. Ambedkar's life which stands as his legacy.

---

62. Id.

3

Dr. Ambedkar-His Social Philosophy and its Relevance

- Basava Prasad Kunale &Kaushik Basu***

3.1 Introduction

Dr. Ambedkar, who is considered to be the author of our Indian Constitution, a strong nonconformist, says in his daily newspaper "Mooknayak", the dumb hero[1] ,

"Swaraj wherein there were no fundamental rights guaranteed to the depressed classes would not be the swaraj. For them it would be new kind of slavery."

This statement of Babasaheb, sums up the ideology he followed, the ideology of 'Social Equality'. He felt that more than political freedom we need to have social freedom, we need to have a society where equality is guaranteed to every member, irrespective of whether it is religious, social, political or economic. He would even go on to contend that if the Caste Hindus are justified in fighting the British for their political rights, then the depressed classes are thousand times more justified in fighting the caste system to achieve their social justice. He felt that political independence would not only be detrimental to the depressed classes but would be a great disaster to India.[2] He felt that each diverse community or each group in India, which is suffering

*Basawa Prasad Kunale,Third Year law B.A.LLB ,Gujarat National Law University ,Gandhinagar.

** KaushikBabu, Third Year law B.A.LLB ,Gujarat National Law University ,Gandhinagar.

1. DHANANJAYKEER, DR. AMBEDKAR: LIFE & MISSION 42 (3rd ed., 1971)
2. Christophe Jaffrelot, Dr. Ambedkar's Strategies Against Untouchabilty And The Caste System, Indian Institute Of Dalit Studies, (July. 06, 2015, 03:30 PM), available at: http://www.dalitstudies.org.in/wp/0904.pdf.

from many of the disabilities like untouchability, religious tension, low representation, political control etc., would be able to consolidate itself at each stage, in the transfer of power from the British. This would help the Indian society to be stronger, which ultimately will help the country to become politically and economically powerful. This is the reason why he denounced the idea of Swaraj, the independence.[3]

There is difference between colonialism and imperialism. Colonialism refers to the process wherein a foreign country establishes its political control in other country and frames policies and laws which favour their own country. Under colonialism, there might be situation where the ruling country may also frame policies which will benefit the ruled country and colonialism indirectly may also help in achieving unity and fraternity among the people of the ruled country.[4] Like for example, it was because of the entry of British in India that led to proper education system, which helped in spreading the ideas of the West, of revolution and egalitarian society. Though most of the policies of British were detrimental to India, some of the policies taught Indians the systematic functioning of any institution.[5]

Imperialism is much more barbaric and ruthless control of small handful of elite class over the larger servitude class. Imperialism can be exercised by the people among one's own country. It is a further form of colonialism, where the thought process of the members of the society is completely controlled. The people are not given any chance of having a life of dignity. The policies and

---

3. Ramdas V., Ambedkar And National Politics, Department Of Adult Education And Extention Service, Calicut, (July. 06, 2015, 03:40 PM), available at: http://shodhganga.inflibnet.ac.in:8080/jspui/bitstream/10603/28174/11/11_chapter%206.pdf.

4. Prabhat S., Difference Between Colonialism And Imperialism, Difference Between.net (July. 06, 2015, 03:40 PM), available at: http://www.differencebetween.net/miscellaneous/difference-between-colonialism-and-imperialism/.

5. Rayan Brown, The British Empire In India, Ashbrook (July. 06, 2015, 03:40 PM), available at: http://ashbrook.org/wp-content/uploads/2012/06/2010-Brown.pdf.

law framed are of such a nature that it leads to a loss for a huge number of people.[6]

The caste system can be said to be an ideology which is imperialistic, in nature. The unique Indian caste system oppressed more than half of the humankind in India, forcing them to live in filth and completely denied their life and liberty. This graded institution named a group of community as "untouchables" and denied them every basic human right. Their social status was not recognised at all. Every member of the society was known by his caste rather than his character and personality, by virtue of this system.

Dr. Ambedkar strived to destroy this imperialism of caste, as an institution. On the Indian Caste system, Dr. Ambedkar says,[7]

"One caste enjoys singing a hymn of hate against another song as much as the Germans did in singing their hymn of hate against the English during the last war. The literature of Hindus is full of caste genealogies in which an attempt is made to give a noble origin to one caste and an ignoble to other caste." And further goes on to say that,

"This anti-social sprit is not confined to caste alone. It has gone deeper and has poisoned the mutual relations of the sub castes as well. In my province the Golak Brahmins, Deorukha Brahmins, Karada Brahmins, Palshe Brahmins, and Chitpavan Brahmins all claim to be sub-divisions of the Brahmin caste. But the anti-social spirit that prevails between them is quite as marked and quite as virulent as the anti-social spirit that prevails between them and other non-Brahmin castes. There is nothing strange in this.An anti-social spirit is found wherever one group has "interest

---

6. Prabhat S., Difference Between Colonialism And Imperialism, Difference Between.net (July. 06, 2015, 03:40 PM), available at: http://www.differencebetween.net/miscellaneous/difference-between-colonialism-and-imperialism/.

7. Dr. Ambedkar, The Annihilation of Caste, Columbia Center For New Media Teaching And Learning (Aug. 23, 2014, 10:04 AM), available at: http://ccnmtl.columbia.edu/projects/mmt/ambedkar/.

of its own" which shut it out from full interaction with other groups, so that its prevailing purpose is protection of what it's got. This anti social spirit, this spirit of its own protection is as much a marked feature of the different castes in their isolation from one another as it is of nations in their isolation."

He believed that it was necessary to establish a society which is based on the ideals of 'Liberty, Equality and Fraternity'. He would also justify his stand, that he borrowed this idea not from the French revolution which was fought for the same ideals, but from the religious revolution of Buddha. He felt that for the society to remain strong either sanction of law or sanction of morality, should be there and in all societies law plays a very small part, people might not accept the law, therefore it is the morality which holds the society together and this morality can be achieved through religion, the religion which has morality as its base and only Buddhism has morality as its base.[8]

This distinctive ideology of Babasaheb forces us to look at his background, to see what impact it had on him to have such unique thinking. Dr. Ambedkar, was born in Mahar caste, an "untouchable" community, on 14th April, 1891 in Mhow village, MadhyaPradesh. He faced caste discrimination till his last breath. During his childhood he would have to ask his elder sister to cut his hair, as the barber would refuse to touch him, because of the caste he was born in.[9]

The most famous incident that changed Dr. Ambedkar's perspective of thought and to fight for justice, was when he was just 9-11 years old. He was to visit his father along with his brother. The location of his father's work place was far from the railway station, and no cart man was willing to take them on a bullock cart. One cart man agreed with the condition that the boys would have to drive the cart while he would sit behind. Throughout this escapade which lasted through the night, the

8. SANGHARAKSHITA, AMBEDKAR AND BUDDHISM 76 (1st South Asian ed., 2006).
9. DHANANJAYKEER, DR. AMBEDKAR: LIFE & MISSION 13 (3rd ed., 1971).

boys went hungry because they could not get pure water to drink, even though they had plenty of food. Their inability to get water was of course due to the fact that untouchables were barred from using public wells. This incident had a very important place in Dr. Ambedkar's life and it left an indelible impression on his mind.[10]

Another life event which made him fight against the caste system was when he went to Baroda after being appointed as the Military Secretary to the Baroda State. Though highly educated but an "untouchable" he could not get accommodation in Baroda. He found a quarter in a Parsi boarding house and assumed a Parsi name, so that no one would recognize him. At work, the Brahman clerks and subordinates kept their distance and threw files and papers on him to avoid his touch. In the club, he was not allowed to take part in games. No clear assignment was given to him, though he was a Military Secretary. When the Parsis discovered his identity, they threatened to beat him and forced him to leave the place. These events in Dr. Ambedkar's life did not make him weak or force him to accept the oppression, but instead every single incident of discrimination and injustice in his life made him stronger and encouraged him to fight against the system.[11]

He was a critique of M.K. Gandhi, who propagated for political freedom and wanted to establish an Indian society based on the Varnashram Dharma, the Sanskrit word for the Indian caste system.[12] Gandhi was a strong protagonist of the caste system, he would call upon the Hindus to follow the Varna system, he said

"The law of Varna teaches us that we have each one of us to earn our bread by following the ancestral calling. It defines not our rights but out duties. It necessarily has reference to callings

10. Id. at 12.
11. DHANANJAYKEER, DR. AMBEDKAR: LIFE & MISSION 34 (3rd ed., 1971).
12. M.K. Gandhi (Complied By R.K.Prabhu), India of My Dreams, Bombay SarvodayaMandal& Gandhi Reserch Foundation (July. 06, 2015, 10:04 AM) available at: http://www.mkgandhi.org/ebks/india_dreams.pdf.

that are conductive to the welfare of humanity and to no other. It also follows that there is no calling too low and none too high. All are good, lawful and equal in status. The calling of a Brahmin-spiritual teacher- and a scavenger are equal, and their due performance carries equal merit before the God and at one time seems to have carried identical reward before man."[13]

Maybe such statements made by Gandhi, forced Dr. Ambedkar to say "There have been many Mahatmas in India whose sole object was to remove untouchability and to elevate and absorb the depressed Classes, but every one of them has failed in his mission. Mahatmas have come, Mahatmas have gone. But the Untouchables have remained as Untouchables."[14] To critically evaluate the statement of Gandhi, there is too much flaw in it. To decide one's life based on the ancestral calling is very much impracticable. Each individual is unique and has his own way of looking at life and trying to achieve his or her goal, the society or religious texts, cannot impose upon the individual to live a particular way of life, which is detrimental to his personal development, this is nothing but suppressing the creativity and individuality of a man.

The Varnashram Dharma of Gandhi is an imperfect ideology, not suited for a progressive society. The theory of Gandhi is based on the idea that the society must be static and under his theory there is no room for change. Society needs to change, whether positively or negatively; it cannot remain static all the time. Through negative change in the society, the path of positive change opens up and an egalitarian society can be established, and through positive change, the path leads to perfection. Therefore we need have constant change in the society, there must be new ideas evolving every time and based on these ideas the society develops. The VarnashramDharma is completely opposite to this idea of

13. Dr. Ambedkar, The Annihilation of Caste, Columbia Center For New Media Teaching And Learning (Aug. 23, 2014, 10:04 AM) http://ccnmtl.columbia.edu/projects/mmt/ambedkar/.

14. Siddhartha Dash, Dr. B.R. Ambedkar: The Messiah of the Downtrodden, E-Magzine Orissa Review (Aug, 23rd, 2014, 11:00AM), available at: http://orissa.gov.in/e-magazine/Orissareview/2011/may/engpdf/31-33.pdf.

change; it thrusts upon the society to live in the same old primitive way of living. Dr. Ambedkar criticized this VarnashramDharma, where the ancestral calling is to be followed, he says,

"Everybody wants social stability and some adjustment must be made in the relationship between individuals and classes in order that stability may be had. But two things, I am sure nobody wants. One thing nobody wants is static relationship, something that is unalterable, something that is fixed for all times. Stability is wanted but not at the cost of change when it is imperative. Second thing nobody wants is mere adjustment. Adjustment is wanted but not at the sacrifice of social justice. Can it be said that the adjustment of social relationship on the basis of caste i.e. on the basis of each to his hereditary calling avoids these two evils? I am convinced that it does not. Far from being the best possible adjustment I have no doubt that it is of the worst possible kind inasmuch as it offends against both the canons of social adjustment- namely fluidity and equity."[15]

His idea of fighting the social freedom instead of political freedom is very unique. He used the help of British to fight the caste system and protect the human rights of the depressed classes, rather than fighting colonial power to establish political democracy in the country.[16] His acceptance of invitation to the discussion with Simon Commission and 1st Round Table Conference led to furious anger among the masses in India, who were fighting for political freedom. Dr. Ambedkar was called as British Stooge,[17] However, a man of great character as he was, Babasaheb never bothered about these tags and names and carried on his work of achieving justice. Dr. Ambedkar replied very strongly, to these allegations, when he said,

15. Dr. Ambedkar, The Annihilation of Caste, Columbia Center For New Media Teaching And Learning (Aug. 23, 2014, 10:04 AM) http://ccnmtl.columbia.edu/projects/mmt/ambedkar/.

16. CHRISTOPHEJAFFRELOT, DR. AMBEDKAR AND UNTOUCHABILITY: ANALYSING AND FIGHTING CASTE 95 (1st ed., 2000).

17. DHANANJAYKEER, DR. AMBEDKAR: LIFE & MISSION 116 (3rd ed., 1971).

"I hate injustice, tyranny, pompousness and humbug, and my hatred embraces all those who are guilty of them. I want to tell my critics that I regard my feelings of hatred as a real force. They are only the reflex of the love I bear for the causes I believe in, and I am in no wise ashamed of it. For these reasons I tender no apology for my criticism of Mr. Gandhi and Mr. Jinnah, the two men who have brought India's political progress to a standstill" and concludes, by saying,

"However strong and however filthy be the abuses which the Congress Press chooses to shower on me, I must do my duty I am no worshiper of idols. I believe in breaking them. I insist that if I hate Mr. Gandhi and Mr. Jinnah-I dislike them, I do not hate them-it is because I love India more. That is the true faith of a nationalist. I have hopes that my countrymen will someday learn that the country is greater than the men, that the worship of Mr. Gandhi or Mr. Jinnah and service to India are two very different things and may even be contradictory of each other."[18]

3.2 The Philosophy of Conversion

Hinduism has a peculiar social structure called the Chaturvarnya. It is an institution which is based on the idea of inequality. The society is divided into four classes, the Brahmin, Kshatriya, Vaishya and Shudra further there is another class of people who are called the Ati-shudra, who are outside the Hindu fold, they are the "untouchables". Each of these five classes have a determined occupation by the Hindu scriptures and one class cannot transgress the social order by following the occupation of another class.[19]

This Chaturvarnya is the base for the birth of millions of castes in India, each just confined to its own group and trying to

18. Dr. Ambedkar, Ranade, Gandhi and Jinnah, Dr. B.R. Ambedkar Who tried to turn The Wheel Of The Law Toward Social Jusitice For All (Aug 22, 2014, 1:00 AM), available at: http://www.columbia.edu/itc/mealac/pritchett/00ambedkar/txt_ambedkar_ranade.html.

19. Prabhu Narayan Khalkho, Ambedkars Critique of the Indian Social System, Articles In Philosophy (July. 06, 2015), available at: http://snphilosophers2005.tripod.com/prabhu.pdf.

protect its "superiority" by forbidding inter marriage, inter dinning and other rituals. It has divided the Hindus among themselves and has spread hatred among them. The biggest beneficiary of this caste system are the Brahmins, whereas the "untouchables" are the ones who suffer the most under this system of slavery.[20]

The Holy Scripture of Hindus, The Rig Veda sanctions upon the Hindu society to have a stratified way of living. A study of the Chaturvarnya must in its turn start with a study of the ninetieth Hymn of the Tenth Mandala of the Rig Veda[21] - a Hymn, which is known by the famous name of PurushaSukta.

"11. When (the gods) divided Purusha, into how many parts did they cut him up? What was his mouth? What arms (had he)? What (two objects) are said (to have been) his thighs and feet?

12. The Brahmana was his mouth, the Rajanya was made his arms; the being called the Vaishya, he was his thighs; the Shudra sprang from his feet.

13. The moon sprang from his soul (manas), the sun from the eye, Indra and Agni from his mouth and Vayu from his breath.

14. From his navel arose the air, from his head the sky, from his feet the earth, from his ear the (four) quarters; in this manner (the gods) formed the worlds.

15. When the gods, performing sacrifices, bound Purusha as a victim, there were seven sticks (stuck up) for it (around the fire), and thrice seven pieces of fuel were made.

16. With sacrifices the gods performed the sacrifice. These were the earliest rites. These great powers have sought the sky, where are the former Sadhyas, gods."

20. Id.

21. COMPILATION BY VASANT MOON, DR.BABASAHEBAMBEDKAR WRITINGS AND SPEECHES VOL. 7, WHO WERE THE SHUDRAS? HOW THEY CAME TO BE THE FOURTH OF INDO-ARYAN SOCIETY? 2-3 (1st ed., 1

This Hymn tries to justify the status of different classes in the Hindu society. The Brahmin from the Brahmas mouth makes him superior among the all the four classes, therefore his is to be the philosopher class, the Rajanya or Kshtriya is born form shoulders, therefore this class his military class, the Vaishya are born form the thighs, therefore they do the trade and business and the Shudra's are from the feet, therefore they do the menial jobs.[22]

This way the Caste Hindus justified there act of oppression over the untouchables and denied there basic human rights. Dr. Ambedkar, after studying the status of Shudras under the Hindu scripture, summarizes as follows,[23]

"(1) That the Shudra was to take the last place in the social order.

(2) That the Shudra was impure and therefore no sacred act should be done within his sight and within his hearing.

(3) That the Shudra is not to be respected in the same way as the other classes.(4) That the life of a Shudra is of no value and anybody may kill him without having to pay compensation and if at all of small value as compared with that of the Brahmana,Kshatriya and Vaishya.

(5) That the Shudra must not acquire knowledge and it is a sin and a crime to give him education.

(6) That a Shudra must not acquire property. A Brahmin can take his property at his pleasure.

(7) That a Shudra cannot hold office under the State.

(8) That the duty and salvation of the Shudra lies in his serving the higher classes.

(9) That the higher Classes must not inter-marry with the Shudra. They can however keep a Shudra woman

---

22. Dr. Ambedkar, The Annihilation of Caste, Columbia Center For New Media Teaching And LEARNING (July. 06, 2015, 07:00 PM), available at: http://ccnmtl.columbia.edu/projects/mmt/ambedkar/.

23. COMPILATION BY VASANT MOON, DR. BABASAHEBAMBEDKAR WRITINGS AND SPEECHES, 89-91 (1st . ed., 1987).

as a concubine But if the Shudra touches a woman of the higher classes he will be liable to dire punishment.

(10) That the Shudra is born in servility and must be kept in servility forever."

The status of the untouchables was even worse than that of Shudras. The condition of the "untouchables" can be briefly understood by what Manu writes in his *Manusmriti:*[24]

"X. 51. But the dwellings of the *Chandalas* and the *Shvapakas* shall be outside the village, they must be made Apapatras and their wealth (shall be) dogs and donkeys.

X. 52. Their dress (shall be) the garments of the dead, (they shall eat) their food from broken dishes, black iron (shall be) their ornaments and they must always wander from place to place.

X. 53. A man who fulfils a religious duty, shall not seek intercourse with them; their transactions (shall be) among themselves and their marriages with their equals.

X. 54. Their food shall be given to them by others (than an Aryan giver) in a broken dish; at night they shall not walk about in village and in towns.

X. 55. By day they may go about for the purpose of their work, distinguished by marks at king's command, and they shall carry out the corpses (of persons) who have no relatives; that are a settled rule.

X. 56. By the King's order they shall always execute the criminals, in accordance with the law, and they shall take for themselves the clothes, the beds, and the ornaments of (such) criminals."

Such was the condition of the Shudras and the "untouchables", the servitude class of this country. This systematic oppression of these classes still continues in the present time.

Dr. Ambedkar tried his level best to destroy the Hindu social order, which had kept millions of people in dark, but he

24. Id. at 95.

failed to achieve his goal. He realised that the Caste Hindus, denied the lower castes entry into the temple, they were denied the use of the public tank, they were not allowed to have property, overall they were not allowed to live a happy life, but still the lower castes were recognized as Hindus. He felt that when the untouchables are not treated as one among the Hindus, then they cannot be called as Hindus at all. Therefore he decided that the untouchables can achieve their goal of social justice and social equality only through conversion to other religion that protects their interest and treats them equally and recognizes their basic human rights.[25]

According to Dr. Ambedkar the struggle between the Hindus and the Untouchables is a permanent phenomenon. It is eternal, because the religion which has placed the untouchables at the lowest level of the society is itself eternal, according to Caste Hindus. The untouchables are at the lowest rung of the ladder today and they will remain lowest forever. This means that the struggle between Hindus and Untouchables shallcontinue forever. Therefore to survive this struggle, Dr. Ambedkar says there only three solutions,[26] i.e. the Man power, the financial power and the mental strength.

With regard to man power and financial power, the untouchables are weak. The untouchables are a minority community in India, even though they are minority they are not completely organized and united to fight the power, the caste system has further divided them into sub castes. Therefore the untouchables have no man power. With regard to financial power, the untouchables are in very bad condition. They form the poorest among the poor population in the Indian society, in the present 21st century there is emergence of middle class "untouchables", but even that is in very low in number. Therefore, Dr. Ambedkar says the only solution for the "untouchables" to emancipate and win the struggle against the Caste Hindus, is through gaining mental strength which can be achieved through conversion.[27]

25. Dr. Ambedkar, Why go for Conversion? (Aug 22, 2014, 1:00 AM), available at: http://www.angelfire.com/ak/ambedkar/BRwhyconversion.html.

26. Id.

27. Id.

The mental strength can be achieved when the society enables its members to have liberty over thought and action. The individual would be able to discover himself and achieve his goal and objectives. The Hindu religion sanctioned upon the members of the Hindu society, to have a life of rules, which was just confined to the working of castes. The religion had degraded the untouchables to the highest level that it was hard for them to get up and fight. Therefore conversion to a religion which does not sanction inequality and is based on the idea social justice, Dr. Ambedkar says, is the correct and only path to be free from the shackles of slavery for the "untouchables".

This stand of Dr. Ambedkar shows the importance he gave to the social development of the "untouchables" rather than the political or economic development. Though he fought for the reservation of seat in the legislature for the untouchables, for him the more important task for the emancipation of the "untouchables", i.e. the social equality, through which the individual can himself achieve political and economical equality.

Dr. Ambedkar on conversion says,[28]

"Most of the present day Sikhs, Muslims and Christians were formerly Hindus, majority of them are from the Shudra and Untouchable community. Do these critics mean to say that those, who left the Hindu fold and embraced Sikhism or Christianity, have made no progress at all? And if this is not true, and if it is admitted that the conversion has brought a distinct improvement in their condition, then to say that the untouchables will not be benefited by conversion, carries no meaning.

After giving deep thought to the problem, everybody will have to admit that conversion is necessary to the Untouchables, as self-government is to India. The ultimate object of both is the same. There is not the slightest difference in their ultimate goal. This ultimate aim is to attain freedom. And if the freedom is necessary for the life of mankind, conversion of Untouchables which brings them complete freedom cannot be called worthless

28.Id.

by any stretch of imagination..." He conclude the speech by saying,

"Convert, for getting organized. Convert, for becoming strong. Convert, for securing equality. Convert, for getting liberty. Convert, for that your domestic life may be happy."

According to Dr. Ambedkar the real development of the depressed class would be to come out of the yoke and strive to achieve justice for them, rather than living in filth and fighting from inside, for the simple reason that no matter what rights and privileges are given to the depressed classes, they will be deprived of it by the Caste Hindus, but through conversion the depressed classes can form their own platform and develop themselves socially which will ultimately help them in achieving the political and economical development.

3.3 Dr. Ambedkar and Buddhism

Revolution is a process wherein the society moves towards a change. It is a process where the people unite against the old beliefs and ideals and overthrow, in order to establish newly recognized ideas. Revolution can be in any form 'Political, Economical or Social'. The methods used to achieve might be violent or non-violent. The impact of revolution might last for a long time or its impact might just be there for a short period. A revolution is hard to begin, harder to sustain and even harder to win, but the main difficulties comes when a revolution is won.[29]

According to Dr. Ambedkar, Buddhism in India was a revolution. Though it was religious in nature, later it turned out to be political and social revolution. The ancient Buddhist society in India destroyed all the old beliefs of Brahminism of superstitions, the Vedas, the status of women etc. The ideology tried to establish an egalitarian society based on the principles of 'Liberty, Equality and Fraternity'.[30]

---

29. LauraNeitzel, What is Revolution?, Columbia Center For New Media Teaching And Learning, available at: http://www.columbia.edu/cu/weai/exeas/asian-revolutions/pdf/what-is-revolution.pdf (July. 06, 2015, 10:04 PM)

30. COMPILATION BY VASANT MOON, DR. BABASAHEBAMBEDKAR WRITINGS AND SPEECHES

To eradicate the vicious caste system and the social slavery imposed by it, Dr. Babasaheb, tried his very best to change the Hindu social order. His first attempt to change this social graded inequality was the Mahad Satyagraha. On March 20th, 1927, way before Gandhi started his Salt Satyagraha in the March 12th, 1930, Babasaheb with his thousands of untouchable followers marched towards the Chowdar Tank to exercise their right over it, which was protected by the resolution passed by the Bombay Legislative assembly, but the Caste Hindus refused to allow any of the untouchables to drink water from that tank. Treading through the streets of Mahad in a disciplined and peaceful manner, the procession reached the Chowdar Tank. Dr. Ambedkar asserted his right over the tank by bending down on his keens and drank the water and thousands of his followers followed him. Then the procession peacefully returned back to the venue of conference. By now the rumors had been spread that Dr. Ambedkar with his follower would be entering the village temple and this lead to a furious angry mob among the Caste Hindus. The unarmed men, women, children and old, who had come for the Conference, were beaten up by the Caste Hindus. Inspite of all this undue beating and humiliation, Dr. Ambedkar advised his followers to remain calm. Soon the orthodox Hindus performed the purification ceremony of the tank, as it was polluted by the touch of the thousands of "untouchables". The Mahad municipality also revoked the right of drinking water over the tank, to the "untouchables". This hurt Dr. Ambedkar very much. He returned to Mahad in December, this time to ceremoniously burn the Manusmriti, the book which he referred it as the "bible of slavery".[31]

Dr. Ambedkar, to restructure the Hindu religion led another Satyagraha in the year 1930, in Nasik. The object of this Satyagraha was to establish the right of the untouchables, to enter the Hindu temples. The venue was the Kalaram temple, Nasik. He contended that if the untouchables are Hindus, then they have right to enter the Hindu temple. The Satyagraha began on March 2nd,

31. DHANANJAYKEER, DR. AMBEDKAR: LIFE & MISSION 97 (3rd ed., 1971).

and continued for more than a month. When on April 9th, the day of the chariot procession of the idol of Rama, some satyagrahis attempted to go near the image, the Caste Hindus lost their senses and ambushed untouchables with stones and lathis. A larger number of them, including Dr. Ambedkar, were injured.[32] After such a failure, Dr. Ambedkar says,[33]

"Why should an Untouchable beg for an admission, in a place from which he has been excluded by the arrogance of the Hindus? This is the reason of the Depressed Class man who is interested in material welfare. He is prepared to say the Hindus, to open or not to open your temples is a question for you to consider and not for me to agitate. If you think, it is bad manners not to respect the sacredness of human personality, open your temple and be a gentleman. If you rather be a Hindu than a gentleman, then shut the doors and damn yourself for I don't care to come."

These two incidents show how Dr. Ambedkar tried to achieve and bring about social and religious equality to the untouchables. He tried to change the Hindu social system, in order to make it more egalitarian and moral, by not only protecting the interest of the untouchables but also to see to it that there is no division among them and the caste Hindus.

Facing failure in these two agitations, to unite the divided Hindus, Dr. Ambedkar was left in disgust. The hard core base of the Hinduism, the caste system, was unbreakable. All his efforts proved fruitless. With all the failures, Dr. Ambedkar, summoned a Conference of his people at Yeola on October 13th, 1935, where he furiously said "Unfortunately, I was born a Hindu. It was beyond my power to prevent that but I solemnly assure you that I will not die as a Hindu".[34] He further said, "Time had come to decide if it was not better for them to abjure Hinduism

---

32. Id.

33. Dr. AMBEDKAR, What Congress and Gandhi Have done to the Untouchables?, Ambedkar.Org (JULY 7, 2015, 1:00 AM)available at: http://www.ambedkar.org/ambcd/41E. What% 20Congress% 20and% 20 Gandhi% 20 CHAPTER% 20IV.htm

34. D.C. AHIR, DR. AMBEDKAR ON BUDDHISM 10 (1st ed., 1982).

and embrace some other faith that would give them an equal status, secure a position and rightful treatment."

This statement of Dr. Ambedkar left the whole nation in shock. The protagonists of Hinduism ridiculed Dr. Ambedkar and accused of him misleading the untouchables. Some claimed that the untouchables would remain untouchables, even if they changed religion, and conversion was not the solution. But at the same time other religious groups like the Sikhs, Muslims, Christians and even Buddhists approached him to prove that their religion was better than any other, and it would be better for Dr. Ambedkar and his followers to choose their religion.

The religious leaders of Muslims, Christians and Sikhs tried to induce him to embrace their respective religions by offering enormous funds and other amenities not only for himself but for his followers as well.[35] But he refused it. Although he knew that conversion to religion like Islam or Christianity, he would gain political power, he did not go for it. He wanted something more important to emancipate the untouchables, that through social liberty, which he knew could be achieved only by way of conversion to right religion.

After studying, debating and discussing all the religions, with leaders and priests, he decided to convert to Buddhism. On October 14th, 1956, was the day when Dr. Ambedkar converted to Buddhism with millions of his followers and friends. This day was chosen because it was the auspicious day of Vijaya Dashami, the day on which the Emperor Asoka has embraced Buddhism and had declared that he would conquer the people by love instead of by force.[36] Dr. Ambedkar after the Diksha ceremony said,[37]

"I started the movement of renouncing the Hindu religion in 1935 and since then I have been continuing the struggle. This conversion has given me enormous satisfaction and pleasure unimaginable. I feel as if I have been liberated from hell."

---

35. Id. at 11.
36. DHANANJAYKEER, DR. AMBEDKAR: LIFE & MISSION 496 (3rd ed., 1971)
37. D.C. AHIR, DR. AMBEDKAR ON BUDDHISM 11 (1st ed., 1982).

This shows that Dr. Ambedkar tried his best to change the Hindu social order and because of the hard crust of the Hindu religion or the caste system, Dr. Ambedkar failed to achieve his goal, therefore the only solution for him to break the chains of slavery of millions in India, was conversion, which, he was of the opinion that, secured social respect, and which he found it in the religion of Buddha, the Buddhism or Buddha's Dhamma.

Having found no scope for self development in Hinduism, Dr. Ambedkar after careful study of all the religions, converted to Buddhism. There were many reasons for choosing Buddhism. First of all was the personality of Buddha, which made him completely different for other religious preachers. Buddha never taught his followers that he was either the son of God, the messenger of God or he was the God himself. The three most influential persons with regard to religion are Jesus, Mahommed and Krishna. Jesus preached that he was the son of God and in order to enter the kingdom of heaven, the people should refer him as son of God, Mahommed even went further and contented that he was not only the messenger of God, but instead his was the last messenger and whereas Krishna, crossing the limits, claimed himself to be the God.[38]

Buddha never claimed himself to be related to god in any way. He claimed to be a common man among the common and was satisfied with it. He would force the people to not treat him as someone superior but instead to treat him as one amongst them. He never claimed to have supernatural powers nor did he perform some miracle to prove his supernatural origins, he lived as a common man amongst the common people.[39]

Jesus and Mohammed claimed that their teaching was infallible and it cannot be challenged or changed, they contended that their teachings were directly acquired from the teachings of God, therefore they are permanent. Krishna claimed that he was God himself, therefore his teachings were permanent and whatever

38. Dr.Ambedkar,Whygo for Conversion?, Anglefire (Aug 22, 2014, 1:00 AM) http://www.angelfire.com/ak/ambedkar/BRwhyconversion.html

39. Id.

he uttered were the words of god.[40] Whereas this was different in case of Buddha, Dr. Ambedkar says,[41]

"In Mahaparinibbana Sutta, Buddha told Ananda that his religion was based on reason and experience and that his followers should not accept his teachings as correct and binding merely because they emanated from him. Being based on reason and experience they were free to modify or even to abandon any of his teachings if it was found that at a given time and circumstances they did not apply. He wished, is religion not to be encumbered, with the dead wood of past."

It is true that that the followers look up to the man who follows what he preaches and Buddha followed what he preached. The character and the personality of Buddha was unique and very appealing in nature. People were forced to follow him, his new ideas and thinking of liberty, equality and fraternity demolished the old rituals and ideology of the caste system and superstitions, made Buddha acceptable by everyone.[42]

The spread of Buddhist ideas in the ancient India society werethose of new thinking and development. It was a kind of revolution that made people to question the authority and question themselves, as whether the life they were living was in fact the correct way of living. The ancient Indian society, before the spread of Buddhism, was filled with hatred, corruption and bigotry. The Aryan community had completely degraded the Indian society into the lowest scale. The society was steeped in the worst kind of debauchery: social, religious and spiritual.[43]

One of the social evils prevalent at that time was gambling, which was wide spread. Every King had a hall of gambling attached to his palace. The King had an expert gambler in his employment

40. Id.

41. DR. AMBEDKAR, BUDDHA AND THE FUTURE OF HIS RELIGION 2 (MAHA BODHI 1950).

42. VenrableNaradMahathera, The Buddha and His Teachings, Buddhadharma Education Association, available at: http://www.buddhanet.net/pdf_file/buddha-teachingsurw6.pdf

43. Id.

as a companion to play with. Gambling was not just fun, but was played with heavy stakes. They staked kingdom, dependents, relative, salves, servants etc. Mahabharat is the best example to prove how rampant gambling was, Yudhisthira, the Dharma Raja, staked everything he had even his and his brothers wife, Draupadi.[44]

Drinking was another evil which had spread over whole of ancient Indian society. The Mahabharat mentions an occasion when both Krishan and Arjuna were dead drunk. That shows that the best among the Aryan society were not free from drinking habit but they drank heavily. Even the Aryan women were addicted to drinking.[45]

The priestly profession in the ancient Aryan society was monopolized by the Brahmins. None except a Brahmin could become a priest. The Brahmins were the guides of the people in moral and spiritual matter. But the Brahmins were not themselves clean and able enough to lead the people. They were addicted to visiting shows like Nautch dances, combats of elephants, horses, buffaloes, bulls etc. They were addicted to games like throwing dice, hitting a short stick with large ones etc. Brahmins earned their living by low arts like vowing gifts to a God if a certain benefit be granted, fixing a lucky site for dwelling, ceremonial bathing, offering sacrifice etc.[46]

During such a period of Dark Age in the Indian history, the teachings of Buddha spread like a wildfire in the forest. The teachings were of such a nature, that the Aryan society had never heard, for example, before if any member of the society wanted to be a Buddhist, then undertaking to observe certain moral precepts or the Panch Sila had to be made. These Panch Sila were :[47]

- Not to Kill
- Not to steal

---

44. COMPILATION BY VASANT MOON, DR. BABASAHEBAMBEDKAR WRITINGS AND SPEECHES 153 (1st ed., 1987).
45. Id.
46. Id., at 158 - 164(1st ed., 1987)
47. Id., at 187,188.

- Not to lie
- Not to be unchaste
- Not to drink intoxicants

For the Monks, there were 5 additions precepts, they were:

- Not to eat at forbidden times
- Not to dance, sing, or attend theatrical or other spectacles
- To abstain from the use of garlands, scents and ornaments
- To abstain from use of high or broad beds
- Never to receive money

Such were the teachings of Buddha, which transformed whole of ancient Indian society to be based on the principles of morality. Buddha was completely against the caste system, practised by the Aryan society. He did what the Aryan society refused to do. The Shudra or any low caste man could never have the status that of a Brahmin, but Buddha not only preached against caste but admitted the Shudra and the low caste to the rank of a Bhikku who held the same rank as that of Brahmin.[48]

The status of women in the Aryan society too was in a very bad condition. They were placed in the same position as that of Shudra. Both of them were denied of the basic human rights by the Brahmins. Buddha broke this rule and even advocated for the women to become Bhikku, this was taking her to the highest level in the society.[49]

Dr. Ambedkar's social philosophy is based on the this ideals of Buddha of liberty, where each individual had the right to critically evaluate the teachings, Equality, where every member had the right to enjoy his basic right to life, and he is known by his character and not birth and Fraternity; by breaking the shackles of caste system, Buddha tries to spread the message of brotherhood, among the member of the society.

3.4 Ambedkar, Democracy & Social Philosophy

Dr. Ambedkar is known for his strong stand for democracy. He believed that through democracy, a great revolution can be

48. SunilXess, Ambedkars views on Untouchability, Articles In Philosophy (July. 06, 2015), available at: http://snphilosophers2005.tripod.com/sunil.pdf
49. COMPILATION BY VASANT MOON, DR. BABASAHEBAMBEDKAR: WRITINGS AND SPEECHES 187, 188 (1st ed., 1987).

achieve without any bloodshed, the society can be revived into a better one, where the basic ideals of the society are 'Liberty, Equality and Fraternity'.

There are many scholars who have given the definition for democracy,according to R.K. Kshirsagar, democracy is a form of Government in which the people rule themselves either directly or indirectly or through their elected representatives. In democracy sovereignty vests with the people in general.[50] According to J.R. Lewis, democracy exists basically not as a form of Government, but a form which exists to supply and maintain a better society and to provide the maximum amount of liberty for individual consistent with the attainment of order and security within the State.[51] The most famous definition of all can be said to be that of Abraham Lincoln, who said, democracy is for the people, by the people and of the people.[52]

Dr. Ambedkar had a different view on democracy. He said, democracy was not just about "Adult Suffrage" or "Representative Government", it was more than that, he says democracy is an ideology, on which a society is based and follows the principles of liberty, equality and fraternity. According to him, to have political democracy, we need to have social democracy, without which, the democracy would be just a top dressing over the disease of tyranny and oppression. Dr. Ambedkar states that, political democracy rests on four premises. They are :[53]

- The individual is an end in himself.
- The individual has certain inalienable rights which must be guaranteed to him by the Constitution

---

50. KSHIRSAGARRAMCHANDRAKAMAJI, POLITICAL THOUGHT OF DR.BABASAHEBAMBEDKAR53 (1st ed., 1992).
51. I.R. LEWIS, DEMOCRACY THE THEORY AND PRACTICE 14 (1st ed., 1966).
52. KSHIRSAGARRAMCHANDRAKAMAJI, POLITICAL THOUGHT OF DR. BABASAHEBAMBEDKAR53 (1st ed., 1992).
53. Sandesh M. Wagh, Dr. Ambedkar's thoughts on Democracy, Indian Streams Reserch Journal (Aug 24, 2014, 01:30 pm) available at: http://www.isrj.net/UploadedData/3318.pdf.

- The individual shall not be required to relinquish any of his constitutional rights as aprice of any privilege.
- The state shall not delegate power to private persons to govern others.

Dr. Ambedkar believed in having a democracy based on the democratic society. The political democracy would be of no value and it would be a great disaster in the working of democracy, if the society is not democratic. He said that the politicians should realise that democracy is not merely a form of political government instead, it is a form of society, where each and every individual follows the principle of democracy, which is based on the idea ofliberty, equality and fraternity.[54]

The principles of 'Liberty, Equality and Fraternity' are important for the working of a country. Liberty of thought and mind, where each individual is not sanctioned to follow particular set of rules and has a right to critically evaluate and propagate his ideas, Equality is the social equality where no member of the society is denied of his human rights and is given the opportunity to find and achieve his goal, without prejudice to colour, caste, religion, economic power, gender or anything that demarcates man and Fraternity is brotherhood among the members of the society, without which Equality and Liberty are futile.[55]

Any given society is bound to have differences in it, whether on the basis of caste, religion, colour etc. and even if the society is free from differences still that society will have difference in gender. Therefore to form a good government we need have a good relationship among the "differences", if not, the majority, under a dictatorship or democratic form of govt., is bound protect the interest of the majority, at the cost of the interest of the minority and the weak communities. Therefore the feeling of brotherhood is important to have a stable and just society, i.e. the society based on Fraternity.

Therefore Dr. Ambedkar felt that if the society is democratic in nature then automatically there would be no issue or problem

---

54. Id.
55. GailOmvedt, Dr. BabasahebAmbedkar's Vision of a New Social Order, available at: http://www.ambedkar.org/research/LibertyEquality.htm.

with the political functioning of the country. His words are so much relevant in the present context. The absence of social democracy in India has made the India political scenario a joke. The political parties in India, with no fellow-feeling among the masses, are continuing to divide the people on the basis of caste, religion, ideology etc. People kill each other in riots and communal violence based on religion. Dr. Ambedkar was correct in his words, when he said in his final speech, after presenting the Constitution of India, which still echoes in the Parliament[56] today, he said,

"The third thing we must do is not to be content with mere political democracy. We must make our political democracy a social democracy as well. Political democracy cannot last unless there lies at base of it social democracy. What does social democracy mean? It means a way of life which recognizes liberty, equality and fraternity as the principles of life. These principles of liberty, equality and fraternity are not be treated as separate items in a trinity. They form a union of trinity in the sense that to divorce one from the other is to defeat the very purpose of democracy. Liberty cannot be divorced from equality and equality cannot be divorced from liberty. Nor can liberty and equality be divorced from fraternity. Without equality, liberty would produce supremacy of few over many. Equality without liberty would kill individual initiative. Without fraternity, equality and liberty could not become natural course of things. We must begin by acknowledging the fact that there is complete absence of two things in Indian society. One of these is equality. On the social plane, we have in India a society based on the principle of graded inequality which we have a society in which there are some who have immense wealth as against many who live in abject poverty. On the 26th of January 1950, we are going to enter into a life of contradictions. In politics we will have equality and in social and economic life we will have inequality. In politics we will be recognizing the principle of one

56. COMPILATION BY VSANT MOON, DR. BABASAHEBAMBEDKAR WRITINGS AND SPEECHES; DR. AMBEDKAR: THE PRINCIPLE ARCHITECT OF THE CONSTITUTION OF INDIA 1216, 1218 (1st ed., 1987).

man one vote and one vote one value. In our social and economic life, we shall, by reason of our social and economic structure, continue to deny the principle of one man one value. How long shall we continue to live this life of contradictions? How long shall we continue to deny equality in our social and economic life? If we continue to deny it for long, we will do so only by putting our political democracy in peril. We must remove this contradiction at the earliest possible moment or else those who suffer from inequality will blow up the structure of political democracy which is Assembly has to laboriously built up." He continues,

"The second thing we are wanting in is recognition of principle of fraternity. What does fraternity mean? Fraternity means a sense of common brotherhood of all the Indians- if Indians being one people. It is the principle which gives unity and solidarity to social life. It is a difficult thing to achievethere can be no gainsaying that political power in this country has too long been in the monopoly of a few and the many are not only beasts of burden but also beasts of prey. This monopoly has not merely deprived them their chance of betterment, it has sapped them of what may be called the significance of life. These downtrodden classes are tired of being governed; they are impatient to govern themselves. This urge of self realization in the downtrodden classes must not be allowed to develop into class struggle or class war. It would lead to a division of the House. That would indeed be a day of disaster. For, as has been well said by Abraham Lincoln, a House divided against itself cannot stand very long. Therefore the sooner room is made for the realization of their aspiration, the better for the few, the better for the country, the better for the maintenance of independence and better for the continuance of democratic structure. This can only be done by the establishment of equality and fraternity in all spheres of life. That is why I have laid so much stress on them."[57]

These final words of Dr. Ambedkar proves the importance he gave to the ideals of liberty, equality and fraternity, for the establishment of democracy and to have a just society. Every law

57. Id

made by the Parliament must be recognized by the society, if not then the proper functioning of that law will be at jeopardy. A law protecting the interest of the depressed classes will only be recognised by the majority, if there is fraternity among the two classes, and this fraternity will lead to liberty and equality among, which ultimately fulfil the elements of ideal society, which is 'Social Democracy', based on the principle of liberty, equality and fraternity.

3.5 Conclusion

Article 1 (1) of the Indian Constitution states as follows: "India, that is Bharat, shall be a Union of states".[58]

The founding fathers of the Indian Constitution chose the word "India" as well as "Bharat", because one view was in favor of retaining the international name of the country, while the other insisted on replacing it by the ancient name, "Bharat".

Internationally, India is the largest democratic country in the world. It is the fastest economically growing country and is said be a role model to many developing and underdeveloped countries. Many world powers like the Great Britain, the USA, Russia etc. keep a close eye on the ongoing internal and external activities of India, so that they won't be threatened and aim at keeping a good relationship with India. Many of the foreign countries are attracted towards India, for the cheap and best labor it gives, and also because our country is the best place for raw materials. Though in the present time the economic condition of India is in the stage of slump of the business cycle,but still in the international scenario there is respect and fear over the growth of the country.[59]

Such is the position of India, but is the situation of "Bharat" thesame? By "Bharat", I mean the socio-political nature of the country. There is an urgent need to answer this question, for the simple reason that no matter how big India grows economically, if "Bharat" is socially backward then the economic growth is of no use.

---

58. INDIAN CONSTITUTION. art. 1.
59. K.R. GUPTA & J.R. GUPTA, INDIAN ECONOMY 83 (1st ed., 2008).

Better education, health facilities, the better position of the deprived sections of the society, etc. will not only lead to the development of each of the individual, but this development will eventually lead to economic growth. The economic growth of the country might just indicate the growth of few rich capitalists, but this growth neglects a very vast majority of people in the society, who suffer due to the acts of these few capitalists. Economic development is the nomenclature for inclusive growth, is not the development of single individual or a group, but the development of every member of the society.[60]

"Bharat" ranks 136, in Human Development Index, among 187 counties around the world.[61] This poor ranking shows that our country is in a very bad state. The ranking shows that there is low literacy, less sex ratio, no good health care; overall the people of this country are facing the situation which was faced by the citizens governed under the Emperor Nero, who ruled while Rome burnt.

The country's main problems lie elsewhere, particularly in the lack of attention that is paid to the essential needs of the people, especially the underprivileged and oppressed sections of the Indian society. One of the biggest failures has been the very inadequate use of the public resources generated by economic growth. There is a continued inadequacy both of social services such as schooling, medical care and immunization, and of physical services such as the provision of safe water, electricity, drainage and sanitation. Even as India has overtaken other countries in its rate of growth, because of these inadequacies of "Bharat", India has fallen behind many of the same countries, in the quality of life.

Dalits, are a major section of the Indian society who are not part of and are left out of the larger economic growth of the

60. LIONEL ROBBINS, THE THEORY OF ECONOMIC DEVELOPMENT., MISES INSTITUTE, (July. 7, 2015, 09:00 AM) https://mises.org/sites/default/files/The%20Theory%20of%20Economic%20Development_2.pdf

61. MadhaviRajadhyaksha, India Ranks 135 in Human Development Index: UNDP, THE TIMES OF INDIA, JULY 24, 2014, at A1.

country. They are more than one sixth of India's population, who live a precarious existence, shunned by the society because of their rank as "untouchables" or as Dalits, which means broken men, who are at the bottom of the Hindu social order.[62]

The condition of Dalit community in "Bharat" is a pity. The Human Rights Watch, an independent, international organization that works as part of a vibrant movement to uphold human dignity and advance the cause of human rights for all, released a report, based on the research conducted in the year 1998. The report, in its summary, says as follows:

"Most Dalits continue to live in extreme poverty, without land or opportunities for better employment or education. With the exception of a minority who have benefited from India's policy of quotas in education and government jobs, Dalits are relegated to the most menial tasks, as manual scavengers, removers of human waste and dead animals, leather workers, street sweepers and cobblers. Dalit children make up the majority of those sold into bondage to pay off debts to upper-caste creditors. Dalit men, women and children numbering in tens of millions work as agricultural labourers for a few kilograms of rice or Rs. 15 to Rs. 35 a day. Their upper caste employees frequently use caste as a cover for exploitive economic arrangements: social sanction of their status as lesser beings allows their impoverishment to continue."[63]

The National Human Rights Commission Report on the Prevention and Atrocities against Scheduled Castes, 2002 gave the following facts and figures on the condition of the Dalit communities:[64]

Every 18 minutes:

- A crime is committed against a Dalit
- Social and Economic condition of Dalits

---

62. Human Rights Watch Report, Broken people-Caste violence against India's untouchables, (Aug. 24, 2014, 09:00 AM), available at: http://www.hrw.org/reports/1999/india/

63. Id.

64. Justice A.S. Anand, Report on the Prevention of Atrocities against Schedule Castes (National Human Rights Comission)(2004).

- 37% of Dalits living below poverty in India
- More than half (54%) of their children are undernourished in India
- 83 per 1000 live birth children born in Dalit community would probability die before the first birthday
- 45% of Dalits do not know read and write in India
- Dalit women burden double discrimination (gender and caste) in India
- Only 27% of Dalit women give institutional deliveries in India
- About one third of Dalit households do not have basic facilities
- Public health workers refused to visit Dalit homes in 33% of villages
- Dalits were prevented from entering police station in 27.6% of villages
- Dalit children had to sit separately while eating in 37.8% of Govt. schools
- Dalits didn't get mail delivered to their homes in 23.5% of villages
- Dalits were denied access to water sources in 48.4% of villages because of segregation & untouchabilty practices
- Half of India's Dalit children are undernourished, 21% are severely underweight & 12% DIE before their 5th birthday
- Literacy rates for Dalit women are as low as 37.8% In Rural India

Such is the plight of the Dalit community in "Bharat". They are the rejected, refused and an oppressed community of this country.

In such kind of a situation it has become very much necessary to not reject the ideology of social justice and social Philosophy of Dr. Ambedkar. It has become necessary for us to build a society based on liberty, equality and fraternity. The absence of brotherhood among the Indians, because of the presence of caste, has made us still a backward country. In India there is lack of social unity among the people which has lead to economic and political difference among them. Therefore now it has become for us of vital importance to reconstruct our society, by respecting the rights and following our duty towards the depressed classes, women, tribals, minorities etc. We need to focus more on the social development of the individuals rather than economic development, which can be achieved through providing education, hospital facilities, better living conditions, better working of public distribution system rather than concentrating in the development of roads, industries and trying to increase the GDP rate.

A system has to be established, wherein each individual is able to develop his personality, in order to become a perfect human being. An individual must get every opportunity to explore the strength in him, irrespective of who that individual is. That individual must not only be able to contribute towards the society, according to his ability, but also must be able to receive the benefits, according to his needs. He should be free from all ideas, that are antithetical to the scientific temperament and should be rationale in every . This is what the social philosophy of Dr. Babasaheb Ambedkar, teaches us.

4

Ambedkar's Sublime Ideology in the Context of Foundation of Socio-Democratic Institutions

- Chanakya Sharma &Alok Vajpeyi***

4.1 Introduction

"Indifferentism is the worst kind of disease that can affect people"

Dr. Bhimrao Ramji Ambedkar (1891-1956), 'a symbol of revolt' (as mentioned by Pandit JawaharlalNehru, the first Prime Minister of independent India), was among the key thinkers who influenced the objectives of the Indian Constitution.[1] Dr. Ambedkar was a renowned scholar, masterly statesman, powerful debater, valiant upholder of human rights, social reformer, the foremost fighter of the cause of depressed classes. He was an eminent economist, renowned democrat, a committed patriot, dedicated educationalist and known for high quality of character and integrity.[2] The leader, throughout his life, fought for dalit rights and other socially backward classes.[3] Dr. Bhim Rao Ambedkar was a great

*Chanakya Sharma, Second Year , B.A.LLB (Hons) ,Ram ManoharLohia National Law University, Lucknow

**AlokVajpeyi, B.A.LLB (Hons) Institute of Law, Nirma University, Ahmedabad.

1. BEJOY NARAYAN MAHAVIDYALAYA & SHYAM PURSIDDHESWARI MAHAVIDYALAYA, B.R AMBEDKAR AND HIS PHILOSOPHY ON INDIAN DEMOCRACY: AN APPRAISAL, JOURNAL OF EDUCATION AND PRACTICE 74, 74-82 (2011).
2. PROF. G. MANOHERRAO, DR. AMBEDKAR AND THE INDIAN CONSTITUTION vii (2d ed., 2009).
3. M.LSHAHARE, DR.BHIMRAOAMBEDKAR: HIS LIFE AND WORK 111, (1 ed., 1987).

son of India. As the architect of Constitution, he remains unmatched. The acceptance of the constitution on January 26, 1950 is a tribute to the trials and tribulations undergone by him for he dedicated, with determination, his all to treat the ailing India for a healthy and rejuvenated life of endless embarkment into the future.[4] His inducements and indictments will always keep the unprivileged inspiring and the atrocious deterred. The "Bharat Ratna" to him was really well deserved. But, no amounts of awards or laurels can match his personality, pursuits and performances.[5]

The Ambedkar statue that is planted on the commons and rallied around always holds a book in its hand. Significantly, that book is not Annihilation of Caste with its liberating, revolutionary rage. It is a copy of the Indian Constitution that Ambedkar played a vital role in conceptualising the document that now, for better or for worse, governs the life of every single Indian citizen. Modern society remembers Ambedkar as the leader of the Dalits or as chief architect of the Indian constitution. But his thoughts and ideologies offered much more, the essay discusses those ideologies of Ambedkar in their true sense and how those ideologies and his vision is relevant in today's India.

4.2 Democracy: Political and/or Social?

"Democracy is not merely a form of Government but essentially it is a form of Society"

As per Britannica Encyclopedia, social democracy (also revisionism) is political ideology that advocates a peaceful, evolutionary transition of society from capitalism to socialism using established political processes. Based on 19th-century socialism and the tenets of Karl Marx and Friedrich Engels, social democracy shares common ideological roots with communism but eschews

4. Mahendra Kumar Nayak, Contribution of Dr. B.R. Ambedkar in the Making of the Constitution of India, Odisha Review, (2014).
5. Id.
6. Arundhati Roy, The Doctor and the Saint, The Caravan- Journal on Politics and Culture (March 2014).

its militancy and totalitarianism.[7] Dr. Ambedkar never undermined the importance of political democracy but at the same time believed that 'Social Democracy' is a sine qua non for political democracy to flourish.[8] He opined that Social Democracy means a way of life which recognizes that Liberty, Equality and Fraternity are intermingled and interdependent virtues which go hand in hand.[9]

He asserted that liberty, equality and fraternity are not 'mutually exclusive' and for any Democracy to progress they must coexist intertwined with each other. He corroborates this by explaining that liberty without equality would result into supremacy of few over many, and equality if divorced from liberty would destroy individual initiative, and even if equality and liberty exist in absence fraternity, 'Equality & Liberty' together would become 'mere' principles and it would require a constable to enforce them.[10]

According to him, economic inequalities are inherent in the capitalist economy which makes political equality assured by democracy worthless. Thus, according to Ambedkar, the failure to recognize that political democracy cannot succeed where there is no social and economic democracy has vitiated parliamentary democracy.[11] Ambedkar maintained therefore that though "parliament democracy developed a passion for liberty, it never made a nodding acquaintance with equality. It failed to realize the significance of equality and did not even endeavour to strike a balance between liberty and equality, with the result that liberty swallowed equality and left a progeny of inequalities".[12]

In light of the above ideas he warned Constituent assembly of one big contradiction that was there on eve of adoption of

7. Social Democracy, BrittanicaEncylopedia, available at https://www.britannica.com/topic/social-democracy.
8. DR. AMBEDKAR, B.R.AMBEDKAR: WRITING AND SPEECHES 168.
9. DR. AMBEDKAR, B.R.AMBEDKAR: WRITING AND SPEECHES41.
10. CONSTITUENT ASSEMBLY DEBATES,- Vol. XI, (25th November, 1949.
11. SHYAMPUR SIDDHESWARI MAHAVIDYALAYA, B.R.Ambedkar and his Philosophy on Indian Democracy:An Appraisal, No. 5, Issue 2, 74 (2011), available at www.iiste.org/Journals/index.php/JEP/article/download/500/ 385.
12. Supra note 1.

Constitution of India. He said "We must begin by acknowledging that there is complete absence of two things in Indian Society. One of these is equality. On the social plane, we have in India a society based on the principle of graded inequality that is a society in which there were some who had immense wealth as against many who lived in abject poverty".[13] He warned that the day the Constitution came into force, India was going to enter into a life of contradictions. In politics it would have equality and in social and economic life it will face inequality.[14] In politics it will confer on citizens the principle of one man one vote and one vote one value but in social and economic life, because of social and economic structure, it will continue to deny the principle of one man one value.[15] He vehemently asked that how long can India support such a contradictory approach and also warned that if it 'continued' to deny it for long, it would put political democracy at stake so much so that it might sink until its foundation is based on Social Democracy.[16] He appealed that this contradiction must be corrected at the earliest possible moment or else those who suffer from inequality will blow up the very structure of political democracy which the Constituent Assembly was laboriously trying to build up.[17]

Hence he had unshakeable faith in Democracy, both Political and Social.Social democracy alone can assure to the masses the right to liberty, equality and fraternity. So, democracy is not only a form of government but a way of life through which social justice can be established. Social justice ensures that society should promote the welfare of all. Democracy is a dynamic attitude towards human life.[18]

13. DR. AMBEDKAR, B.R.AMBEDKAR: WRITING AND SPEECHES 295.
14. JEAN DREZE., AMARTYA SEN, INDIA: DEVELOPMENT AND PARTICIPATION, P-375, (2002).
15. OBSERVE AMBEDKAR JAYANTI AS DALIT RIGHTS DAY, PEOPLES DEMOCRACY, available at http://peoplesdemocracy.in/2015/0412_pd/observe-ambedkar-jayanti-dalit-rights-day.
16. Supra 10.
17. DAYALKESHAV, MAKERS OF INDIAN CONSTITUTION 90 (2013).
18. DR.JATAV, THE SOCIAL PHILOSOPHY OF AMBEDKAR 32 (1965).

4.3 Ambedkar: The Realistic Socio-Economist

"I like the religion that teaches liberty, equality and fraternity."

Dr. Ambedkar's contribution in economics is huge and certainly cannot be ignored.[19] Dr. Ambedkar wrote three scholarly books on economics namely, *'Administration and Finance of the East India Company', 'The Evolution of Provincial Finance in British India', and 'The Problem of the Rupee: Its Origin and Its Solution'.*[20] In the second book he criticizes the British tax system and in another two works he describes how Indian economy was manhandled by the British.[21] In hindsight we realize that Ambedkar was an economist who foresaw the economic crisis that India would face because as early as in 1918, Ambedkar said that industrialization would resolve the problems of agriculture sector. He felt that both agriculture and industrial sectors should be given equal priority.[22]

Dr. Ambedkar had always maintained that for individual freedom to prevail the dictatorial, tyrannical, and anarchical tendencies must be abandoned and it is paramount that Parliamentary democracy prevails in letter and spirit.[23] His vision of State socialism meant that the State shall not treat an individual as a 'means' but as an end in itself, hence anything that curtails an individual's basic, inalienable right i.e. Right to life, equality, and liberty is void ab initio.[24]

As an economic thinker, by and large his orientation is that of a socialist but he did not agree with Karl Marx whose ideas

19. Dr. R.P Saharia, Economics thoughts of Dr. B.R Ambedkar, 14(54) The Economic Challenger 77-78 (2012).
20. Dr.K.S.Ingole, Ambedkarian Perspective For Economic Development, in National Seminar on the theme: Social Justice:Gandhi, Nehru and Ambedkar (2006).
21. GAILOMVEDT, AMBEDKAR TOWARDS AN ENLIGHTENED INDIA 116 (Penguin Viking, 2004).
22. SUKHDEOTHORAT, RESERVATION IN PRIVATE SECTOR 19 (2005).
23. B.R.Ambedkar: Writing and Speeches, Vol-1 .p-409.
24. BADAL SARKAR, DR. B.R. AMBEDKAR'S THEORY OF STATE SOCIALISM, NO. 8, ISSUE 2, 38-41 (2013), available at http://www.isca.in/IJSS/Archive/v2/i8/6.ISCA-IRJSS-2013-113.pdf.

and method supported violence. Dr. Ambedkar was in favour of a mixed economy where there will be a shrewd combination of State control and liberty but also maintained the opinion that there must be 'State Control' in transformation of agriculture and nationalisation of major industries which would play a great role in equitable distribution of resources and thereby remove economic inequalities.[25] On 10th Oct-1927 in Bombay Legislative Council Dr. Ambedkar argued that the "the better method is to introduce cooperative agriculture and to compel owners of small strips to join in cultivation". Against this argument there was a criticism by libertarians who said that State Control would unnecessarily curtail the liberty of producers.[26] Ambedkar justified his argument by highlighting the risks of dictatorial tendencies and deftly responded to this by saying that "liberty from State Control is another name dictatorship of the private employers".[27] Hence he sought a balance between 'Individual Liberty and Social Equality' by means of a mixed economy.[28]

On Rupee, exchange system and its functions his contribution is immense. He critically examined the ideas of Keynes in his book "The problem of Rupee-its origin and its evolution", and he said the to stabilize Rupee, stabilization of its purchasing power is a must.[29]

In present context it would be apposite to say that Economic liberalization regimes in India cannot afford to ignore the bitter realities of unequal and discriminatory structure of its social life and chronic poverty. Any action to rephrase the economy without the hard-core social realities would lead to serious repercussions on Indian polity and society as well as its economy. And it is in this manner that the idea of economic liberalization, social and political fabric must operate in tandem.

25. NarendraJadhav, Neglected Economic Thought of BabasahebAmbedkar, 26(15) Economic and Political Weekly 980-982 (1991).

26. A NEW RESONANCE, FRONTLINE, available at http://www.frontline.in/static/html/fl1915/19151150.htm.

27. Id.

28. Supra 24.

29. DR.AMBEDKAR, B,R, AMBEDKAR WRITINGS AND SPEECHES, 328 (1989)..

4.4 Impediments for Ambedkar

"To leave inequality between class and class, sex and sex, which is the soul of Hindu Society, and to go on passing legislations relating to economic problems is to make a farce of our Constitution and to build a palace on a dung heap"

Dr. Ambedkar was a true liberator and maverick for he was never scared of anyone and always spoke from his conscience. As Law Minister post-independence India, he worked for once on a draft of 'The Hindu Code Bill'. He believed that the caste-system advanced itself by controlling women, and one of his major concerns was to make Hindu Personal Law more equitable for women.[30] The Bill he proposed sanctioned divorce and expanded the property rights of widows and daughters. The Constituent Assembly Draft dragged its feet over four years(1947-1951) and then blocked it.[31] The then President Dr. Rajendra Prasad threatened to stall the bill's passage into law. Hindu Sadhu laid siege to Parliament. Industrialists and Zamindars warned they would withdraw their support in coming elections.[32] Eventually Ambedkar resigned as law minister. In his resignation speech he said " To leave inequality between class and class, sex and sex, which is the soul of Hindu Society, and to go on passing legislations relating to economic problems is to make a farce of our Constitution and to build a palace on a dung heap".[33]

One cannot but recall how various ambiguous objections were raised when Dr. Ambedkar was asked to address the Jat-Pat Todak-TodalMandal. The Annual Conference was to be held at Lahore, under the presidentship of Baba Saheb at the headquarters of the Mandal. The Conference was to meet at Easter, but was subsequently postponed to the middle of May 1936. The Reception

30. AMBEDKAR, CASTES IN INDIA: THEIR MECHANISM, GENESIS AND DEVELOPMENT, INDIAN ANTIQUITY (1915).
31. SHARMILAREGE, AGAINST THE MADNESS OF MANU 207, 191-255 (2013).
32. Id. at 209.
33. Id. at 241.

Committee of the Mandal arbitrarily cancelled the Conference. The notice of cancellation came long after the Presidential address had been printed. In a continuous conversation with Dr. Ambedkar the commission requested him to alter various parts of his speech and specifically those that might hurt the sentiments of Hindu members of the Commission.[34] He after a several talks finally told the commission " I request you to announce immediately that the Session of the Conference which was to meet under my Presidentship is cancelled. All the grace [period] has by now run out, and I shall not consent to preside, even if your Committee agreed to accept my address as it is, in toto".[35]

4.5 Relevance of Ambedkarite Ideology in Present Context

4.5a Dalit Population and the Discrimination

Dr. Ambedkar fought hammer and tongs to eradicate the social evils of caste discriminations. But even today, almost sixty-five years ahead of Independence Indian Society is stuck with gruesome discrimination towards the Dalit Community. Even today, around thirteen lakh people belonging to Dalit population have to engage in manual scavenging of latrine trenches to earn bread.[36] Due to manual scavenging, many Dalit girls, aged as young as 10 years, drop out of school which is why states such as Bihar, Rajasthan, Madhya Pradesh and Uttar Pradesh have a very high school dropout rate. It is as high as ninety-five percent among some age groups in Bihar and over sixty percent in other states.

For this job Municipal Corporations pay a mere amount of 5000 rupees per month while those hired by private contractors get a minuscule amount of 2500 rupees.[37] Contrary to what

---

34. ANNIHILATION OF CASTE, ANNIHILATION OF CASTE WITH A REPLY TO MAHATMA GANDHI, available at http://www.ambedkar.org/ ambcd/02.Annihilation%20of%20Caste.htm.

35. B.RAMBEDKAR, ANNIHILATION OF CASTE (2nd ed.).

36. 13 Lakh Dalits Still Engaged In Manual Scavenging: Thorat, INDIAN EXPRESS, October 8th , 2013.

37. Id.

Babasaheb wanted as women's position in society,[38] most of these dalit women cannot even count their money let alone education. Despite sanctions of budget for women and people from SC & ST backgrounds, the money hardly reaches them.

4.5b Economic Crises

The present Indian Economy is in bad shape today. Value of 'Indian Rupee' has fallen continuously and increasingly due to many reasons such as persistent inflation, huge deficit etc. On February 17th , 2014 Finance Minister Mr. P. Chidambaram claimed that it is expected that current account deficit (CAD) is expected to go down to $45billion from $85 billion as in 2013, which was 4.5 percent of GDP.[39]

India faces teeming poverty and a huge section of society still struggles to make both their ends meet. Stagnation has been corroding market liquidity and despite regular changes in Monetary Policy, Government and Reserve Bank have failed to control inflation. Unemployment too has reached its crescendo, it is two percent in rural area and three percent in urban areas. By January-1, 2012 the number of unemployed has increased to 10.8 million.[40]

In hindsight all this may be construed as a consequence of our politicians becoming oblivious of 'just' and pragmatic economic ideologies of Dr. Ambedkar. A more detailed study of his ideas clearly reveal that he had foreseen such situations and he was correct when he said that to ensure stability of money its purchasing power must be stabilized.[41] Another teaching by him that is ignored is his idea of 'Sate Socialism' where he believed that the State should hold full control of the natural resources and the key sectors to ensure socio-economic justice to the downtrodden

38. M.N. FARUQUI, CASTE SYSTEM: A MAJOR IMPEDIMENT TO THE DEVELOPMENT OF DALITS IN INDIA, AMBEDKAR ON LAW, CONSTITUTION AND SOCIAL JUSTICE 76-87 (2005).

39. Vote on Account 2014:Current account deficit to be $45 billion this year, says P Chidambaram, THE ECONOMIC TIMES, February 17th, 2014.

40. N.D. Shiva Kumar, Unemployment Rate Increases In India, THE TIMES OF INDIA (Bangalore), June 23rd, 2013.

41. Supra note 20.

sections of people. It had affected Indian economy in form of unprecedented increase in price levels of special commodities such as petrol and electricity.

Even on neo-liberal reforms he had warned that complete liberty would give unnecessary freedom to market players and have its direct impact on 'Social' fabric, and even this teaching by him can now be traced to be ignored when we see that post-1991 despite a steady growth rate, due to capitalist structure, the lower strata of society is being ignored and laws to protect interests of minorities have become defunct.

4.6 Other Issues in Contemporary India-

4.6a Water Policy

Dr. Ambedkar's views on water policy are also very much apposite in present context. India is one of those blessed countries which have huge geographical diversity and when there is drought in one state, simultaneously there are floods in other two states, still there is bloodshed for water lying in contiguous zones such as 'Kaveri' water dispute between Tamil Nadu, Karnataka and Kerela or 'Krishna' water dispute between Maharashtra, Karnataka and Andhra Pradesh. And in relation to these disputes, Ambedkar's policy to interlink rivers to transfer surplus water to deficient regions is bearing fruits, albeit slowly.[42]

4.6b Prohibiting Prohibition

Ambedkar was very critical of provinces for not tapping its resources.[43] He was a strong critique of complete prohibition of liquor. This contention was very practical and he justified by saying that a complete ban on liquor will not cease people from drinking rather it would give rise to illicit sales of liquor which would affect economy in three ways. Firstly, flow of black money in market will rise and secondly the revenue of the government will suffer, thirdly the revenue that will be spent from State's

42. P Abraham, Notes On Ambedkar's Water Resource Policies, Economic And Political Weekly 4772-4774 (2002).
43. R.G.BBhagvath Kumar, "Tensions in Centre-State Relations" in Dr.Ambedkar and Empowerment: Constitutional Vicissitudes (1993).

exchequer on policing to enforce prohibition will be a futile exercise and that too at cost of corrupt practices.[44]

In present context Gujarat can serve as best example. In Gujarat liquor is banned but still according to surveys it ranks amongst top liquor consuming states.[45]

4.7 Conclusion

Dr. B.R Ambedkar was indeed a prophetic reformer, transformer, and a true Liberator. He was a paragon of philosophy both democratic and social, an anthropologist and a spiritual thinker who rekindled the Buddhist imagination of a humanitarian society of Indian nation.[46]

After a detailed study of his principles it is observed that his shrewd combination of social economic and democratic principles present a circular reasoning between 'State Control' 'Economic upliftment of deprived sections' and 'Social Equality' because if 'State Control is used for uplifting the deprived, then social equality will automatically achieved and if 'Social equality' is attained absolute 'State Control' is inevitable. This proves that his reasoning and intentions aimed at collectively achieving equality and rule of law, both of which are the rudiments of any efficient democracy.

---

44. AMBEDKAR, THOUGHTS ON LINGUISTIC STATES 33 (1955).
45. AshleshaaKhurana, Surat: The Booze capital of Gujarat, TIMES OF INDIA April 3, 2010.
46. OMVEDT GAIL, BUDDHISM IN INDIA: CHALLENGING BRAHMINISM AND CASTE (2003).

5

Contributions of Dr. Ambedkar for Women Empowerment and Their Liberty

- Shruti Kamble &Avadhut Joshi ***

5.1 Introduction

The Indian society which we today observe has witnessed a large number of revolutions, reformatory movements, agitations protest, etc. The decades after 1900 are remembered largely for freedom movements, but in the same period the air, which was blowing in India had also an essence of change for the half of population. It was the time when most of the parts of the world were in favor of caging women and there were very few who were in support of providing women the opportunity to breathe in the air of freedom. In India the process to distribute the rights began with the draft of the Indian Constitution, and the most optimistic approach towards gender equality was to give all the rights to the women that a man possesses which kept both the sexes at an equal footing. Hence it gets clear that, if the constitution was framed by people who did not respect the human values, who were anti-feminist or were hardcore followers of the orthodox gender discriminatory principles, then the Indian structure would have taken a totally different form. Therefore, this is the reason one cannot forget the remarkable contribution of Dr. Bhim Rao Ambedkar in the context of journey of Indian women's liberty. It would be wrong to equate his works merely in the field of dalit rights because he devoted his life for Dalits as well as for women

*ShrutiKamble, Third year B.A.LLB(Hons), MATS Law School, MATS University, Raipur.

**AvadhutJoshi ,Fourth year B.A.LLB(Hons), MATS Law School, MATS University, Raipur.

of this country. And for the visible changes in the position of women in India and their empowerment, Dr. Ambedkar is a protagonist.

Since the very beginning of the civilization women were the weaker section of the society. In most part of the world women did not have the very basic fundamental rights. They did not enjoy any political, economic or social status. Every religion be it Christianity, Islam or Hinduism, every culture and every tradition placed them at an inferior position. The portion of the world which we consider to be the developed one where women enjoy equal status, even their past consists of a long history of events and revolts in favor of women. In India, Hinduism was prevalent and the later Vedic period and the epic period, lead to the relegation of women to adevastated position.[1] It was a period which gave rise to various social evils like denial of education, child marriage, female feticide, sati immolation, devadasi or sevadasi system.[2] The customs, tradition, and culture of the Indian society bound the feet of Indian women. These sets of customs, tradition, and culture etc. are being followed by both men and women since very long and put women into such a drastic situation that they became totally dependent on others and lost their liberty.

Dr. B. R. Ambedkar was an eminent jurist of modern era and many people are unaware of the fact. He was an extraordinarily intellectual personality who conducted extraordinary research on the position of women in the Indian society and the reasons why they were subjected to such position. He did a detailed analysis on Hinduism and concluded that the position of women in society was the gift of the moral values served to them by the ancestors. This can be understood from the lines of Manusmriti, which Dr. Ambedkar quoted and criticized in his book on "Women and Counter revolution":

Day and night a woman must be kept in dependence by males, and, if they attach themselves to sensual enjoyments, they must be kept under ones control. Her father protects in childhood, her husband

1. ACHLA SHARMA, Status of Women: A Socio-Historical Analysis in Different ages of Indian Society, RESEARCH JOURNAL OF LANGUAGE, LITERATURE AND HUMANITIES, Vol. 1(1), 10-14, January (2014),www.isca.in, www.isca.me

2. Id.

protects in youth and her sons protect her in old age, a woman is never fit for Independence.[3]

Laws of Manu on the status of women, legitimizes the denial of independence, freedom, self-respect, etc. to women. Dr. Ambedkar attacked Manusmriti by ascribing an eminent apotheosis to women.[4]

Similarly in his book "Pakistan and the Partition of India" he has expressed his views about Muslim women and their rights and 1traditions, about wearing veil, and their marriages, etc. Thus, his vision was to humanize the nation and to develop a society on the basis of humane principles which is against any kind of discrimination. The Constitution of India has given equal status to women, which was the result of the visionariness, where Dr. Babasaheb Ambedkar played a major role.[5]

5.2 Dr. Ambedkar, Constitution of India and Women Empowerment

Dr. B. R. Ambedkar is well known as the chief architect of the Indian constitution. He was the chairman of drafting committee of the constituent assembly. In fact he played an exclusive role in it. For this reason Shri. T. T. Krishnamachari, a colleague of his in the drafting committee said in one of his speeches:

"The house is perhaps aware that of seven members nominated by you, one has resigned from the house and was replaced, and one had died. One was away in America and his place was not filled up and another person was engaged in state affairs. One or two persons were far away from Delhi and perhaps the reason of health did not

---

3. Dr. B.R. AMBEDKAR, Dr. B.R. AMBEDKAR SAMPURNA VANGMAYA, Vol. 7, NariAurPratikranti, 331, (DrAmbedkarPratishthanKalyanMantralaya Bharat Sarkar, 1998)
4. KB USHA, Dr. BR Ambedkar-the Champion of Womens rights, SAMYUKTA A JOURNAL OF WOMEN'S STUDIES, Sat, 11/14/2009, http://samyukta.info/site/node/225
5. Dr. B.R. AMBEDKAR, Dr. B.R. AMBEDKAR WRITINGS AND SPEECHES, Vol 8, 225-248 (Education Department Government Of Maharashtra 1990)

permit them to attend. So it happened ultimately that the burden of drafting this constitution fell upon Dr. Ambedkar."[6]

The valuable principles of equality, right to life, liberty are the base of Indian Constitution. Equality is given the status of fundamental right and is enshrined in the Constitution of India under Article 14, which states that 'the state shall not deny to any person equality before the law or the equal protection of the laws within the territories of India', is the reflection of his idea of gender equality. Further Article 15 of the Constitution of India favors women by prohibiting discrimination on the grounds of religion, race, caste, sex or place of birth. Also special provisions were part of the constitution which empowered the state to formulate special laws for the upliftment of women, such provisions include Article 15(3), Article 39 equal means of livelihood i.e. equal pay for equal work for men and women; Article 42, human conditions for work and maternity relief, Article 46, Article 47,[7] etc. All the statutory[8] provisions made thereafter in India were in accordance with the constitutional provisions. Thus now, the women have a legal shield to protect themselves against any discrimination. He did not confine his work merely to the special provisions in the statues but he implemented it into practical life. He used to encourage women to free themselves from the customary clutches, get educated and participate and contribute in the political arena also. Thus many times we may encounter equal participation of women as part of many of his important movements.

5.3 Struggle for Women Rights

The various instances from his life suggests his respect and modest behavior towards women. He has always appreciated equal participation of women with men in every sphere of life. This is

6. DR. B.R. AMBEDKAR, DR BABA SAHEB AMBEDKR WRITINGS AND SPEECHES, DR AMBEDKAR THE PRINCIPLE ARCHITECT OF CONSTITUTION OF INDIA, Vol 13, v, (Education Department Government Of Maharashtra, 1994)
7. Id.
8. Id.

the reason each of his protests, meetings or conferences witnessed the presence and active participation of women. In any of the conferences he could easily address the women in a friendly manner. The incidences like Mahad Chavdar Talab Satyagrah of 1927, where there were 500 women present at the protest.[9] After the Mahad Chavdar Talab incidence on December 25, 1927, Dr. Babasaheb Ambedkar made the bonfire of the Manusmriti. The fight against the societal structure which enslaved women started from the day when the Manusmriti was immolated. There were around 50 women who registered their presence with Dr. Ambedkar.[10] On its third day Dr. B. R. Ambedkar addressed a meeting of about 3000 women.[11] He expressed his views that the 'Depressed Class Women' should stop wearing silver ornaments and should bring decency in their outfits and clothing as is done by the women of higher caste women, so as to diminish the differences between the lower caste women and the higher caste women which could be easily identified by the their attire. He also added that the girls should be equally educated as boys, and suggested women not to feed their spouse and son if they are drunk.[12]

Similarly in Kalaram Temple Entry Satyagrah at Nasik in 1930, again 500 women marched alongside men.[13] Many of them were even arrested with men and ill-treated. To face tortures along with their men, women also organized their 'Samta Sainik Dal'.[14] Every time when Dr. Ambedkar approached the masses

---

9. DR. M.R.SINGARIYA, Dr B R Ambedkar and Women Empowerment in India, QUEST JOURNALS JOURNAL OF RESEARCH IN HUMANITIES AND SOCIAL SCIENCE, Volume 2, Issue 1 (2014), 2, http://www.questjournals.org/jrhss/papers/vol2-issue1/A210104.pdf

10. K.B. USHA, Dr BR Ambedkar, the Champion of Women Rights, SAMYUKTA A JOURNAL OF WOMEN'S STUDIES, Sat, 11/14/2009 http://samyukta.info/site/node/225

11. GAIL OMVEDT, AMBEDKAR: TOWARDS ENLIGHTENED INDIA, 32 (Penguine Books, 1st ed., 2004)

12. Id.

13. Id. at 10

14. Id.

to stand for their rights, he not only addressed men but also the women to come out of their houses, to break the bondage, to attain freedom, liberty and equality of status. When Dr. Ambedkar returned to India after attending the round table conference in 1932, hundreds of women were present for the committee meetings. At various places depressed classes women's conferences were held and they began to present their demands assertively. The encouragement was given by Dr. Ambedkar to empower women and to speak out their feelings in a bold manner. As Radhabai Vadale said in a press conference in 1931, *"We should get the right to enter the Hindu temples, to fill water at their water resources. We call these social rights. We should also get the political right to rule, sitting near the seat of the Viceroy. We don't care even if we are given a severe sentence. We will fill all the jails in the country. Why should we be scared of lathi-charge or firing? On the battlefield does a warrior care for his life? It is better to die a hundred times than live a life full of humiliation. We will sacrifice our lives but we will win our rights."*[15]

In depressed class women's conference held at Nagpur on July 20, 1942,[16] Dr. Ambedkar presented a memorable speech where he projected his beliefs for women, separately. He said that "I am a great believer in women's organizations. I know what they can do to improve the condition of society if they are convinced. In the eradication of social evils they have rendered great services." He further stated that, "since I have started working among Dalits, it been a routine to include women with men". Further putting forward his liberal views he said, "I measure the progress of a community by the degree of progress which women have achieved, whenever I observe this meeting, I get happy and satisfied that we have progressed."[17]

---

15. DR. VIJAY G. MORE, Dr. B. R. Ambedkar's Contribution for Women's Rights, MULTI- DISCIPLINARY E-RESEARCH JOURNAL Vol.-02, Issue-I, August 2011, http://ghrws.in/charity/Variorum/Variorum%20Vol.-02%20Issue%20I,%20August%202011/Dr.Vijay%20More-15-0.pdf

16. NANAK CHAND RATTU, BABASAHEB DR. AMEBDKAR SANSMARANA URSMIRITIYA 109 (Samyak Publication, 3rd Ed., 2007).

17. NANAK CHAND RATTU, BABASAHEB DR. AMEBDKAR SANSMARANA URSMIRITIYA 109 (Samyak Publication , 3rd Ed., 2007).

In his speech he focused upon the points that the women should learn to be clean and keep themselves away from vices. They should educate their children and instill high ambition in them. Speaking on marriage and parental responsibilities, he advised women to get married only when they are financially able. They should stand by their husband as a friend and an equal and refuse to be his slave. He reminded them that having too many children is a crime. The paternal duty lies in giving each child a better start than its parents had. He concluded his address by saying that, "I am sure if you follow this advice, you will bring honor and glory to yourselves".

His major fight against the unjust system which snatched away women's right was the codification of Hindu personal laws.[18]

5.3a Women Education

Dr. Ambedkar belonged to one of the backward castes. He was the holder of B.A. from Bombay University, M.A. from Columbia University, M.Sc. from London School of Economics, Ph.D. form Columbia University, D.Sc. form London School of Economics, Barrister- at-Law from Gray's Inn. London, L.L.D. from Columbia University and D.Litt. from Osmania University; at the time when the dalit people cannot think of studying as they were so socially depressed that they were not even touched. His studies made him to reach to the conclusion that education is the chief requirement in the society. He emphasized the education of women as a way to women's liberty, and believed that if a boy gets education, he is the only person to get educated in the family, but if a girl child is educated in the family the whole family is benefitted. He said that "it is the education which is the right weapon to cut the society's slavery and it is the education which will enlighten the downtrodden masses to come up and gain social status, economic betterment and political freedom."[19]

---

18. SANJEEV KUMAR, Women Empowerment In India and Dr. B R Ambedkar, INTERNATIONAL JOURNAL IN COMMERCE, IT & SOCIAL SCIENCES, http://ijmr.net.in/download.php last accessed August 3,2015

19. Dr. Navjot, Education and Vulnerable Communities-Reading B R Ambedkar's Vision, International Journal of English Language, Literature and Humanities, http://ijellh.com/education-and-vulnerable-communities-reading-b-r-ambedkars-vision/

When he was in Colombia University, he wrote to a friend on the need to educate the depressed classes, especially the womenfolk. To quote him: "We shall see better days soon and our progress will be greatly accelerated if male education is pursued side by side with female education".[20] Dr. Ambedkar perceived education as a catalyst for a movement for self-respect and self-help.[21] During his tenure of member of Governor General's Executive council, with a view to improving the educational and economic condition of the Schedule Castes, the Government of India decided to give scholarship for the year 1946-47 to the students belonging to these classes in British India who wish to pursue their studies in scientific and technological subjects beyond the Matriculation stage. At the same time women students offering Arts subjects in the Intermediate and Graduate courses were also made eligible for the awards of scholarships.[22]

5.3b Voting Rights for Women

Right to vote which is now is considered one of the greatest rights in a democracy was vehemently debated in constitunal assembly debates. Dr. Ambedkar was part of First Round Table Conference, where he discussed aspects of adult suffrage. Dr. Ambedkar strongly opposed the ideas of having limited franchise in India on the ground that people are not fit for it.[23] He believed that suffrage could not be given merely on the parameters of higher class, intellectuality or propertied class and leave, the lower classes at their mercy. There were many members who were

---

20. DHANANJAY KEER, Dr BABA SAHAB AMBEDKAR JEEVANCHARIT, 29, (Popular Publication New Delhi, 1996)

21. Id. at 10

22. Dr. B.R. AMBEDKAR, Dr. BABA SAHEB AMBEDKAR WRITINGS AND SPEECHES, Vol.10, Dr. Ambedkar as member of the Governor-General's Executive Council, 1942-46, 392 (Education Department Government of Maharashtra, 1991)

23. DR. B.R. AMBEDKAR, DR. BABA SAHEBAMBEDKAR WRITINGS AND SPEECHES 562, (Dr. Amebedkar In The Bombay Legislature, With The Simon Commision, At The Round Table Conferences) (Dr. BabasahebAmbedkar Source Material Publication Committee, Government Of Maharashtra, 2005).

supporting the franchise of literacy. Dr. Ambedkar in response called such system a fancy franchise as he was aware of the fact that literacy in India was unevenly distributed where few communities would have all the right towards it and others wouldn't have been left with anything.[24] If the principle of franchise of literacy were to be adopted in India, then the role of women in the democracy would have diminished to null as a result of low literacy rate among women. Dr. Ambedkar was advocating for separate electorate for minorities but it could not be achieved. In his speech he said that "unless I know that every man and every woman in the Depressed Class Community will be able to exercise their voting right and to determine the destiny of the candidate who is going to represent mass of people in the country, I certainly, am not going to consent to the joint electorate."[25]

Thus his focus in the matter of right to vote was not concentrated on the men but he equally identified women's right in this regard. The Adult suffrage in India consists of the efforts of Dr. Babasaheb Ambedkar. And it is amazing that in many of the countries it took women centuries to gain this fundamental right. In the countries like Saudi Arabia,[26] the battle to gain the right to vote for women was won just a year ago. And again still in many countries which we call the developed one namely, the United Arab Emirates and the Vatican City women are still struggling for their political rights.[27] Ambedkar's efforts ensured that the women in our country enjoy this right since the birth of republic. since men got this right. This serves as the great ideology of the gender equality of the chief architect of the Constitution of India.His major fight was against the unjust system which snatched away women's right.

24.Id.

25.Id.p.563

26.Women in Saudi Arabia to vote and run in elections, BBC NEES, 25 September 2011, http://www.bbc.com/news/world-us-canada-15052030

27.Daniel Tovrov, Saudi Women Vote; Which Countries Still Don't Allow Women's Suffrage?, INTERNATIONAL BUSINESS TIMES, September 26 2011 9:53 AM, at: http://www.ibtimes.com/saudi-women-vote-which-countries-still-dont-allow-womens-suffrage-318260

5.4Dr. Ambedkar's Contribution to Hindu Code Bill

"Dr. Baba Saheb Ambedkar was a symbol of revolt against all oppressive features of the Hindu Society."[28]

- Pandit. Jawaharlal Nehru

Hindu code bill is one of the most debated and controversial bills in the history of India. The idea behind the bill was to bring reforms in the Hindu Dharma. The reform movements had already started taking shape. Prior to the Hindu Code Bill ('the Bill'), the Act modifying Hindu Law related to women were the Caste Disabilities Removal Act, 1850; the Hindu Widow Remarriage Act, 1856; the Indian Succession Act, 1925; the Native Convert's Marriage Dissolution Act, 1866; the Indian Majority Act, 1875; the Hindu Gains of Learning Act, 1930, Hindu Women's Right to Property Act, 1937. The enactment of constitution of India provided equal status to both the genders, it provided a legal background to bring women at par with men, thus in order to convert thought into reality, there was an immediate demand to bring further reforms in personal laws. The so called customs and established societal structure among Hindu culture and tradition were a kind of obstacle in the path of women especially for their political and socio-economic betterment also.

Thus the Hindu Code bill was the remedy to the disease that the Indian System was suffering from. The Bill was welcome by the visionaries, who were in favor of national development and the followers of the humanitarian principles but was very brutally opposed by the followers of orthodox and blindfolded members of the Hindu Community as they found the Bill as interference in the religious matters of Hindu Society.[29] The importance of this Bill could be understood from the incident that, Pandit. Jawaharlal Nehru on being asked by a journalist that what would be the most important success in his tenure as a Prime Minister, he enthusiastically replied that it would be the Hindu Code Bill.[30]

---

28. Id. at 10
29. SARLA MAHESHWARI, SAMAN NAGRIK SANHITA, 28 (R. K. Publishing Pvt. Ltd. 1st Ed. 1997)
30. L. R. BALI, DR. AMBEDKAR LIFE AND MISSION, (BhimPatrika Publication, 2012).

It was suggested by Dr. Ambedkar in the constituent assembly debates that the Bill was aimed to codify the rules of Hindu law which are scattered in innumerable decisions of High Courts and Privy Council.[31] To a Hindu woman the Bill was a key to her liberty. The Hindu society had several oppressive features which kept the women in clutches. Even though women had all the equal rights as provided in the Constitution , but it was difficult to attain that without any positive support and for this, the Bill was a helping hand which opened the path for socio-economic development. It was a symbol of liberty and equality. The principles of codification covered right to property, order of succession to the property, maintenance, marriage, divorce, adoption minority and guardianship.

5.4a Inheritance and Economic Stability of Women

One of the drawbacks for women was regarding denial of their right to inheritance. There was no provision to make them economically stable in the absence of her relatives on whom she was dependent. The lack of such provision in the society blurred her status as an individual. As per the views of Dr. Ambedkar, the two schools of Hindu Law: Mitakshara and Dayabhaga created and sustained inequality. The Mitakshara School treated the property of Hindus, as belonging to a co-parcenary by reason of the birth of sons, grand-sons and grand-grand-sons. The property passed by survivorship under Mitakshara whereas Dayabhaga recognized the rule of personal interest and capacity to dispose off the property by the person having interest in it.[32] In this system the interest of the women in the property was never recognized. So the Bill, in an attempt to eliminate the gender differences came forward to recognize women's right in property with regard to the inheritance.[33] The remarkable changes in favor of women that were introduced by the select committee also

31. DR. B.R. AMBEDKAR, DR. BABASAHEBAMBEDKAR WRITINGS AND SPEECHES 5, (Dr. Ambedkar and the Hindu Code Bill) (Education Department, Government of Maharashtra, 1995).

32. Id.

33. Id.p.6

included succession to a deceased Hindu. The widows, the daughter, the widow of predeceased son, all were given the same rank as the son in the matter of inheritance. Also it was proposed that, daughter shall also be given the share in her father's property; her prescribed share was the half of the share of the son.[34] In the present Hindu Code Bill the number of female heirs recognized was much larger than under either in Mitakshara and Dayabhaga Schools.[35]

Also under the old Mitakshara and Daybhaga, discrimination was made among the female heirs, as to whether a particular female was rich or poor in circumstances at the death of testator, whether she was married or unmarried, or whether she was with issue or without issue.[36] All these consideration which led to discrimination of female heirs were now abolished by the way of Hindu Code Bill. Now a woman who had right to inherit had such right by the reason that she was declared to be an heir irrespective of any other considerations.[37] The last change in the matter of inheritance was made to the rule of inheritance in Dayabhaga School. In Dayabhaga School the father succeeded in preference to mother, the Hindu Code Bill altered the position so that the mother would succeed before the father.[38] Thus, the changes in that Bill suggested were purely to aid women.

5.4b Women's Property Under the Bill

Prior to the Bill under consideration the Hindu woman's property was categories into two categories; first, the stridhan which was again subdivided into numerous categories and the second was woman's property. The Bill consolidated the different categories of stridhan into single category of property and laid down a uniform rule of succession. The second change was that the son was now also given a right to inherit the stridhan and was given half of the share to which the daughter would be entitled[39]

34. Id.
35. Id.
36. Id.
37. Id.
38. Id.
39. Id.

Regarding woman's estate, Dr. Ambedkar clarified that the earlier a woman inheriting the property could just get the life estate. She could enjoy the income of property, but she could not deal with the corpus of the property except for legal necessity, the property after her death could pass to the reservoirs of husband. Then the Bill proposed to convert the life estate of a woman in property into an absolute estate and it abolished the right of reversionary to claim the property after widow.[40] Further, the Bill was also in favor of the proposition that the property which is given as dowry to the girl on the occasion of marriage shall be treated as trust property, the use of which shall inure to the woman and she would be entitle to claim that property after the age of 18. Thus the husband or his relatives seized to have any interest in her property, and they were disabled to waste such property and to make her disabled rest of her life.[41]

5.4c Separate Maintainance for Women

The Bill also provided for the right of wife to claim separate maintenance if she lived separate from her husband. The bill was in favor of separate maintenance for woman by husband if, he was suffering from a loathsome disease, if he kept a concubine, if he was guilty of cruelty, if he had abandoned her for two years, if he had converted to another religion and any other cause justifying her living separately.[42]

The provisions of inheritance, stridhan, and separate maintenance were an aid to the economic stability to the women. Sucheta Kriplani, one of the members in the committee praised the Bill and said that, "Much was said about the protection that is given to the unprotected women in the joint family. I know that in the past in a joint family unprotected women did get the protection. Even now some of them do get the protection but at the same time we know that hundreds of women, who failing to get any shelter in joint family, having no economic resources of

40. Id.
41. Id.
42. Id .p.9

their own, are hounded to a life of degradation and shame. Many of us woman, who are doing the social work come across such innumerable cases. Therefore, it is not only right, it is not only just to give woman her portion but it is absolutely essential to give her share if you want to safeguard the Hindu society about which you speak so loudly."[43]

5.4d Debate on Hindu Marriage and Esssentials

Those were the decades, when the individuality of a woman was not valued. For the general people the identity of a woman was glued either to her father or other elder member or her husband. For marriage as an institution Dr. Ambedkar gave it a very serene definition. He said that "the relationship between the husband and the wife should be one of the closest friends." As he was given the task to codify personal laws, the provisions regulating marriages could not be left out.

The bill also aimed to regulate the marriages and recognized two types of marriages the 'Sacramental' marriages and the 'Civil' marriages.[44] Each of the provisions of Bill was to bring the oldest institution of marriage into a more civilized form. Even after independence, the women could not enjoy her individual identity and were totally dependent on her father before marriage and after marriage were considered as the property of her husband. It was a social stigma that the unmarried woman was regarded as the burden on her father's head and the father the 'Karta' of the family, saw the marriage of his daughter, as the only way to remove the burden. This was the reason; the custom of child marriage came into existence. Child marriage was a social evil and was a hindrance to women development. Further there was another social disorder related to marriage dowry. The parents were ready to get her daughter married to a very old person or a lunatic or an idiot person, to escape from this burden. To be valid marriage firstly the Bill fixed the minimum age of bridegroom as 18 years

---

43. Id. at 11.

44. Hindu Code Bill, A Dalit- Bahujan Media, http://www.ambedkar.org/ambcd/64A1.%20On%20The%20Hindu%20Code%20Bill. htm (last accessed Sep. 14, 2014).

and of bride as 14 years.[45] It gave the girl and the boy enough opportunity to develop physically and mentally as marriage as an institution brings responsibilities to the spouse. Further the Bill suggested marriage between the two Hindu individuals, thus it also provided a room for inter-caste marriage.[46] Dr. Ambedkar was a genuine supporter of inter-caste marriage. In his 'Annihilation of Caste' he has suggested inter-caste marriage to be one of the remedies to end the caste system prevailing in our country. But the views generated anger among the other members and it faced opposition.[47]

5.4e Monogamy V. Polygamy

Where the old Hindu law allowed polygamy not actively but as in the manner prescribed by Manusmriti (Dr. Ambedkar has explained this in women and counter revolution), the new law preferred monogamy. The second condition was that neither of the parties should have spouse living at the time of marriage.[48] Monogamy was preferred over polygamy as two or more wives reduced the woman's rights and put her in a vulnerable position.

Even the proposal of monogamy angered the carriers of core Hindu sentiments. Dr. Mukherjee supported that the provision should not be made compulsory but should be left to the will of people. He tried to show his inclination towards this proposal but simultaneously raised doubts whether the government has the courage to impose the rule of monogamy over Muslims also.[49]

Shrimati Jaishree strongly opposed the views of Dr. Mukherjee and answered that in terms of rights, Muslim women have many basic rights in these matters than the Hindu women, which Hindu

45. Id. at 31 p.59, Section 7(3), Draft Hindu Code Bill as proposed to the Select Committee
46. Id. section 7, Hindu Code Bill as proposed to the Select Committee
47. DR. B R AMBEDKAR, DR.BABASAHEB AMBEDKAR WRITINGS AND SPEECHES Vol. 1, 67 (Education Department Government of Maharashtra 1979)
48. Id. at 31 p.59 Section 7(1),Hindu Code Bill as proposed to the Select Committee
49. SARLAMAHESHWARI, SAMANNAGRIKSANHITA 56 (R. K. Publishing Pvt. Ltd. 1st Ed. 1997).

law denies or does not provide. She questioned him where the Hindu marriage is qualified as pious obligation, whether it is followed in that pious and strict manner. In a Hindu society a man can have as many number of marriages as he wants and each of the oaths that are taken during a marriage are binding only on women.[50] There are instances where a man's marriage is fixed in front of his wife's dead body.[51] Where a marriage of a man is conducted in such situation and so easily how can one raise the argument that Hindu marriage is a pious tie between the two. She clarified the situation with an example from a judgment given by a court in Madras where the judge suggested that Hindu Law permits beating a wife.[52]

The third and the fourth condition restricted marriage within very close relationship and within the Sapinda relationships[53] as such kind of marriage brought bad health issues. The fifth condition was that neither of the spouse should be a lunatic or an idiot.[54] The Code even considered bigamy as an offence and penalized it.[55]

5.4f Conflicting Concept of Divorce and Sacramental Institution

Hindu Marriage is considered to be a Sacramental marriage, where it is a religious obligation. Prior to the Bill the Hindu marriage had the status of being indissoluble. The thought of dissolution of marriage as a provision was a cause of anger among the society . The Bill had the provision to consider a marriage either void or voidable at the option of parties and also related to dissolution of marraiage.[56] There were two grounds proposed by which the marriage could be declared null and void.First,if the

50.Id.

51.Id.

52.Id.

53.Id. at 31 p. 59 Section 7 (4) & 7(5) Hindu Code Bill as proposed to the Select Committee

54.Id. Section 7(2) Hindu Code Bill as proposed to the Select Committee .

55.Id. p. 77,Section 25 Hindu Code Bill as proposed to the Select Committee

56.Id.

party had a living spouse at the time of marriage and second if the parties were in prohibited degree of relationship the marriage declared null and void,[57] secondly to have declared marriage to be invalid, and thirdly to have marriage dissolved.. Four grounds were proposed to declare the marriage voidable. If either of the party was lunatic at the time of marriage, if the parties belonged to prohibited degree of relationship, if the bride has not completed the age of 16 years and if the guardian's consent was obtained by force.[58]

And the suit for invalidation of marriage could be filed within 3 years from the date of marriage. It also suggested that the children born out of invalid marriage to be the legitimate children. And at the end seven grounds were put forward on which divorce could be obtained. The seven grounds are: (1) Desertion, (2) conversion to another religion, (3) keeping a concubine or becoming a concubine, (4) incurably unsound mind, (5) virulent and incurable form of leprosy[59] The provisions of Divorce in the Hindu Code Bill again caught critic's eyes. Dr. Mukherjee in his speech in the assembly while opposing the Bill said that "Piousness, unbreakably and continuity are the characteristics of a Hindu marriage which suggests that a Hindu Marriage can never be dissolved. In the Select Committee appointed to discuss the Bill, support was only given by two members out of thirty three members. A single Section of the Bill was debated for almost seven days.[60]

The tool of divorce gave women an opportunity to dissolve marriage in case they were treated in an inhuman way. All the grounds that were listed up were based on very genuine requirement as in many instances women are beaten, ill-treated, sometimes made to do unfavorable acts against their respect inside the four walls of the house. Many members of the house were strictly against divorce. According to them the concept like divorce would

---

57.Id. at 15.

58.Id. p. 83, Section 29 Hindu Code Bill as proposed to the Select Committee

59.Id. p. 85, Section 30 Hindu Code Bill as proposed to the Select Committee

60.Id.at 29 p.47

mar the old established Hindu values of marriage . Dr. Ambedkar presented the most valid reasons in support of divorce.[61] He said that the shudra community since ages has been following the pattern of customary divorce. The whole shudra community comprised of ninety per cent of the total population of Hindus, and it would be wrong to impose the laws of ten per cent population over the population of ninety per cent. Further he also discussed about the Narad Smriti and Parshara Smriti which recognized that the women can divorce her husband when he has abandoned her, when he died or when he has taken parivrijya.[62]

5.4g Adoption Under Hindu Code Bill

The Bill favored that if the husband wanted to make an adoption it was necessary to obtain consent of his wife.[63] The widow could only adopt if there were positive instructions left by the husband authorizing her to adopt, also the evidence of such instruction should be by registered deed or by provision in will. Dr. Ambedkar presented his intension and said that the adoption is the fruitful sources of litigation in this country, where all sorts of oral evidences are manufactured, concocted; witnesses are suborned; widows are fooled. Few would take the benefit that they have made an adoption and the others shall make avowal that they had not.[64] Thus the registration of adoption was also necessitated.

While concluding his speech in parliament Dr. Ambedkar expressed that he does appreciate anarchy in terms of religion. He said that *"our society is an inert society. Society has never accepted its own power and its responsibility in molding its social and legal life"*. While to make the Hindu Code Bill a reality Dr. Ambedkar

---

61. L. R. BALI, DR. AMBEDKAR LIFE AND MISSION, 332 (BhimPatrika Publication, 2012)

62. DR. B.R. AMBEDKAR, DR. BABA SAHEBAMBEDKAR WRITINGS AND SPEECHES 271, (Dr. Ambedkar and the Hindu Code Bill) (Education Department, Government of Maharashtra, 1995).

63. Id. p. 107 Section 54 Hindu Code Bill as proposed to the Select CommitteeSupra note 15.

64. Id.

disinclined to bear a child for any reason whatsoever, she must be in a position to prevent conception and bringing forth a progeny should be entirely dependent on the choice of women. Only those children who are welcome by their parents can be of social benefit, and hence every woman must be enabled to prevent conception quite easily.[69]

Few of the members were of the view that introduction of late marriages would help to check the birth rate. But again on practical terms Dr. Ambedkar's view was that even late marriages in this regard would not be successful and there were less chances of population being checked. According to him more children would live up to the mature ages and hence there is an increase and not a decrease in the rate of growth of population. Also prostitution is encouraged by people who are unable to marry at an appropriate age, and other evil consequences also follow there by. Other contentions by other members included that the economic independence of women will hamper the growth of population but Dr. Ambedkar gave an example of women from lower classes and said that the women from lower classes are actually helping their families with their own earnings but that does not seem to affect family limitation to any extent.[70] Meanwhile the members insisted that the people should follow the principle of self-control.[71] Mr. Roham rebutted the above statement by considering it to be impractical and illogical. In the assembly he then read a part of pamphlet by Mrs. Sarojini Mehta: *'How many lessons on continence can pupils find in the Mahabharat, the Bhagwat and the Puranas? How can an age, that never knew what continence was, inspire us to observe that virtue? How is it possible to consider that age to have observed continence in which there were incidents like the story of King Dushyanta, who first*

---

69. Id.
70. Id. p. 272
71. DR. RAJENDRA D. JEUR , Relevance of B.R. Ambedkar's Thought on Family Planning, RESEARCHJOURNALI'S JOURNAL OF SOCIOLOGY, Volume 2, No. 1 January, http://www.researchjournali.com/pdf/336.pdf

misled an innocent and guileless girl living in the hermitage of a sage and then discarded her when she was pregnant?[72]

The issue of birth control was important in respect of many aspects. Dr. Ambedkar in the speech highlighted the health status of women and the child's overall development. The issue of birth control was not merely confined to the National problem of population growth but according to Dr. Ambedkar, it was taken to the grass root level of family system. The thought of giving women their reproductive rights was innovative and a revolutionary concept. It was a step forward towards the dignity of women. The will and the consent of women were recognized by his vision. Dr. Ambedkar advocated the introduction of new measures for birth control.[73] He suggested that vasectomy would be useful in the case.[74]

The other important legislation in the field of women rights by Dr. Ambedkar was Mines Maternity Benefit Act and the amendment proposed by him.

5.5 The Question of Women's Identity

Since the emancipation of women is a journey, this journey consisted of several small and large steps. Even in the immediate decades after independence, lack of awareness still prevailed among women. There were some instances where few sections of women were protesting the Hindu Code Bill, of which the major part was only for empowering women. After independence, India adopted the principle of adult franchise where women were also given the right to vote as an individual citizen. When it came to their enrollment into the voter's lists, the situation went problematic

72. Dr. Ambedkar in the Bombay Legislature, A Dalit- Bahujan Media, http://www.ambedkar.org/ambcd/13D.% 20Dr.%20 Ambedkar % 20in% 20the% 20Bombay% 20Legislature% 20 Appendix.htm (last accessed Sep. 17, 2014).

73. Id .at 71

74. Dr. B.R. Ambedkar, Dr. BABA SAHEB AMBEDKAR WRITINGS AND SPEECHES, Vol. 2, Dr. Ambedkar In the Bombay Legislature, With the Simon Commission, At the Round Table Conference, Dr. BabasahebAmbedkar Source Material Publication Committee, 263, Government of Maharashtra, 2005)

as in many of the places they were not enrolled by their individual names but by the names of their husband or father. On 25th September 1951, on behalf of Shrimati Renuka Ray, Shrimati Durgabai raised the question that whether the omission of names of women voters of Rajasthan was due to the fact that their proper names were not initially put down by the officials who prepared the list or whether the officers for the particular work did not get instructions to take proper names of women concerned which resulted in the omission of their names from electoral roll.[75] Defending the officials Dr. Babasaheb Ambedkar said that at the very initial level the officers were unable to get the real names of women in the particular states. To answer the question he presented two very genuine and practical situations, he said it was either due to the disinclination of women and in many times their relatives did not disclose their names.[76] As the law minister he had concerns towards the problem as the situation would have left the political participation of women in the statue books only. But in the assembly he assured that the election commission had issued specific instructions to the state governments that women voters must be registered by their proper names and not as 'wife of' or 'daughter of' and so.[77] The state governments were also instructed to make every effort through governmental agencies to ascertain the real names of women voters who were not registered on the rolls by actual names. The public were so invited to assist in this task. It was not due to lack of proper instructions that the names could not be entered in the rolls in the prescribed manner.[78] Thus these incidents present his view towards the empowerment of woman that they should be recognized by their own individual names and not by the name of their husband or father.

---

75. Dr. B.R. Ambedkar, Dr. BABA SAHEB AMBEDKAR WRITINGS AND SPEECHES, Vol. 15, Dr. Ambedkar as Free India's First Law Minister And Member of Opposition In Indian Parliament from 1947 to 1956, 1085 (Education Department, Government of Maharashtra,)

76. Id.

77. Id.

78. Id .

5.6 Conversion to Buddhism

"I was born Hindu, I had no choice. But I will not die a Hindu." [79]

- Dr. B. R. Ambedkar

On 14 October 1954, Dr. Bhim Rao Ambedkar adopted Buddhism along with lakhs of his followers He spent his whole life reforming the typical social structure whose foundation was based on the system of caste. His conversion was a reflection of his ideas of equality and liberty.

Dr. Ambedkar in his detailed article Rise and Fall of Hindu women, he countered an argument in an article published in eves weekly, which held the Buddha responsible for the fall of Hindu women. In the article he said that all the comments against Buddha in this regard are false. Buddha has never neglected or disrespected women. Before the phase of Buddha the women were denied of the very basic right that a human should enjoy. They had no right to read or study or get educated. It was by the way of Buddha Dhammma, the women could turn into a 'parivrajaka'.[80] Accepting women as parivrajaka was a revolution in itself, which gave the women the right to have academic excellence and gain intellectuality as that of men. He further added that, ideology of Manu was against theprinciples of Buddha, and Manu was the one to put numerous restrictions on women.[81] His ideologies were restraining the growth of Buddhism as a religion. Concluding his article he wrote that if someone is responsible for fall of position of Indian women in society, it was Manu and not Buddha.[82]

When the gender aspects of the Buddhism are observed, Buddhism has no place for any kind of discrimination based on sex. As per Henry Steel Olcott, in Buddhism the place of a woman is nowhere different than a man. In Chulla Veda, Buddha has

---

79.VASANT MOON, DR BABA SAHAB AMBEDKAR, National Book Trust of India, 96, (2nd, 1997)

80.Id .p.377-378

81.Id.

82.Id.

said that the way to attain arhat (spiritual position) is equally destined for a woman like a man, and she can also attain it.[83] He suggested that Buddhism as religion was based on scientific principles which has no place for any kind of inequality and discrimination. The conversion of his religion from Hinduism to Buddhism was a symbol of liberation from the discrimination on the basis of caste and also on the basis of gender.[84] In his book "Buddha and his Dhamma" he has presented several thoughts of Buddha regarding marital code of conduct, respect towards women, and importance of education for both the sexes and other moral and humanitarian principles.[85] One of reason behind his conversion was that he spent whole of his life struggling against the conservative and orthodox discriminatory principles present in the society and he found that Buddhist philosophies were based on the principles of equality and parity.[86]

5.7 Conclusion

Looking into the life of Dr. Bhim Rao Ambedkar and his work towards women, few may even consider him a hardcore feminist, who has worked on the grass root level. In the course of empowerment of women, he has worked in various fields ranging from drafting of Constitution, giving structure to the Hindu personal laws, labor welfare laws like Maternity Benefit Act, etc. He was the champion of social justice which included social, political and economic justice. He attacked the social evils of the society in order to safeguard the principle of social justice. Hindu Code Bill was his one attempt towards it. Dr. Ambedkar said that his fight was not against the Hinduism but against those principles which were pulling back the society. His speech in the assembly in the topic of birth control depicted his modern approach to mould the society into a better shape. He has recognized the reproductive rights of women which are still under debate in the present scenario. He emphasized the importance

83. HENRY S. OLCOTT, BUDDHIST CATECHISM- BUDDHA AND HIS DHAMMA SOCIETY OF INDIA 71 (2nd ed., 2003).

84. Id.

85. DR B.R. AMBEDKAR, BUDDHA AUR UNKA DHAMMA, 220, 264 (Buddha aurunkaDhamma Society of India (Reg.) SamtaPrakashan, 2001)

86. Id. at 87

of women education in the society. He majorly contribution in the field of voting rights of women. It must be noted that Indian women in the twenty-first century possess all these rights.In the present day, we have a long list of women who have progressed extraordinarily in their lives and contributed to society like Smt. Pratibha Patil former President of our country, Smt. Meera Kumar the present Loksabha Speaker, Kumari Mayawati former Chief Minister of Uttarpradesh, Sania Mirza Star tennis player, Aishwarya Rai former Miss world and the leading actress, Lata Mangeshkar in the field of art and music and so on. This liberty and freedom is achieved by the constant struggle and great ideologies. We are very well aware of the fact there still exist countries where women do not enjoy basic human rights. Malala Yousofzai's struggle for the right to education is one of the recent examples. But also due to illiteracy the social evils still prevail. The Indian social structure has become very rigid and complex that on one side we have women who have rised high in their lives and on the other side we have the profiles of the women under the veil. This section of the society is under developed and is afraid to raise their voices. For this Dr. Ambedkar had quoted- "so long as you do not achieve social liberty whatever freedom is provided by the law is of no avail to you".[87]

In the long journey of liberty that the women have achieved, definition of which still cannot be restricted to a few words, and the definition of which is ever-expanding with the progress of time, in that liberty includes immense efforts of Dr. Ambedkar which is remarkable and unforgettable. When a person in the world is asked to think about an Indian woman he will portray her as a women covered in sari doing household work with children all around. Now there is the time for us, to change this portrait of Indian women in our minds. To set free that section of women behind the veil, from traditional and illogical custom bounds, so that these women can spread their wings and get ready to fly in their sky of dreams.

87. Frances W. Pritchett, , What Path to Salvation, Columbia University, http://www.columbia.edu/itc/mealac/pritchett/00ambedkar/txt_ambedkar_salvation.html (last updated on Sep. 22, 2014).

6

The Hindu Code Bill, the Concept of Social Justice and Ambedkar's Role in Women Empowerment

*- Shashank Singh **

"I measure the progress of a community by the degree of progress which women have achieved."

\- Bharat Ratna B.R. Ambedkar. (1891-1956)

6.1 Introduction

'Women Empowerment' has been an area of academic research and forethought since the commencement of the feminist movement in the 1970s. Though the topic came into light later on, the initiatives started in the pre-independence era.

'Empowerment' itself as a tool of emancipation can have heterogeneous interpretations.[1] A widely accepted construal has been the social and economic unification of the disabled wherein power and authority develop a harmonious relationship.

While a number of politicians and activists campaigned for the liberty of women from the manacles of social obligations and compulsions, Ambedkar was arguably the most successful. This was mainly due to his multi-faceted talents. He was a reformer, an eminent jurist and a distinguished scholar. His credentials were well acknowledged and he held the office of Chairman of the Drafting Committee of the Constitution and was actively involved in the Constituent Assembly debates.

---

*Shashank Singh Fourth Year, B.A., L.L.B. (Hons.)W.B. National University of Juridical Sciences, Kolkata.

1. AndreBeteille, Empowerment, 34 Economic and Political Weekly 589 (Mar. 6-19, 1999).

Through this essay, the author attempts to elaborate upon Ambedkar's vision of a gender neutral society and his initiatives towards the same. The essay has been divided into three major parts, each expounding upon the vast and expansive work done by Ambedkar in the field of women empowerment. This includes 1) Constitutional assurances of emancipation of women. 2) Codification of Hindu Law and introduction of women's rights orchestrated by removal of religious compulsions and 3) Ambedkarite vision for humanity and means of achieving social justice.

6.2 Constitutional Gurantees

Ambedkar was intrinsically linked to the formation and deliberation of the Constitution of India in his capacity as the Chairman of the Drafting Committee of the Constitution. His position gave him ample opportunity to extend constitutional guarantees towards emancipation of women. His footprints can especially be traced in those parts of the Constitution that provide for the promotion of women's rights and the emancipation of the 'Depressed Classes'. There were several provisions that Ambedkar attempted to instil in the Constitution in order to safeguard women's rights. His concept of 'constitutional morality' later went on to form the basis for entrenchment of the Fundamental Rights ("FR") in the Constitution.

Ambedkar started by guaranteeing equality among the sexes as under Article 14.[2] This equality has a broad connotation and includes parity in social, economic and political spheres. Article 14 is supplemented by Article 15,[3] which prohibits discrimination

---

2. Constitution of India, Article 14 "Equality before law: The State shall not deny to any person equality before the law or the equal protection of the laws within the territory of India Prohibition of discrimination on grounds of religion, race, caste, sex or place of birth."

3. Id., Article 15 "Prohibition of discrimination on grounds of religion, race, caste, sex or place of birth

(1) The State shall not discriminate against any citizen on grounds only of religion, race, caste, sex, place of birth or any of them.

(2) No citizen shall, on grounds only of religion, race, caste, sex, place of birth or any of them, be subject to any disability, liability, restriction or condition with regard to:

on grounds of sex but allows affirmative action in favour of women. Ambedkar was in favour of reservation and he sought affirmative action not only for the 'Depressed Classes' but also for women as he felt that equality of opportunity was essential to reconcile the traditionally inherent inequalities in Indian society.[4] He favoured universal adult franchise for transcending the psephological and sociological barriers faced by a neo-democratic country as it would give women a voice in the democratic system. In his opinion, universal adult franchise formed the bedrock of democracy.

By placing these natural rights of equality and justice for all citizens under Part III of the constitution which formed the FRs, Ambedkar essentially ensured that they are not tampered with. The Constitution provides for Right to Equality as an FR which has been held as a constituent of the 'basic structure doctrine' thereby implying that the parliament does not have the power to amend or take away this right.[5]

Ambedkar placed special emphasis on Directive Principles of State Policy ("DPSP"). The DPSP are a set of special provisions which form the high moralistic stage that our country has always been renowned for. The DPSPs have a particular solicitude for the weaker sections of society and women. Ambedkar resolutely defended any amendment which sought to exclude women from the purview of the rights accessible through the Constitution.[6]

(a) access to shops, public restaurants, hotels and palaces of public entertainment; or

(b) the use of wells, tanks, bathing ghats, roads and places of public resort maintained wholly or partly out of State funds or dedicated to the use of the general public.

(3) Nothing in this article shall prevent the State from making any special provision for women and children.

(4) Nothing in this article or in clause (2) of Article 29 shall prevent the State from making any special provision for the advancement of any socially and educationally backward classes of citizens or for the Scheduled Castes and the Scheduled Tribes."

4. CONSTITUENT ASSEMBLY DEBATES, Vol. VII p. 699.

5. IR Coelho v. State of Tamil Nadu, AIR 2007 SC 861: See generallyKesavanandaBhartiSripadagalvaru v. State of Kerela, AIR 1973 SC 1461.

6. Supra note 4, at 504.

Article 39[7] which gives constitutional status to 'equal pay for equal work' was incepted through the intellectual reformist ideology of Ambedkar. He thought that for women to achieve true liberty, economic freedom was of paramount significance. Their wellbeing and health was also given due importance as a woman forms the nucleus of a family. Article 42[8] thus underscores this aspect allowing maternity relief as a constitutional right for women.

Throughout his life Ambedkar denounced religious practices that acted as a detriment to women's' liberties. Article 44[9] holds a unique position in Indian democracy as it reaffirms the State's 'endeavour for a uniform civil code'. Ambedkar staunchly supported a uniform civil code as he believed that "religion shouldn't be given a vast and expansive jurisdiction, so as to cover the whole of life and to prevent the legislature from encroaching upon that field."[10] He opined that the liberty of a woman was curtailed by the discriminatory and unequal practices followed by most religions. His bravest adventures include the codification of Hindu Law.

---

7. Supra note 2, Article 39 "Certain principles of policy to be followed by the State: The State shall, in particular, direct its policy towards securing:

(i) that the citizens, men and women equally, have the right to an adequate means to livelihood;

(ii) that the ownership and control of the material resources of the community are so distributed as best to subserve the common good;

(iii) that the operation of the economic system does not result in the concentration of wealth and means of production to the common detriment;

(iv) that there is equal pay for equal work for both men and women;

(v) that the health and strength of workers, men and women, and the tender age of children are not abused and that citizens are not forced by economic necessity to enter avocations unsuited to their age or strength;

(vi) that children are given opportunities and facilities to develop in a healthy manner and in conditions of freedom and dignity and that childhood and youth are protected against exploitation and against moral and material abandonment."

8.Id. Article 42 "Provision for just and humane conditions of work and maternity relief The State shall make provision for securing just and humane conditions of work and for maternity relief"

9.Id.Article 44 "Uniform civil code for the citizens The State shall endeavour to secure for the citizens a uniform civil code throughout the territory of India."

10. ChristopheJaffrelot, Ambedkar And The Uniform Civil Code, OUTLOOK (New Delhi) March 7, 2013.

6.3 Codification of Hindu Law

At the time of independence, the country was dominated by Hindus, but unlike Pakistan which declared itself an Islamic State, India sought to choose the higher moral ground of secularism. This meant that the personal laws of each religion had to be accommodated within the ambit of our Constitution. It was no hidden fact that while in power the British wanted to codify Hindu law,[11] but due to the unfavourable political situation in India at that point in time, the idea was shelved. Hindu law as it stood after independence was disadvantageous to women as it followed the concept of 'sacramental' marriage which inherently allows limited property rights and no divorce rights to women. Further, the social status of women in rural areas was wretched as polygamy was prevalent and female infanticide was widely practiced.[12] Manusmriti which dealt with Hindu law before its codification was extremely prejudiced against women.[13] Other scriptures of pious importance to Hindus too discriminated against women as they fastened the Hindu society into a patriarchal social system wherein women were depicted inferior to men.[14]

Through major judicial decisions new women's' rights were introduced and applauded by the progressive sections of society. However, the lack of awareness at the grass root level impeded the enforceability and efficacy of these rights. Therefore, after

11. In 1937 the Women's Right to Property Act (also known as Deshmukh Act) was passed which created judicial ambivalence as the interpretations were ambiguous. Thus, the first Hindu Law Committee was formed in 1941 under the chairmanship of Sir B.N. Rau (later he went on to become the Constitutional Advisor to the Constituent Assembly). The Committee suggested that Hindu laws regarding marriage and succession should be codified. Consequently, the Second Hindu Law Reforms Committee was formed which reiterated the same recommendations in the submission made in 1946 which was then referred to as the Hindu Code Bill.
12. O.P. Diwiedi, Hinduism:Historical Settling in The Wiley Blackwell Companionto Religion and Social Justice, page 119 (2012).
13. See generally Manusmriti
14. SambuddhaGhatak,GenderMarganilization: A Discourse on the Status of Women in South Asia in The Developing World:Critical Issues in Politics and Society (E Ike Udogu ed.) 70 (2012)

independence Nehru revived the process of codification and appointed Ambedkar as the custodian of its reformation. Ambedkar in his capacity as Law Minister along with a Select Committee[15] took it upon himself to codify Hindu law by amalgamating the views of liberal and modern thinkers and disregarding unreasonable and perverse orthodox practices.

Ambedkar moved the contentious Hindu Code Bill in the Constituent Assembly[16] itself as he felt that the constitutional guarantees regarding gender equality would be imperfect without such a law.[17] The bill consisted of eight parts.[18] Despite the name 'Hindu Code Bill' the bill was to apply to Sikhs, Buddhists, Jains and all castes and sects of the society excluding Muslims, Christians, Parsi and Jews.[19]

The bill differed from classical Hindu Law in many ways. 1) It provided for separation and dissolution of marriage on certain grounds such as cruelty, infidelity, incurable disease, conversion of religion etc. which was a clear egress from the Hindu concept of sacramental marriage. 2) It eliminated the Mirtaksara[20] joint

15. The Select Committee which originally discussed the Hindu Code Bill under Dr. B.R. Ambedkar included ShriAlladiKrishnaswami, Dr. BakshiTek Chand, Shri L. AnantihasayanamAyyangar, Shrimati G. Durgabai, Shri L KrishnaswamiBhatathi, Shri U. SrinivasaMallayya, ShriMihirLalChattopadhyay, Dr. P.S. Deshmuks, ShrimatiRenuka Ray, Dr. P.K. Sen, BabuRamnayaran Singh, ShriKishorimohanTripathi, ShrimatiAmmuSwaminadhan, PanditBalkrishna Sharma, ShriKhurshedLal, ShriBrajeshwar Prasad, Shri B. Shiva Rao, ShriBaldeoSwarup, Shri V.C. KeshavaRao.

16. The British government has composed the Constituent Assembly comprising of Indians in 1946 to draft the Indian constitution.

17. Supra note 4, Vol. I at 41.

18. Part I defined 'application of the law'. Part II dealt with marriage. Part III dealt with adoption. Part IV dealt with guardianship. Part V elaborated upon the controversial joint family property. Part VI had provisions relating to women's property. Part VII dealt with succession and finally Part VIII dealt with maintenance.

19. Hindu Code Bill, 1948, § 2.

20. Mitaksara School of Hindu Law is a more conservative school and practiced in large parts of India excluding West Bengal, north-eastern states and some parts of Bihar. Under this system the son gets a birth right over the joint family property and can ask for a partition. The widow cannot become coparceners and cannot demand property rights. There is unity in ownership. This school of Hindu Law awards deprives women of property rights.

family system and prescribed the Dayabhaga[21] system for all Hindus. 3) It gave inheritance rights to daughters in intestate succession. 4) It sought to give widows absolute property rights along with alienation rights. 5) The wife was granted maintenance in situations where in the husband was cruel to the wife, took a concubine, had a loathsome disease or deserted her for more than two years.[22] 6) It made monogamy obligatory and not optional.[23] This was hailed as an 'egalitarian pluralist legislation' which would help in the long term social inclusion of women the country.

The bill sought to provide more equal rights to women which included absolute rights in the affairs of marriage, property, inheritance, guardianship and minority.[24] Ambedkar was the first to propose eradication of dowry through a legislative enactment. He labelled dowry as a 'scandalous affair' and sought to give women absolute rights over the property they received by way of gift or stridhan.[25] He realised that the social stigmas such as female infanticide, sati, and dowry demands are intrinsically linked with one another. He believed that the traditional Hindu family consciously desired a male child in order to continue the customarily established Mitaksara joint family system and thus maintain the family lineage and inheritance rights.[26] Therefore, granting women property rights had truly empowering implications for women.[27]

---

21. Dayabhaga School of Hindu Law is practiced in West Bengal, north-eastern states and some parts of Bihar. Under this system the son has no right over the joint family property. Women as well as men are given a right to demand partition and can further alienate their interests. Widows can become coparceners and are given property rights. This is a far more progressive school of law than Mitaksara School.

22. RinaVerma Williams, Hindu Laws and Personal Laws in HINDUISM AND LAW- AN INTRODUCTION 110 (ed.TimothyLubin, Donald R. Davis Jr, Jayanth K. Krishnan).

23. Id.

24. NANDINICHAVAN&QUTUBJEHANKIDWAI, PERSONAL LAW REFORMS AND GENDER EMPOWERMENT: A DEBATE ON UNIFORM CIVIL CODE 105.

25. SeeB.R. AMBEDKAR, THE ESSENTIAL WRITINGS OF B.R. AMBEDKAR 495 (Valerian Rodrigues ed., 2002).

26. Id.

27. Id.

The line of inheritance could continue with daughters, women wouldn't have to be dependent on men while taking decisions regarding property which would further lead to financial emancipation of women in India. Ambedkar denounced the traditionalist interpretation of Shastras and argued that the Holy texts didn't give the husband an 'unfettered, unqualified right to polygamy'.[28]

The bill was staunchly opposed by Hindu fundamentalists who thought that spiritual validity of these laws would destroy the Hindu system[29] and some Muslim leaders as they thought that over the course of time the government would codify Muslim Law which would contravene and encroach upon their religious practices.[30] The opposition to the bill was immense as the Hindu fundamentalist parties called it 'anti-Hindu' and 'anti-India'.

Ambedkar's vision could not be fulfilled while he was the Law Minister as Nehru's political aspirations had to be balanced in light of the general elections scheduled in 1951. Ambedkar felt 'misled and betrayed' by Nehru and consequently resigned from the post of Law Minister.[31] His efforts did not go in vain as subsequently the original Hindu Code Bill was broken up but diluted into the Hindu Marriage Act, 1955; Hindu Succession Act, 1956; Hindu Minority and Guardianship Act, 1956; and Hindu Adoptions and Maintenance Act,1956 and was passed by the Parliament.

However, these ensuing legislations passed by the Parliament were a departure from the laws that Ambedkar had suggested as: 1) While the original Hindu Code Bill, 1948 substituted the Mitaksara joint family system with Dayabhaga joint family system, the final version re-established the Mitaksara system. 2) The dissolution of marriage was allowed but only after three years of

28. B.R. AMBEDKAR, THE ESSENTIAL WRITINGS OF B.R. AMBEDKAR 495 (Valerian Rodrigues ed., 2002)

29. Supra note 4, Vol.VII, at 543-6.

30. Id.

31. UpendraBaxi, Emancipation of Justice in CRISIS AND CHANGE IN CONTEMPORARY INDIA 128 (UpendraBaxi, Bhikhu C Parekh ed.).

marriage unlike Hindu Code Bill, 1948 where no time limit was prescribed. 3) It also reinstated the customary law which was abolished in the original bill. 4) The adoption rights of women were severely restricted. 5) The property rights which were at the heart of contention were harshly confined to only half the share as opposed to the earlier version which gave daughters equal rights as compared to the sons in intestate succession.[32]

Even though the abovementioned legislations significantly differed from the initial bill recommended by Ambedkar, their provisions were a progressive step towards the evolution of a gender neutral law as maybe observed in recent statutes that contain a watermark of Amedkarite values.

Ambedkar's vision wasn't restricted to emancipation of Hindu women; he was deeply sympathetic towards women of other religions as well.

"No words can adequately express the great and many evils of polygamy and concubinage, and especially as a source of misery to a Muslim woman. Take the caste system. Everybody infers that Islam must be free from slavery and caste. [While slavery existed], much of its support was derived from Islam and Islamic countries. While the prescriptions by the Prophet regarding the just and humane treatment of slaves contained in the Koran are praiseworthy, there is nothing whatever in Islam that lends support to the abolition of this curse. But if slavery has gone, caste among Musalmans [Muslims] has remained."[33]

Thus, his vision of a uniform civil code comes into picture and the history of subsequent years shows the profound affect that it has had on women's rights in the country.

6.4 Ambedkarite Vision for Women- The Concept of Social Justice

Ambedkar believed that women should practice defiance as it acts an effective catalyst for social justice. His relentless tirade for securing social justice with the help of law elevated the societal

32. Supra note 20, 115, 116.
33. B.R. AMBEDKAR, PAKISTAN OR THE PARTITION OF INDIA 215-219 (1946)

condition of women in the country. He had a special affiliation towards the 'Depressed Classes' but he never let his personal beliefs curtail or encroach upon the rights of other groups. He wanted women to be the vanguard of his patented philosophical vision of social justice.

"I measure the progress of a community by the degree of progress which the women have achieved. There cannot be an occasion of greater happiness to anyone interested in advancement of the depressed classes than to witness a gathering of women. Women should give education to their children, learn to be clean, keep away from all vices, instil ambition in children that they are destined to be great, remove from their minds all inferiority complexes, not to be in a hurry to marry in respect to themselves and their children unless they both are financially able to meet the liabilities arising from marriage, bear in mind that to have too many children is a crime, that the parental duty lies in giving each child a better start than its parents had and above all let each girl who marries stand up to her husband, claim to be his friend and equal acid refuse to be his slave."[34]

Ambedkar, in his journals Mooknayak (1920) and Bahishkrit Bharat (1927) condemned the the Hindu Brahminical order which is based on the chauvinistic socio-cultural construct of gender. Under his advocacy, there was a demand for new jurisprudential principles carved in the experience and image of women to emancipate them from sustained subjugation and domination. Women demanded rights to enter Hindu temples and to fill water from common supply. They asked for political representation so that they could be a part of the deliberative democracy and ensure gender mainstreaming by participating in policy formulation. Ambedkar argued that one must not be content with mere political democracy. We must make sure our political democracy a social democracy as well." In his own words,"What does social democracy mean? It means a way of life which recognizes liberty, equality and fraternity as the principles of life. These principles of liberty,

34. B.RAmbedkar, Addressing India Depressed Classes Women's Conference, The Awakening of Women (July 20, 1942)

equality and fraternity are not to be treated as separate items of trinity."[35]

Ambedkar's concept of social justice developed from the discrimination he faced throughout his life.[36] Despite his of brilliance and tenacity, Ambedkar was treated with disdain in the name of caste since his birth. His interpretation of 'social justice' was unswervingly linked to social contentment. For him, a just social system would spontaneously remove disabilities and help change the hierarchical social order into an egalitarian plain.

A distinguishing aspect of Ambedkar's social justice system is that its patronage lay in legal framework. Ambedkar was a constitutionalist and thus believed that articles in the Constitution enshrining principles of equality were essential for true realization of social justice. The Constitution is a gender neutral document and under Article 23,[37] property rights are seen as a symbol of independence and after comprehensively advocating for absolute property rights for women through the Hindu Code Bill, Ambedkar provided for Article 31[38] which contains a specific provision in regard to the fundamental right to property. By securing Article 38 in the Constitution Ambedkar ensured that free legal aid is provided to all and securing justice is not denied to any citizen by reason of economic, gender or caste disability.

Women empowerment as is not about short term appeasement by about protracted inclusion through economic freedom and social equality. Introduction of right to work, to education and

---

35. DR. AMBEDKAR,DR.BABASAHEBAMBEDKAR: WRITINGS AND SPEECHES 216 (Vol. 13, 1994)

36. Supra note 26.

37. Supra note 2, Article 23 "Prohibition of traffic in human beings and forced labour (1)Traffic in human beings and begar and other similar forms of forced labour are prohibited and any contravention of this provision shall be an offence punishable in accordance with law.

(2) Nothing in this article shall prevent the State from imposing compulsory service for public purpose, and in imposing such service the State shall not make any discrimination on grounds only of religion, race, caste or class or any of them."

38. Article 31 was repealed by the 44th Amendment to the Indian Constitution.

public assistance under Article 41 form an integral part of empowerment and social justice. Article 42 provides women with the right to maternity relief so as to not hinder their professional obligations due to societal, familial and health concerns. Article 46 emphasizes the importance of the promotion of educational and economic interests of the weaker sections of the society who have been previously discriminated. The ideal of social justice that Ambedkar formulated is seen as a benchmark while statutes are legislated.

In later years of his life, Ambedkar converted to Buddhism which promotes equality among sexes, self-respect and education.[39] In Buddha Dharma, Ambedkar found that women were treated in parity with men, they were venerated and loved, unlike Manusmriti, where they were treated with contempt and condescension. He felt that Hindu culture clogged the way to women empowerment. He favoured conversion to Buddhism and in his enlightening memoir The Buddha and His Dhamma, Ambedkar dedicated an entire part to the 'Conversion of Women' to Buddhism.[40] He publically deplored the hierarchical order entrenched in the Hinduism and consequently mass conversion ceremonies were held throughout the country.

The Ambedkarite concept of social justice has been successful in shaping consciousness about gender issues to the judicial class which has over the past few decades interpreted existing laws in the favour of women with due respect to the changing socio-political context in India. Ambedkar's vision has also influenced the political class with varying degrees of success into introduction of more women's rights.

6.5 Conclusion

Ambedkar made significant contributions toward rebuilding the country after independence. His intellectual prudence is widely acknowledged and applauded by the society. Ambedkar's vision of social justice still resonates in judicial verdicts which attempt

39.See generallyB.R. AMBEDKAR, THE BUDDHA AND HIS DHAMMA (1974).
40.Id.

to amplify the rights of citizens. Being the Chairman of the Drafting Committee of the Constituent Assembly provided Ambedkar with a platform from where he could advocate and provide constitutional guarantees towards gender equality. His unequivocal support for a uniform civil code has persevered after his life time and today's reformist are arguably inspired by his vision.

His arguments concerning gender equality are hailed by feminist groups and have inspired many social movements. He is rightly revered as the 'Father of the Constitution' where he successfully tried to incorporate women's rights.

Ambedkar's philosophical vision inspired many contemporary sociologists who highlight his viewpoint in the fight against gender discrimination. He was a supporter and defender of women empowerment. His work reforming personal laws has been of significant importance for the country. He fought for women's rights and ultimately brought about progressive laws regarding property, inheritance, minority, marriage, divorce etc. legislated in favour of women.[41] He is commonly referred to as the 'modern Manu' for his expansive and progressive interpretation of Manusmriti.

Even today the legislations passed in the Parliament today are in sprit of Ambedkar's concept to social justice and emancipation of the down-trodden. If not in literature, in action Ambedkar is definitely comparable to many feminist stalwarts.

41. ANJANI KANT, WOMEN AND LAW 355 (2008).

7

Dr. Ambedkar's Quest for Gender Equality

*- Tanvi Dubey * &Sachin Sharma ***

8.1 Introduction

A woman is the calm of a hurricane's eye, where a man finds tranquillity as the storm passes by. A woman is the pillar of a temple foundation, where a man comes and goes with renewed inspirations. A woman is the cloud that carries the rain, giving life to man's soul parched from anxiety and pain. But as we step into the past, we find that she never felt the frisson of dancing in the rain, never breathed the air of freedom, never became the person she could have been, without any fault of her, but only because she was a 'GIRL'. Her life was surrounded by a cloud of despair, pain and misery. She had lost all hopes and dreams.

But, suddenly she saw a new beam of light glorifying her depressed life. And that beam of light originated with the birth of 'Dr. B.R. Ambedkar '. Born on 14th April 1891 to RamjiMaloj Sankpal and BhimBai at Mhow. He was the saviour of the untouchables and depressed. The life of woman was constantly marginalised and ignored. With the rise of the Polar star from tatters in Maharashtra, named Dr. B.R. Ambedkar, women got their real emancipator. Ambedkar regarded 'Empowerment' as the process of increasing the spiritual, political, social and economic strength of individuals and communities.

8.2 The Mahad Tank Struggle

Dr.Ambedkar considered Gender Equality,Gender Mainstreaming, networking leadership and financial freedom as

*TanviDubey ,Advocate and Associate at ShardulAmarchand and Mangaldas&Co

**Sachin Sharma LL.M, NALSAR University of Law,Hyderabad.

the 'pillars of women empowerment'. The first revolutionary change was brought by Dr. B.R. Ambedkar and that was the changein the attitude of Dalit Women. In December, 1927 during the 'Mahad Tank Struggle',Ambedkar brought the Dalit women into the struggle. On the first day of the procession women marched along with the men. On the second day, Dr.Ambedkar exclusively day, Dr.Ambedkar exclusively addressed the women.[1] He arose the passion in them to participate in the struggle against the tyranny of gender inequality. This step of Ambedkar marked a progressive change in the lives of women as they were now prepared for a 'cultural change'.Dr.Ambedkar encouraged them to change their style of dressing, to do away with unwanted ornaments and send their girl child's to school. His speech was so effective that women dropped the unwanted ornaments in the meeting itself.[2]

Dr.Ambedkar started his movement in 1920. He started a fierce propaganda against Hindu Social Order and launched a journal 'MookNayak'in 1920 and 'Bahishkrit Bharat' in 1927 for this purpose. Dr.Ambedkar raised the global feminist demands which covered right to education, equal treatment with men, right to property and involvement in the political process. Dr.Ambedkar had the habit of working for more than eighteen hours a day without any difficulty. His reading habits helped him to understand the feminist developments in different cultures and across the world. In 1924, 'BahishkritHitkarniSabha' was formed marking another step of Ambedkar towards social-political equality of women.

8.3 All India Dalit Mahila Conference, 1942

Dr.Ambedkar dared to speak against the unpardonable boundaries imposed on women in Indian society. Another step of Ambedkar to the mainstream, got its start on 20th July 1942, when a historic women's conference was held at Nagpur. Some

1. Mathew, Thomas : Ambedkar : Reform or Revolution , Segment Books , New Delhi, 1991.
2. Heywood, Andrew : Political Ideologies : An Introduction, Macmillan Press London, 1998

25,000 Dalit women were part of the gathering.Dr.Ambedkar encouraged the women to be progressive, abolish traditionalism, ritualism and customary habits which were detrimental to their progress. Since Ambedkar himself was a victim of oppression and discrimination in all its severity, his views about women oppression and equal rights are more useful than anyone else, whose theory is based on mere observation.

8.3a A Way Towards Women Education

Master of Arts and Doctorate in economics, Columbia University; Master of Science and Doctorof Science ,London School of Economics and Political Science; Barrister at Law , Grey Inn, London. For anyone to attain so many degrees is impressive, but for an untouchable, born in a small rural town in a colonial country at the end of the 19th century it is even more. This superior education helped to propel Ambedkar to the leadership of a growing movement of India's downtrodden. Dr.Ambedkar's bitter experience in his early days, made him a relentless critic of a caste based society. Spiritual, Social, political inequality and the cultural-religious forces that generated it, became the defining framework of his life and its eradication, the focus of his career.Ambedkar stood as the 'fountainhead of wisdom and knowledge'.

Empowerment envelops developing and building capacities of individuals, communities to make them part of the main-stream society. Dr.Ambedkar regarded 'Education' as the only means by which women can grow out of oppression and mark towards democratic participation and involvement. Over the centuries, women in Indian society were denied the opportunity to educate themselves. Dr.Ambedkar put all his efforts to guarantee educational opportunities to women in Indian society.[3] Dr.Ambedkar regarded 'Education' as the only means by which women can grow out of oppression and mark towards democratic participation and involvement. Over the centuries, women in Indian society were denied the opportunity to educate themselves.

3.Ahir, D.C., The Legacy of Ambedkar, Delhi 1990.

Dr.Ambedkar put all his efforts to guarantee educational opportunities without any discrimination to all the citizens of India.[4] In the words of Ambedkar, 'It is the education which is the right weapon to cut the social slavery. It is the education, which enlighten the downtrodden masses to come up and gain 'social statuses, 'economic betterment' and 'political freedom'.[5] According to Ambedkar, society must be based on reason and not on atrocious traditions of the caste system. He found education, intercaste marriage and interdine as methods, which may eliminate patriarchy. Millions of women were enraptured when his endogenous ideas effused. He believed that a real woman is a 'treasure', if treated well.[6]

8.4 Efforts of Geneder Equality through Hindu Code Bill and Constitution

Ambedkar'sdefence for women as the Law Minister of free India appeared in the form of the 'Hindu Code Bill'in Parliament on 11th April, 1947. The Bill was a step towards the codification of Hindu Law, which was in a scattered form. Dr.Ambedkar proposed to reform these laws on seven different matters[7]

I. The right of property of a deceased Hindu dying intestate to both male and female.

II. The order of succession among different heirs to the property of a deceased dying intestate.

III. The Law of Maintenance.

IV. Marriage.

---

4. Government of India: The National Policy for the Empowerment of women 2001, Department of women and Child Development , Ministry of Human Resource Development , New Delhi, 2001.m

5. Omvedt , Gail, 2008 : Ambedkar , Towards an Enlightened India, Vol.1 Issue (2), pp 22-24

6. Ambedkar, B.R. (1987) "Women and Counter Revolution" Riddles of Hindu Women" in Dr. Baba SahebAmbedkar: Writings and Speeches, Vol. 3, Department of Education, Govt of Maharashtra.

7. 'Dr B RAmbedkar and Women Empowerment' byDr.M.R.Singariya, IndiaJournal of Research in Humanities and Social Science, Volume 2- Issue 1 (2014) pp: 8-12

V. Divorce.

VI. Adoption.

VII. Minority Guardianship.

However, due to the opposition of many conservative caste Hindus, the Bill was not passed. But, his efforts did not entirely go waste. Later, the original bill was split into four different Bills with slight changes.[8] Those were passed as the 'Hindu Marriage Act, 1955', 'The Hindu Succession Act', and the 'Hindu Adoption and Maintenance Act, 1956'.Ambedkar emphasized on the political empowerment of women for their all-round development. Ambedkar firmly believed that the relationship between husband and wife should be one of the closest friends.[9] The Hindu Code Bill, reflected Ambedkar's concern to abolish marriage systems prevalent among Hindus and to establish monogamy as the only legal system. It also provided for restitution of conjugal rights and Judicial Separation. Ambedkar's step attempted to unify the Hindu Code in tune with the progressive and modern thought.[10] Ambedkar measured the progress of the community by the degree of progress which women have achieved.[11]

There is undoubtedly, more status of Bhimrao Ramji Ambedkar in India than of any other historical person of the last millennium. They have been raised in every village, on crossroads, in every Dalit urban residential area and in front of education and governmental institutions, throughout the country.[12] They show a stocky man, usually dressed in a western suit and tie, holding a book under his arm. This book represents 'The Constitution of India'. Dr.Ambedkar gave India a living and organic

---

8. Omvedt , Gail, 2008 : Ambedkar , Towards an Enlightened India, Vol.1 Issue (2), pp 28-32
9. Id.
10. Arya, Sudha, (200) Women Gender Equality and the State, Deep and Deep Publications, New Delhi.
11. Gunjal V.R. 2012. Dr.BabasahebAmbedkar and Women Empowerment, Social Work, Vol. XI (1), Pp 88-89
12. KeerDhanraj 1990, Dr. Ambedkar :Life and Mision , Mumbai : Popular Prakashan

Constitution, enshrining in it all those conditions which are necessary to promote fraternity among all the citizens of frees India, including women.[13] He used all his experience and knowledge in drafting the Constitution. He gave free India, its legal framework and the people, the basis of their freedom.[14] His contribution to the Constitution was significant, substantial and spectacular.[15]

The text prepared by Ambedkar provided constitution guarantees and protection for a wide range of civil liberties for individual citizens including the outlawing of all forms of discrimination Ambedkar was Samson of Intellect, many credit him as the father of the Constitution. The article enshrined in the Indian constitution, reflecting the efforts of Dr.Ambedkar in the field of woman empowerment are as follows-

Article 14:-enunciates the general principal of rights of equality and prohibits the state from denying any person equality before law or equal protection of law. Amedekar, reflected the idea that when both expressions are taken together that aim at establishing the equality of status.[16]

Article 15 :- It is more specific instance to right to equality, which prohibits the state from making discrimination against any citizen on grounds only of religion race, sex and place of birth or any of them.[17]

Article 16:-prohibition of discrimination on the basis of sex in matters of employment. Ambedkar strongly supported the point that sex shall not be the sole ground of ineligibility for any post.

Article 21:-Dr.Ambedkar aimed at building India into a self-reliant and strong nation. He believed that nocountry can

---

13. Omvedt , Gail, 2008 : Ambedkar , Towards an Enlightened India, Vol.1 Issue (2), pp 1-8
14. Id.
15. Gunjal V.R. 2012. Dr.BabasahebAmbedkar and Women Empowerment, Social Work, Vol. XI (1), PP 84-85.
16. Constitution of India, Article 14
17. Constitution of India, Article 15

be strong by keeping a section of its own citizens deprived.The birth of a girl is not considered as a matter of pleasure. Even today in many part of India, thousands of female infants are murdered in their mother's womb. Our Constitution makers have taken a step in this respect by incorporating the very breath of the Constitution of India i.e., Article 21.Article 21 guarantees right to life and personal liberty. Dr.Ambedkar emphasised that right to life does mean merely animal existence, but means something more, namely the right to live with dignity.

Special protections under Direction principles of State Policy. To achieve the objective of social and economic justice in order to bring equality of status certain directives have been provided in chapter IV of the Constitution of India, under the following provisions:

Article 38(2):- It reflects the endeavour of the state to eliminate inequality in status, facilities and opportunities.

Article 39:- (i) It provides that the citizens, men and women, equally have the right to an adequate means of livelihood.

(ii) It also secures the right of equal pay for equal work.

Dr.Ambedkar believed that society is not improved unless each member of the society is taken care of. The present directive is thus, an effort in this regard.

(a) Article 42:- It seeks to provide for just and humane conditions for work and maternity relief.

(b) Article 51(A) (C):- It deals with the fundamental duty to renounce practices, derogatory to the dignity of women. Dr.Ambedkar regarded that the power of women is a power no man could live without, because without woman there can be no man.[18]

(c) Article 46:- It also reflects an effort of the Constitutional makers to promote with special care, educational and economic interest of the weaker sections of the people and thus, this marks an effective step towards protection from social injustices and all forms of explanation against women.[19]

---

18. Constitution of India, Article 51 (A) (C)
19. Constitution of India, Article 46

(d) Article 47: It provides that the state shall make an endeavour to raise the level of nutrition and standard of living of its people.

Dr.Ambedkar presented us a great constitution. He tried an adequate inclusion of women's rights in the political vocabulary and Constitution of India. He gave free India, it's legal framework and the people, the basis of their freedom. Ambedkar was a man of humour and courage. He regarded prejudices as a mark of imperfect human evolution. He believed that prejudices are a mark of imperfection, irrationality, arbitrariness, unfamiliarity and un-criticalness. The country which tolerates the scourge of untouchability and discrimination cannot claim to be civilized.

Path to Women Empowerment

Modern life is complex due to rising expectations of men and women. Women, in particular have to face problems due to increasing responsibilities. Society is not improved unless each individual member is taken care of.

Philosophers proclaimed that, 'when nature removes great man million years take for his successor'.But none came and none will be 'Messiah', like Ambedkar. The upliftment of underprivileged and downtrodden was in the very veins of Ambedkar. It was he, who courageously revolted against the existing state of affairs and organized the women so as to knock down those who discriminated unfairly.. There's a dire need of 'Self Realization' on the part of women, otherwise the Constitutional goal can never turn into reality.

Millions of women were enraptured when his ideas effused. Ambedkar's life reflects a story of a man, who gradually rose to become a lawyer of international repute, a founder of Indian Constitution, and a 'founder of a new order of Buddhism'. Dr. B.R. Ambedkar will be revered for centuries, by all lovers of social justice. With his breath of economic and cultural analysis, Ambedkar stood in the forefront of men who shaped India. Ambedkar dreamt of a society in which the women had full freedom to raise their voice against all sorts of discrimination.

He dreamt of an 'Enlightened India' based on the values of 'liberty', 'equality' and 'fraternity'. He believed that empowerment of a woman begins with herself. The power of women becomes even stronger when she finds herself and knows who she is. Ambedkar entertained a dream that political democracy can be translated into 'Social Democracy'. He tried to restructure a totally dilapidated structure. Ambedkar entertained a dream of an 'Enlightened India'.[20]

Authors believe that, though numerous laws have been made, but legal machinery can play a limited role in the social and economic emancipation of women. Law is a 'Fulcrum of Change', but law itself would not help the women to completely address the 'issue of powerlessness'. On account of the patriarchal structure of our society, women have been constantly marginalized and ignored. Dr.Ambedkar, gave Indian women a dream of enlightened future. He gave wings to the dream of thousands of women in the form of 'Constitution of India'. 'Justice to men and women' is the abiding creed in the Constitution of India. Social Justice provides strength to a woman, because she is no more a prisoner of customs and history.[21] Dr.Ambedkar recognised the fact that the lofty ideals expressed in the Constitution would remain as they were, given the nature of contradictions inherent in the society.[22] Law is only an instrument of change and without an active effort of the community; the adequacy of constitutional provisions cannot be questioned. He firmly believed that Emancipation of women is possible only when the matters relating to them are given a serious thought and positive step are taken to improve her social and legal status. Emancipation has to be translated into reality i.e. a public consciousness must be developed so that they are properly informed about their rights and an environment be created so that they are in a position to achieve what has been granted to them by law.

---

20. Omvedt , Gail, 2008 : Ambedkar , Towards an Enlightened India, Vol.1 Issue (2), pp 152-158
21. Journal of Research in Humanities and Social Science, Voulme 2 Issue 1 (2014) pp 1-4
22. Id.

8.5 Conclusion

Through this essay the authors would like to spread a message reflecting Ambedkar's dream, i.e. the dream of an 'Enlightened India'. And his dream can turn into reality only if we come together as an integrated whole and pledge to remove all the in equalities based on gender, and provide women with a dignified life in the society.So let us all come together and join hands towards a 'social change', which is still dream in our so called 'democratic country'. The whole ideas of Ambedkar are represents the true spirit of Feminist thoughts and demands. So from that sense we can credit him as the true feminist activist. Further his ideology has deeply rooted in philosophy of humanity and rationality as supported and argued by great philosophers like J.S. Mill and Kant.

Ultimately we have to remember that *"Lost rights are never regained by begging, and by appeals to the conscience of the usurpers, but by relentless struggle. Goats are used for sacrificial offering and not lions." - Ambedkar.* .

8

Caste and The Constitution

- *Ashok Kumar* *

8.1. INTRODUCTION

Dr.B.R.Ambedkar is considered the father of the constitution of India,he used law as a means to end injustice and considered it as an instrument for social reform. The constitution of India provides the fundamental rights which are antithetical to the age old social system i.e caste, varna. The preamble which is considered as the introduction to the constitution provides. *"Justice, social, economic and political; Liberty of thought, expression, belief, faith and worship; Equality of status and of opportunity and to promote among them all ;Fraternity assuring the dignity of the individual and the unity and integrity of the Nation."*

The concept of justice finds place not only in preamble but it is also enshrined in Part IV (article 39).[1] This concept was overlooked by the Judiciary for a long time and justice for years meant justice as decisions of the court, satisfaction of given set of legal rules or compliance to legal norms or maintenance of integrity of the legal process. It would be erroneous to maintain that justice can be equated with a procedural concept, therefore we must interpret justice as respect for rights or respect of human rights and the Indian constitution must never be viewed as mere tool for administration of nation. The constitution is a document for reformation and contains values which can transform the society.

* Ashok kumar,B.A.LLB(Hons), has graduated from NALSAR and is a independent researcher.

1. The State shall secure that the operation of the legal system promotes justice, on a basis of equal opportunity, and shall, in particular, provide free legal aid, by suitable legislation or schemes or in any other way, to ensure that opportunities for securing justice are not denied to any citizen by reason of economic or other disabilities.

Glanville Austin in his book *"Working a Democratic Constitution"* described the constitution as manifesto for social revolution and according to him one of the objective of the constitution is to achieve fundamental social change. We should note that the struggle for social reform continues seeking to bring Indian society into conformity with what is essentially modern.

Supreme Court in *S.P Gupta case*[2] held that the constitution is an organic instrument intended to endure its provisions,it is not a non-aligned rational charter. It is a document of social revolution which casts an obligation on every instrumentality including the judiciary, which is a separate but equal branch of the State, to transform the status quo ante into a new human order in which justice, social, economic and political will inform all institutions of national life and there will be equality of status and opportunity for all. The ratio in *SP Gupta case* must be read with Supreme Court ruling in *Minerva Mills case.*[3] The apex court said the Indian Constitution is founded on the bed-rock of the balance between Parts III and IV. To give absolute primacy to one over the other is to disturb the harmony of the Constitution. This harmony and balance between fundamental rights and directive principles is an essential feature of the basic structure of the Constitution.[4] The edifice of Indian Constitution is built upon the concepts crystallized in the Preamble, Part III has been put in our Constitution, conferring those rights on the people. Those rights are not an end in themselves but are the means to an end. The end is specified in Part IV,The goals set out in PartIV have, therefore, to be achieved without the abrogation of the means provided for by Part III. It is in this sense that PartsIII and IV together constitute the core of our Constitution and combine to form its conscience.[5]

Dr.Ambedkar wrote extensively on social reform, he found caste to be impediment for societal progress and he said *"turn in any direction you like, caste is the monster that crosses your path. You cannot have political reform; you cannot have economic reform, unless*

2. S.P. Gupta vs President Of India AndOrs. AIR 1982 SC 149
3. Minerva Mills Ltd. and Ors. v. Union Of India and Ors AIR 1980 SC 1789
4. Id.
5. Id.

you kill this monster,[6] caste is harmful for a democratic society and caste,chaturvarnya have spoilt Hinduism, and the sanctity of the shastras which uphold the principle of chaturvarnya be made illegal, Whether you do that or you do not, you must give a new doctrinal basis to your Religion-a basis that will be in consonance with Liberty, Equality and Fraternity, in short, with Democracy. I am no authority on the subject. But I am told that for such religious principles as will be in consonance with Liberty, Equality and Fraternity.[7]

These ideals could also be found in the constitution of India. The fundamental rights which guarantees freedom of choice, expression, employment and other liberties required by an individual for growth of his/her capabilities are also examples of such ideals. The aim of the constitution is to establish a just society based on liberty, equality and fraternity and it would not be possible without annihilating caste.Therefore I attempted to analyse the constitutional provisions which recognise caste along with judgements of the Supreme Court which touch the agenda of the constitution to annihilate caste. This paper is limited to annihilation of caste through inter-caste marriages, reservation and religious conversion.

8.2 Caste Based Reservation and Justice

Castes are closed groups,the membership to a particular caste is only by way of blood i.e by birth and the caste enjoys the sanctity of Hindu religion and castes are concerned about their group interests and Manu the law giver of the ancient time prescribed heavy sentences as cutting off the tongue or pouring of molten lead in the ears of the Shudra who recites or hears the Veda and other penal provisions if one changes his occupation.[8] Most of the occupations in the society are based on castes and also the hierarchical organisation of the caste system responsible for producing a social psychology, which is noteworthy. In the first place it produces a spirit of rivalry among the different castes for dignity. Secondly it produces an ascending scale of hatred

6. Dr.B.R.Ambedkar,Annhilation of Caste.
7. Id.
8. Dr.B.R.Ambedkar,Philosophy of Hinduism

and descending scale of contempt,[9] Caste devitalises by denying to him the right to cultivate vital interest and Caste prevents mobilisation. Caste System is not merely division of labour. it is also a division of labourers and later by the unnatural division of people into water tight compartments.If a Hindu is seen to starve rather than take to new occupations not assigned to his Caste, the reason is to be found in the Caste System. By not permitting readjustment of occupations, caste becomes a direct cause of much of the unemployment we see in the country.[10] The idea of fraternity is absent in caste system in these adverse circumstances reservation in employment and education becomes necessary to balance power and to foster equality, brotherhood and liberty in the society, article 14[11] of the constitution guarantees equality and article 15[12] provides that state must not discriminate one on the basis caste and article 16[13] which guarantees equal opportunities in

---

9. Id.
10. Id.
11. Article 14. Equality before law The State shall not deny to any person equality before the law or the equal protection of the laws within the territory of India Prohibition of discrimination on grounds of religion, race, caste, sex or place of birth.
12. Article 15. Prohibition of discrimination on grounds of religion, race, caste, sex or place of birth(1) The State shall not discriminate against any citizen on grounds only of religion, race, caste, sex, place of birth or any of them(2) No citizen shall, on grounds only of religion, race, caste, sex, place of birth or any of them, be subject to any disability, liability, restriction or condition with regard to(a) access to shops, public restaurants, hotels and palaces of public entertainment; or(b) the use of wells, tanks, bathing ghats, roads and places of public resort maintained wholly or partly out of State funds or dedicated to the use of the general public(3) Nothing in this article shall prevent the State from making any special provision for women and children(4) Nothing in this article or in clause (2) of Article 29 shall prevent the State from making any special provision for the advancement of any socially and educationally backward classes of citizens or for the Scheduled Castes and the Scheduled Tribes.
13. Article16. Equality of opportunity in matters of public employment(1) There shall be equality of opportunity for all citizens in matters relating to employment or appointment to any office under the State(2) No citizen shall, on grounds only of religion, race, caste, sex, descent, place of birth, residence or any of them, be ineligible for, or discriminated against in respect or, any employment or office under the State(3) Nothing in this article shall prevent Parliament from making any law prescribing, in regard to a class or classes of employment or appointment to an office under the Government of, or any local or other authority within, a State or Union territory,

employment or public services, thereby the backward classes such as scheduled castes ,other backward castes and scheduled tribals who are looked down as social inferiors could seek employment through the right enshrined in the constitution, reservation in fact is one of the instruments for annihilation of caste. This is an economical and educational means to destroy caste bit by bit.[14]

The legislative intent of the members of the Constitution Assembly could be understood from Prof. K. T. Shah address in Constitution Assembly recommending reservation provisions for scheduled castes and tribes: *"In regard to the scheduled castes and backward tribes, it is an open secret that they have been neglected in the past; and their rights and claims to enjoy and have the capacity to enjoy as equal citizens happens to be denied to them because of their backwardness. I seek therefore by this motion to include them also within the scope of this sub-clause (2), so that any special discrimination in favour of them may not be regarded as violating the basic principles of equality for all classes of citizens in the country. They need and must be given, for some time to come at any rate, special treatment in regard to education, in regard to opportunity for employment, and in many other cases where their present inequality, their present backwardness is only a hindrance to the rapid development of the country.Any section of the community which is backward must necessarily impede the progress of the rest; and it is only in the interest of the community itself, therefore, that it is but right and proper we should provide facilities so that they may be brought up-to-date so today and the*

---

any requirement as to residence within that State or Union territory prior to such employment or appointment(4) Nothing in this article shall prevent the State from making any provision for the reservation of appointments or posts in favor of any backward class of citizens which, in the opinion of the State, is not adequately represented in the services under the State(5) Nothing in this article shall affect the operation of any law which provides that the incumbent of an office in connection with the affairs of any religious or denominational institution or any member of the governing body thereof shall be a person professing a particular religion or belonging to a particular denomination.

14. KanchaIlaiah , Reservations: Experience as Framework of Debate ,Economic and Political Weekly, Vol. 25, No. 41 (Oct. 13, 1990), pp. 2307-2310 , http://www.jstor.org/stable/4396868

uniform progress of all be forwarded.I have, of course, not included in my amendment the length of years, the term of years for which some such special treatment may be given. That may be determined by the circumstances of the day. I only want to draw your attention to the fact that there are classes of our citizens who may need through no fault of theirs, some special treatment if equality is not to be equality of name only or on paper only, but equality of fact. I trust this will commend itself to the House and the amendment will be accepted." [15]

8.2.a Judicial Interpretation of Caste based Reservation

The first judgement by the Supreme Court against caste based reservation was *Champakam Dorairajan,*[16] the state government of Tamil Nadu wanted to implement an order with respect to reservation, notification G.O.No. 1254 dated 17.5.1948 commonly known as Communal G.O which restricted the number of seats in Government Colleges for certain castes, aggrieved by the above mentioned G.O, The petitioner Smt. Champakam Dorairajan approached the Madras High Court by way of writ petition contending that her fundamental rights guaranteed under Articles 15(1)[17] and 29(2)[18] of the Constitution were infringed, the High Court allowed the petition and set aside the G.O, the State Government appealed against the judgement of the High Court at the Supreme Court but it was dismissed by the court holding that the impugned G.O was ultra vires of article 29(2) of Part III of Constitution .Therefore to mitigate the damage the judgement could have on the reservation scheme the Parliament

---

15. - Volume VII Constituent Assembly Of India, Constituent Assembly Debates On 29 November, 1948
16. State of Madras Vs. Smt. ChampakamDorairanjan AIR 1951 SC 226
17. Article 15. Prohibition of discrimination on grounds of religion, race, caste, sex or place of birth(2) No citizen shall, on grounds only of religion, race, caste, sex, place of birth or any of them, be subject to any disability, liability, restriction or condition with regard to
18. Article 29. Protection of interests of minorities(2) No citizen shall be denied admission into any educational institution maintained by the State or receiving aid out of State funds on grounds only of religion, race, caste, language or any of them

passed the Constitution (First Amendment) Bill[19] Amendment of article 15.

The Supreme Court in the case of *Rajendran vs State of Madras*[20] upheld caste based reservation in educational institutions if the caste(s) are educationally or socially backward,similar approach was taken by the Supreme Court in the case of *S.V. Balaram v. State of Andhra Pradesh*[21] The Supreme Court upholding the reservation in promotion in the case of *State of Punjab vs Hiralal*[22] held that *"It is true that every reservation under Art. 16(4) does introduce an element of discrimination particularly when the question of promotion arises. It is an inevitable consequence of any reservation of posts that junior officers are allowed to take a march over their seniors. This circumstance is bound to displease the senior officers. It may also be that some of them will get frustrated but then the Constitution makers have thoughtof it in the interest of the society as a whole that the backward class of citizens of this country should be afforded certain protection as observed by this Court in A. Peeriakaruppan etc. V. State of Tamil Nadu"*[23]

The judgment delivered by five judge bench of the Supreme Court in *M. R. Balaji & Others vs State Of Mysore*[24] on 28 September, 1962 held that reservation in education shall be less than fifty percent or it cannot exceed fifty percent and it went a further a step by saying that higher standards and competency have to be maintained for the larger interest of the society .

The Supreme Court in the case of *AkhilBharatiya Soshit vs Union Of India & Ors*[25] on 14 November, 1980, decoded the egalitarian provisions of the constitution such as Articles 14 to

19. (First Amendment) Bill Amendment of article 15.-To article15 of the Constitution, the following clause shall be added:-"4) Nothing in this article or in clause (2) of article 29 shall pre-vent the State from making any special provision for the advancement of any socially and educationally backward classes of citizens or for the Scheduled Castes and the Scheduled Tribes.".
20. 1968 AIR 1012
21. 1972 AIR 1375
22. 1971 AIR 1777
23. 1971 AIR 2303
24. 1963 AIR 649
25. 1981 AIR 298

16 and held that the primary aim of these provisions is to enable formation of a casteless and classless society and to eradicate injustice and the age old cultural practises which have enslaved scheduled castes and scheduled tribes, article 46 the directive principles of the state policy which casts a obligation on the state to *"to promote with special care the educational and economic interests of the weaker sections of the people, and, in particular, of the Scheduled Castes and Scheduled Tribes, and shall protect them from social injustice and all forms of exploitation"*. The fifty percent rule in reservation as laid down by the Supreme Court in previous judgements could only be equated as guidelines provided by the judges ,however every case is different and must be decided by the available practical results obtained *by the application of the particular rule of preferential treatment and not with reference to hypothetical results which the application of the rule may yield in the future* and every rule which is just and withstands the scrutiny of the constitutional provisions must be employed to secure the due representation of the Scheduled Castes and Scheduled Tribes in public Services, it is important to highlight that posts which are reserved at the time of recruitment ,promotion and preferential treatment provided to SC/ST /OBC cannot be equated as concession or privileges but it is provided due the enshrined values in the constitution of India which guarantees to all its citizens Justice which is social, political and economical.

The Union Government on 7th, August 1990 planned to implement the Mandal Commission[26] recommendations for providing reservations for other backward castes in government services but the order was challenged in the Indrasawhney[27] case the court allowed twenty seven percent reservation in govt services but it introduced means test or creamy layer, which excluded the economically well OBCs from the ambit of reservation and other important ruling in the judgment was with regard to promotion of SC/ST employees in Govt services, the court

26. Commission appointed by the Janata Government in 1977-79, it was headed B.P.Mandal with a mandate to identify the socially or educationally backward castes.

27. IndiraSawhney&Ors v. Union of India. AIR 1993 SC 477

held *"providing for the reservation of appointments or posts under Article 16(4), the State has to take into consideration the claims of the members of the backward classes consistently with the maintenance of the efficiency of administration. It must not be forgotten that the efficiency of administration is of such paramount importance that it would be unwise and impermissible to make any reservation at the cost of efficiency of administration.* That undoubtedly is the effect of Article 335. Sensing this judgement could have adverse impact on SC / ST reservation the parliament had to amend article 16(4) and A)[28] by (Seventy-seventh Amendment) Act, 1995.

The Supreme Court in the case of *Superintending Engineer, Public Health, U.T. Chandigarh & Others Vs. Kuldeep Singh*[29] *& Others* held that provisions of article 16(4) which provides differential treatment of scheduled caste and tribe employees is not in violation of the equality of opportunity under article 16(1)of the constitution and held that reservation in favour of backward classes and SC/ST cannot only be at the time of appointment ,it shall also be at time of promotions, the court cited *State of Punjab v.Hiralal*[30] and *Akhil Bhartiya Soshit Karamchari Sangh v. Union of India*[31] and the court held the petitioner authority guilty of non-implementing the mandated reservation policy (reservation in promotion) and demanded action against the responsible officers and it also remarked *"Every public servant is a trustee of the society and in all facets of public administration, every public servant has to exhibit honesty, integrity, sincerity and faithfulness in implementation of the political, social, economic and constitutional policies to integrate the nation, to achieve excellence and efficiency in the public administration. A public servant entrusted with duty and power to implement constitutional policy under Articles 16(4), 16(4-A), 15(4) and all inter-related directive principles, should exhibit transparency in implementation and of accountable for due effectuation of constitutional goals."*

---

28. 77nd Amendment act, 1995, Article 16 (4A) Nothing in this Article shall prevent the State from making any provision for reservation in matters of promotion to any class or classes of posts in the services under the State in favour of the Scheduled Castes and the Scheduled Tribes which, in the opinion of the State, are not adequately represented in the services under the State".
29 . AIR 1997 SC 2133
30. 1971 AIR 1777
31. 1981 AIR 298

The Union Government through a notification relaxed the qualifying marks in departmental exam for promotion of SC/ST employees ,the notification to the affect was challenged at the Supreme Court in *S. Vinod Kumar v. Union of India,*[32] the court *held that such relaxations in matters of reservation in promotion were not permissible under article 16(4) of the Constitution in view of the command contained in article 335 of the Constitution. The Apex Court also held that the law on the subject of relaxations of qualifying marks and standards of evaluation in matters of reservation in promotion is one laid down in the case of Indira Sawhney and others Vs. Union of India and others. Para 831 of Indira Sawhney judgment also held such relaxations as being not permissible under article 16(4) in view of the command contained in article 335 of the Constitution.* Subsequently ,the parliament amended the constitution the parliament amended article 335[33] by way of Eighty-Second Amendment Act, 2000.[34]

The Eighty-Fifth Amendment Act, 2001[35] inserting Article 16(4A) of the Constitution retrospectively from 17.6.1995 was challenged in the Supreme Court in *Nagraj&ors vs U.O.I"* for providing reservation in promotion with consequential seniority as being unconstitutional the concerned State will have to show in each case the existence of the compelling reasons namely, backwardness, inadequacy of representation and overall

---

32. (1996) 6 SCC 580

33. Article 335 .Claims of Scheduled Castes and Scheduled Tribes to services and posts The claims of the members of the Scheduled Castes and the Scheduled Tribes shall be taken into consideration, consistently with the maintenance of efficiency of administration, in the making of appointments to services and posts in connection with the affairs of the Union or of a State

34. 82nd amendment of the Constitution (Eighty-second Amendment) Act, 2000 a proviso was "Provided that nothing in this article shall prevent in making of any provision in favour of the members of the Scheduled Castes and the Scheduled Tribes for relaxation in qualifying marks in any examination or lowering the standards of evaluation, for reservation in matters of promotion to any class or classes of services or posts in connection with the affairs of the Union or of a State."

35. The Constitution (Eighty-Fifth Amendment) Act, 2001, Amendment of article 16.-In article 16 of the Constitution, in clause (4A), for the words "in matters of promotion to any class", the words "in matters of promotion, with consequential seniority, to anyclass" shall be substituted.(It shall be deemed to have come into force on the 17th day of June, 1995.)

administrative efficiency before making provision for reservation" but the judgement seems to have overlooked the ruling in Indraswahney which held *"The Scheduled Tribes and the Scheduled Castes are without a doubt backward for the purposes of the clause; no one has suggested that they should satisfy the test of social and educational backwardness".*

The parliament amended the constitution by way of ninety third amendment act[36] with the objective to provide reservation in unaided educational institutions for SC/ST/OBCs and also for OBCs in central educational institutions, the amendment also highlighted there was a inadequate no of seats in Government run professional educational institutions, subsequently the Union Government issued a notification by way of G.O reserving twenty seven percent for OBCs in Central Government Educational Institutions, the notification was challenged In *Ashok Kumar Thakur vs U.O.I,*[37] the court allowed the twenty seven percent reservation and upheld the ratio in Indiraswahney judgement that the creamy layer be excluded from availing reservation and held that after exclusion of creamy layer the backward castes could then satisfy article 15 and 16 for the purpose of reservation.

The recent landmark judgement related to reservation in promotion is Rohit Bankar vs U.O.I,[38] the Supreme Court held *the judgement in Kuldeep Singh is concerned, we find that the matter was decided by this Court having regard to the constitutional provision contained in Article 16(4A). The view taken by this Court in Kuldeep Singh is in accord with constitutional scheme articulated in Article 16(4A). On the other hand, in S. VinodKumar, the Court failed to consider Article 16(4A). As a matter of fact, Article 16(4A) was*

---

36. Constitution (Ninety-third Amendment) Act, 2005.Amendment of article 15.-In article 15 of the Constitution, after clause (4), the following clause shall be inserted, namely:-"(5) Nothing in this article or in sub-clause (g) of clause (1) of article 19 shall prevent the State from making any special provision, by law, for the advancement of any socially and educationally backward classes of citizens or for the Scheduled Castes or the Scheduled Tribes in so far as such special provisions relate to their admission to educational institutions including private educational institutions, whether aided or unaided by the State, other than the minority educational institutions referred to in clause (1) of article 30.".
37. (2008) 6 SCC 1
38. (2014) 8 SCC 872

inserted in the Constitution to undo the observations in IndraSawhney that there cannot be dilution of standards in matters of promotion and it held the judgement in in S.VinodKumar per incuram.

8.3 Constitution, IntercasteMarriages& Annihilating Caste

"Caste in India means an artificial chopping off of the population into fixed and definite units, each one prevented from fusing into another through the custom of endogamy. Thus the conclusion is inevitable that Endogamy is the only characteristic that is peculiar to caste, and if we succeed in showing how endogamy is maintained, we shall practically have proved the genesis and also the mechanism of Caste" As marriage is performed within the caste members i.e endogamous marriages.Dr .Ambedkar held that one of the way to destroy caste system is by way of intercaste marriage, he said "I am convinced that the real remedy is inter-marriage. Fusion of blood can alone create the feeling of being kith and kin, and unless this feeling of kinship, of being kindred, becomes paramount, the separatist feeling-the feeling of being aliens-created by Caste will not vanish. Among the Hindus, inter-marriage must necessarily be a factor of greater force in social life than it need be in the life of the non-Hindus. Where society is already well-knit by other ties, marriage is an ordinary incident of life. But where society is cut asunder, marriage as a binding force becomes a matter of urgent necessity. The real remedy for breaking Caste is inter-marriage. Nothing else will serve as the solvent of Caste"[39]

The existence of social stratification for thousands of years have made the people of Indian subcontinent attach themselves to the caste system and one of their major worry is intercaste marriage would pollute their ritual status, therefore murdering people who undergo intercaste marriage is the evils of the caste system, one cannot change his caste as people are born into a particular caste in Hinduism. To maintain endogamy, violence in the name of honour killing is perpetuated against the couples who marry outside the caste or undergo intercaste marriage, states

39. Dr.B.R.Ambedkar, Annihilation of caste

such as Haryana, Punjab and UP account for about 900 honour killings and another 100 to 300 in the rest of the country.[40]

8.3 a. Constitution The Ray of Hope

Honour killings are violation of fundamental rights. Article 14[41] article 15(1)(3)[42] article 19,[43] article 21[44] and article 38[45] of the Constitution of India mandates and there is obligation on the state to protect the civil liberties and rights of the people undergoing intercastemarraiges.The Supreme Court in the case of *Lata Singh vs State Of U.P.*[46] & Anr held that intercaste marriage is in the national interest and they will result in annihilating caste system and sooner the caste is destroyed it is better for the society and India is a democratic country where the country is guided by the constitution and every individual has his her fundamental rights, therefore any person who attains majority can choose the person he/she likes and held that honour killings are barbaric and shameful actsperpetuated by feudal minded person

40. More than 1000 honour killings in India every year: Experts, available at http://timesofindia.indiatimes.com/India/More-than-1000-honour-killings-in-India-every-year-Experts/articleshow/6127338.cms accessed on August 1,2015
41. Article 14. Equality before law The State shall not deny to any person equality before the law or the equal protection of the laws within the territory of India Prohibition of discrimination on grounds of religion, race, caste, sex or place of birth
42. Article 15. Prohibition of discrimination on grounds of religion, race, caste, sex or place of birth (1) The State shall not discriminate against any citizen on grounds only of religion, race, caste, sex, place of birth or any of them(3) Nothing in this article shall prevent the State from making any special provision for women and children
43. Article 19. Protection of certain rights regarding freedom of speech etc(1) All citizens shall have the right(a) to freedom of speech and expression;(b) to assemble peaceably and without arms;(c) to form associations or unions;(d) to move freely throughout the territory of India;(e) to reside and settle in any part of the territory of India; and(f) omitted(g) to practise any profession, or to carry on any occupation, trade or business.
44. Article 21. Protection of life and personal liberty No person shall be deprived of his life or personal liberty except according to procedure established by law.
45. Article 38. State to secure a social order for the promotion of welfare of the people(1) The State shall strive to promote the welfare of the people by securing and protecting as effectively as it may a social order in which justice, social, economic and political, shall inform all the institutions of the national life
46. (2006) 5 SCC 475

and the court also directed that if any person instigates or issues threat against couple who undergo intercaste marriage must be dealt strictly with criminal proceedings. The court also held that There is no bar to an inter-caste marriage under the Hindu Marriage Act or any other law.

The Supreme Court upheld the LataSingh judgment in *Bhagwan Dass vs State (Nct) Of Delhi*[47] on 9th May, 2011, *it ruled that `honour' killings have become common place in many parts of the country, particularly in Haryana, western U.P., and Rajasthan. Often young couples who fall in love have to seek shelter in the police lines or protection homes, to avoid the wrath of kangaroo courts. We have held in Lata Singh's case (supra) that there is nothing `honourable' in `honour' killings, and they are nothing but barbaric and brutal murders by bigoted, persons with feudal minds. In our opinion honour killings, for whatever reason, come within the category of rarest of rare cases deserving death punishment. It is time to stamp out these barbaric, feudal practices which are a slur on our nation. This is necessary as a deterrent for such outrageous, uncivilized behaviour. All persons who are planning to perpetrate `honour' killings should know that the gallows await them.* The ratio in *Lata Singh* case was also upheld *ArumugamServai vs State of Tamil Nadu*[48] *and Kailas &Orsvs State Of Maharashtra.*[49]

The Supreme Court, based on a news report published in the Business and Financial News dated 23.01.2014 relating to order of KhapPanchayat to assault a woman belonging to the lower caste, took suomotu action and ruled that *"ultimately, the question which ought to consider and assess by this Court is whether the State Police Machinery could have possibly prevented the said occurrence. The response is certainly a 'yes'. The State is duty bound to protect the Fundamental Rights of its citizens; and an inherent aspect of Article 21 of the Constitution would be the freedom of choice in marriage. Such offences are resultant of the States incapacity or inability to protect the Fundamental Rights of its citizens".*[50] the court also upheld the verdict in *ArumugamServai vs. State of Tamilnadu andLata Singh vs State Of U.P. & Another.*

---

47. (2011) 6 SCC 396
48. (2011) 6 SCC 405
49. 1SCI 94, (2011)
50. Supreme Court, SuoMotu Writ Petition (Criminal) No. 24 Of 2014

The Law Commission of India, in its 242nd "Report on Prevention of Interference with the Freedom of Matrimonial Alliances" (in the name of Honour and Tradition)had suggested to reduce thirty notice period to solemnise a registered marriage under the special marriage act and it also suggested that strict action should be taken against members gathered in unlawful assembly for disapproving Inter Caste marriage.

The number of Intercaste marriages taking place across the country have increased over a period of time, the below survey on intercastemarriages seem to yield positive results. Some states are showing more than 20 percent inter-caste marriages. For instance inter-caste marriage in Punjab is 22.36 percent, in Goa it is 26.67 percent and in Kerala it is 21.35 percent.[51] The states showing very low percentages of inter-caste marriages are Jammu and Kashmir (1.67 per cent), Rajasthan (2.36 per cent), Chhattisgarh (3.38 per cent), Madhya Pradesh (3.57 per cent), Bihar (4.60 per cent) and Tamil Nadu (2.59 per cent). The states having moderate to high inter-caste marriages are Haryana (17.16 per cent), Manipur (18.33 per cent), Tripura (17.81 per cent), Maharashtra (17.79 per cent) and Karnataka (16.47 percent).[52]

8.4. Religious Conversion, Judiciary &Annihilation of Caste

Dr.Ambedkar declared "Though, I was born a Hindu, I solemnly assure you that I will not die as a Hindu".

"In a powerful speech to the Bombay Presidency Mahar Conference in 1936, Ambedkar declared that, "religion is for man and not man for religion. For getting humane treatment, convert yourselves. Convert for getting organised. Convert for becoming strong. Convert for securing equality. Convert for getting liberty. Convert so that your domestic life should be happy."According to me, this conversion of religion will bring happiness to both the Untouchables as well as the Hindus. So long as you remain Hindus, you will have to struggle for social intercourse, for food and water, and for inter-caste marriages. And so long as this quarrel continues, relations between you and the Hindus will be of

---

51. Kumudin Das, K. C. Das, T. K. Roy and P. K. Tripathy ,Dynamics of inter-religious and inter-caste marriages in India, available at http://paa2011.princeton.edu/papers/111281
52. Id

perpetual enemies. By conversion, the roots of all the quarrels will vanish thus by conversion, if equality of treatment can be achieved and the affinity between the Hindus and the Untouchables can be brought about then why should the Untouchables not adopt the simple and happy path of securing equality? Looking at this problem through this angle, it will be seen that this path of conversion is the only right path of freedom, which ultimately leads to equality. It is neither cowardice nor escapism." [53]

During the pre-independencedays,certain princely states had anti conversion laws, Rajgarh State Conversion Act of 1936, Patna freedom of Religion ,1942, the Sarguja state apostasy act,1945 and Udaipur state anti conversion act,1946, post-independence the government proposed IndianConverts Regulation and Registration Bill,1954 but it was dropped and the Backward Communities (Religion Protection) Bill was proposed and dropped in 1979, Freedom of Religion Bill seeking official curbs on religious conversion throughout India was proposed and was rejected. After the enactment of the Constitution of India, Right to Freedom of Religion was made a fundamental right, articles such as 25,[54] 26,[55] 27[56] and provides a clear definition of the religious freedom under the constitution, all citizens are free to preach,practise and propagate a religion of their choice.

8.4.a. Conversion, Law & Judiciary

In the contemporary times states such as Madhya Pradesh, Orrisa, Gujarat, Rajasthan, Himanchal Pradesh,Arunachal Pradesh have enacted anti conversion legislations with the objective to prohibit conversion by force, allurement, gratuity and other method by which one may renounce his religion and convert into another

---

53. Translated from Marathi Vasant W. Moon What Path to Salvation?Speech delivered by Dr.Ambedkar to the Bombay Presidency Mahar Conference, 31st May 193,. The typescript of the translation, with handwritten emendations, was presented by the translator to Eleanor Zelliot on 25 January 1988, available at http://www.columbia.edu/itc/mealac/pritchett/00ambedkar/txt_ambedkar_salvation.html

54. Article25. Freedom of conscience and free profession, practice and propagation of religion (1) Subject to public order, morality and health and to the other provisions of this Part, all persons are equally entitled to freedom of conscience and the right freely to profess, practise and propagate religion (2) Nothing in this article shall affect the operation of any existing law or prevent the State from making any law

religion but it is a ground reality that most of the states which intend to or have legislated anti conversion laws have been from tribal and lower caste dominated. Tamil naidu has enacted but it was again repealed in 2004.The anti-conversion legislations have made it a rule that permission of a District Magistrate has to be taken prior to conversion, people wanting to convert to the religion of their choice feel it is one of the bureaucratic hassles to deprive a person to enjoy his right to freedom of religion and many a time the fringe groups owing allegiance to the rightwing have used the anticonversion laws to witch hunt pastors and others who wanted to profess their religion at tribal and dalit hamlets.

In the recent times, the right wing forces in the country have adopted a practise known as Gharwapsi,[57] they are spreading this illegal activity across the country ,the lower castes and other have exercised their freedom to convert to their religion i.eIslam, christinanity, Sikhism, Buddism to escape slavery and untouchability, they are now pressurised to convert back to Hinduism. However in Hinduism there is no concept of shuddi or conversion, even if someone converts back what caste will he adopt? according to the principle of caste one can only take the membership by their birth in that caste.

(a) regulating or restricting any economic, financial, political or other secular activity which may be associated with religious practice;

(b) providing for social welfare and reform or the throwing open of Hindu religious institutions of a public character to all classes and sections of Hindus Explanation I The wearing and carrying of kirpans shall be deemed to be included in the profession of the Sikh religion Explanation II In sub clause (b) of clause reference to Hindus shall be construed as including a reference to persons professing the Sikh, Jaina or Buddhist religion, and the reference to Hindu religious institutions shall be construed accordingly

55. Article 26. Freedom to manage religious affairs Subject to public order, morality and health, every religious denomination or any section thereof shall have the right

(a) to establish and maintain institutions for religious and charitable purposes;

(b) to manage its own affairs in matters of religion;

(c) to own and acquire movable and immovable property; and

(d) to administer such property in accordance with law

56. Article 27 Freedom as to payment of taxes for promotion of any particular religion :No person shall be compelled to pay any taxes, the proceeds of which are specifically appropriated in payment of expenses for the promotion or maintenance of any particular religion or religious denomination.

57.Reconversion

The Supreme Court in *K.P. Manu*[58] case, held that a individual who converted from Hindu religion to Christianity and reconverted to Hinduism is considered valid and he can claim his caste status, the judgement doesn't not establish rationality, it is devoid of sociological or anthropological principles and evidences as the concept of Shuddi i.e conversion doesn't not exist in Hinduism.

There are many reports of preachers being murdered by the right wing fundamentalists, one such gruesome murder was burning alive pastor Graham Stanies[59] in Orissa. The conversion of lower castes to other religions from Hinduism is being stiffly resisted by the upper castes Hindus to maintain the Varnavyavastha and caste system, as conversion of the lower caste would mean their would not be anyone left to take up the menial jobs, an example of conversion which helped the lower castes is that of Pulayas in the state of Travancore which is now in kerala,

From the history of the Pulaya conversion movement in Travancore, what emerges uppermost is the development of social consciousness of a community in the various stages and changes of society in transition. Self-realisation of oppression and slavery naturally lead to finding ways and means of liberation. Forms of protest are evident in traditions, religious rituals, folk arts, and subversionary acts. An ideology of liberation slowly builds up, inspired mainly by the winds of the 19th century change which reach Travancore through the missionaries. The oppressed saw the doors opening for them as a way out of the misery with the success of the anti-slave campaign championed by the missionaries. An alliance is forged. For thousands, conversion was an act of social protest heralding exit from the inhumanity of the caste system.[60]

Dr.Ambedkar publicly converted to Buddism on 14th October, 1956 at Nagpur along with six lakhs of his followers thereafter scores of lower castes have been converting to Buddism and very recently On January 4,2015 around 1,700 Hindus in Bihar have embraced Buddhism citing the religion's emphasis

58. K.P. Manu Vs Chairman ,Scrutiny Committee for Verification of Community Certificate AIR 2015 SC 1402

59. India court backs life term for Graham Staines murderer, available at http://www.bbc.com/news/world-south-asia-12247916

60. GeorgeOommen, Dalit Conversion and Social Protest in Travancore, 1854-1890 availale at http://www.religion-online.org/showarticle.asp?title=1119

on unity and no discrimination among its followers, of these, 1,200 belong to Bainkathpur and Kudarbagha villages in Saran district, about 80 km from here, said a district police official[61] and at least five lakh people from the other backward classes (OBC) have decided to convert to Buddhism from Hinduism in Nagpur as they believe other backward classes and dalits have no respectable space in Hinduism.[62]

In the case of *Mrs. Yulitha Hyde & Ors. vs State Of Orissa &Ors,*[63] The Orrisa government passed anti conversion legislation titled "The Orissa Freedom of Religion Act 2 of 1968," two Christian preachers were tried under section of 3[64]&4[65] of the act, they subsequently challenged the legislation terming violation of the fundamental rights i.e article 19(1)(a)[66], article 25 of the constitution and the state of Orissa did not have the legislative competency to enact the aforesaid legislation, and prayed for quashing the legislation, the High Court validated the contention of the petitioner that that there is no specific entry in Schedule VII of the Constitution dealing with the topic of 'religion' and as such entry 97 of List I of Schedule VII alone must apply. The Act essentially deals with the subject-matter of "religion" and its provisions do not indeed relate to "public order". In Entry I of List II and held the act to be ultravires of the constitution.TheHigh Court made the following observations.

---

61. Bihar: Around 1,700 Hindus convert to Buddhism , http://www.firstpost.com/India/bihar-around-1700-hindus-convert-buddhism-2030339.html
62. Sudhir Suryawanshi,Five lakh Hindu-OBC people to embrace Buddhism by 2016, available at http://www.dnaIndia.com/mumbai/report-five-lakh-hindu-obc-people-to-embrace-buddhism-by-2016-2049100
63. AIR 1973 Ori 116
64. Sec 3.No person shall convert Or attempt to convert, either directly or otherwise, any person fromone religions faith, to another by the use of force or by.-inducement or by any fraudulent means nor shall any person abet any such, conversion.
65. Sec 4. Any person contravening the provisions contained in section 3Shall, without prejudice to anycivil liability, be punishable with imprisonment either description which may extend to one year orwith fine which may extend to five thousand rupees or with both. Provided that in case the offence is committed in respect of a minor a woman, or a, person belonging to the Scheduled Castes or Scheduled tribe the punishment shall be imprisonment to the extent of two years and fine upto ten thousand rupees.
66. Article19. Protection of certain rights regarding freedom of speech etc(1) All citizens shall have the right(a) to freedom of speech and expression

(1) Article 25(1) guarantees propagation of religion and conversion is a part of the Christian religion.

(2) Prohibition of conversion by 'force' or by 'fraud' as defined by the Act would be covered by the limitation subject to which the right is guaranteed under Article 25(1).

(3) The definition of the term 'inducement' is vague and many proselytizing activities may be covered by the definition and the restriction in Article 25(1) cannot be said to cover the wide definition.

(4) The State Legislature has no power to enact the impugned legislation which in pith and substance is a law relating to religion. Entry No. 1 of either Last II or List III does not authorise the impugned legislation.

(5) Entry 97 of List I applies. by this Court in Ramesh Thapper v. The State of Madras(1) that "public order" is an expression of wide connotation and signifies state of tranquility which pre- vails among the members of a political society as a result of internal regulations enforced by the Government which they have established"

In *Rev. Stainislaus vs State Of Madhya Pradesh &Ors,*[67] The Sub Divisional Magistrate, Balodabazar acting on the complaint dated 23-5-1970 made by the Circle Inspector sanctioned prosecution of the petitioner for the offence committed undersections 3,[68] 4,[69] 5(2)[70] and Section 6[71] of the Madhya Pradesh Dharma Swatantrya Adhiniyam, Act 1968, a criminal case was also registered under section 7[72] of the act,aggrieved by the action of the SubDivisional Magistrate and the Circle Inspector, the petitioner challenged the M. P. Dharma Swatantrya Adhiniyam

---

67. AIR 1975 MP 163

68. Section 3 .Prohibition Of Forcible Conversion :No person shall convert or attempt to convert ,either directly or otherwise from one religion to another by the use of force or by allurement or by any fraudulent means nor shall abet any such conversion.

69. Section 4. Punishment For Contravention Of The Provision Of Section 3: Any person contravenening the provisions contained in section 3 shall,without prejudice to any civil liability ,be punishable with imprisonment which may extend to one year or with fine which may extend to five thousand rupees or with both.(Provided that in the case the offence is committed in respect of minor, a woman or a person belonging to scheduled caste or scheduled tribe the punishment to the extent of two years and fine upto ten thousand rupees.)

70. Section 5 :Intimation To Be Given To District Magistrate With Respect To Conversion: (1) whoever converts any person from one religion religious faith to another by performing himself the ceremony necessary for such conversion as a religious priest or by taking part directly or

Act, 1968, for violating the petitioner's fundamental rights guaranteed by Article 25(1)and the state did not have the legislative competency to pass an act as it did not fall within the scope of Entry No. I to List II and Entry No. 1 to List III of the Seventh Schedule. As it falls within Entry No. 97 of List I of the Seventh Schedule and only the parliament had power to pass a legislation on the subject. The High Court dismissed the petition and ruled that the impugned act establishes the equality of religious freedom for all citizens by prohibiting conversion by objectionable activities such as conversion by force, fraud and by allurement and it held that the provision relating to conversion by allurement cannot be challenged either on the ground of legislative competence or on the ground of violation of Article 25(1) of the Constitution.[73]

K.M Munshi addressing the constitution Assembly said regarding the legislative intent for insertion of the word propagate in article 25(1) :

In the present set up that we are now creating under this Constitution, there is a secular State. There is no particular advantage to a member of one community over another; nor is there any political advantage by increasing one's fold. In those circumstances, the word `propagate' cannot possibily have dangerous implications, which some of the Members think that it has.) Moreover, I was a party from the very beginning to the compromise with the minor ities, which ultimately led to many of these clauses being inserted in the Constitution.Speaking frankly, whatever its results we ought to respect the compromise. The Minorities Committee the year before the last performed a great

indirectly in such ceremony shall, within such period after the ceremony as may be prescribed ,send intimation to the district magistrate of the district in which the ceremony has taken place of the fact of such conversion in such form as may be prescribed.(2) If any person fails with sufficient cause to comply with the provisions contained in section sub section(1),he shall be punishable with imprisonment which may extend to one year or with fine which may extend to one thousand rupees or with both.

71. Section 6 Offence to be Cognizable :An offence under this act shall be cognizable and shall not be investigated by an officer below the rank of Inspector of police.

72. Section 7 Prosecution To Be Made With The Sanction Of District Magistrate: No prosecution for an offence under this act shall be instituted except by or with the previous sanction of the District magistrate or such authority not below the rank of Sub divisional office, As may be authorised by him in that behalf.

73. AIR 1975 MP 163

achievement by having a unanimous vote on almost every provision of its report. This unanimity created an atmosphere of harmony and confidence in the majority community. Therefore, the word` propagate' should be maintained in this article in order that the compromise so laudably achieved by the Minority Committee should not be disturbed.[74]

The judgement delivered by the Orissa High Court in *Mrs. Yulitha Hyde &Ors. vs State Of Orissa* and also the M.PHigh Court in *Rev. Stainislaus judgment* was challenged at Supreme Court in *Rev. Stainislausvs State Of Madhya Pradesh &Ors*[75] The Supreme Court reversed the judgement in *Yulitha Hyde And Ors. vs State Of Orissa* and it upheld M.P High Court decision in *Rev. Stainislaus* and it ruled that in *Arun Ghosh v. State of West Bengal*[76] if a particular things disturbs the peace of the life in a community it not only amounts to disturb the life of a individual but the society as whole, there could be communal disturbances on the basis of religious conversion thereby it could cause tranquillity and public order would be jeopardised, in these circumstances the impugned legislations would fall within the purview of entry I of list II of the seventh schedule so as to avoid disturbances to the public order. The Supreme Court seems to have deviated or has not considered the legislative intent or the objective behind article 25(1) of the constitution.

8.5 The Way Forward

The Constitution of India guarantees its citizen fundamental rights and human liberties which are inalienable. It guarantees these rights to the individual even in the wake of majority rule and the state cannot desist the obligation cast on it to protect these liberties enshrined in the constitution. The judgement delivered by the Supreme Court in Balaji[77] and Indrasawhney case[78] is far from satisfactory. If Balaji laid fifty percent cap on reservation, Indrasawhney developed the creamy layer test. These precedences have deviated from the social justice agenda set by the constitution. Granville Austin in his work, "Working a Democratic Constitution" stated that no other Constitution in

74. VOLUME VII ,CONSTITUENT ASSEMBLY OF INDIA - Monday, the 6th December 1948
75. 1977 AIR 908
76. AIR 1970 SC 1228
77. M. R. Balaji And Others vs State Of Mysore ,1963 AIR 649
78. Indira Sawhney&Ors v. Union of India. AIR 1993 SC 477

the world "has provided so much impetus towards changing and rebuilding society for the common good and he considers the Indian Constitution as document for social revolution.

The caste census of present population is not available. Only the 1931 caste census data (enumerated by the British) is available. Therefore the court fixing the fifty percent cap on reservations without examining the empirical data would only amount to travesty of justice if the entire backward classes (SC/ST/OBC) population stuffed in to fifty percent ceiling quota. The cap imposed by the court is devoid of any scientific logic and standard calculations. However there is element of hope as the ruling of the Supreme Court in *Akihil Bhartiya Soshit Karamchari Sangh*[79] held that *the fifty percent rule in reservation as laid down by the Supreme Court in previous judgements could only be equated as guidelines provided by the judges, however every case is different and must be decided by the available practical results.*

A person does not cease to be a backward caste if he is economically empowered in other words economic empowerment does not wash away the caste of an individual. In Hindu Social System, membership in a caste is determined by birth not by economic status. Therefore reservation concept was infused into the constitution to achieve the objective of promoting fraternity, representation and justice. Many social scientists have held that reservation in India means representation or share in the society for the ones who have been subjugated from the portals of education and positions of power for centuries.

KhapPanchayats are rampant across the country posing challenges to the constitutional machinery. We have witnessed the brutal killing of young couples who have crossed the caste lines to marry. The state has not come up with any action plan to weed out these kangroo courts apart from the landmark judgements delivered by Justice Katju's bench to protect inter-caste marriages, we have not witnessed any enthusiasm from the state machinery to promote intercaste marriages. The judiciary should step in to fill the vacuum left by the legislature. Judicial

79.AkhilBharatiyaSoshitKaramchariSanghVs Union (1981) 1 SCC 246

activism is much needed in this segment of social justice. The judiciary, executive and legislature must put up a united front to meet these challenges and ensure protection of civil liberties of the individuals who undergo inter-caste marriage. The law commission recommended that the thirty day (notice)time period in the special marriage act has to be reduced so as to help the couple solemnise their marriage at the earliest and stringent action must be taken against the groups which obstruct inter-caste marriages.

Members of the Hindu right wing are alarmed that conversions would lead to loss of the members of the Hindu religion to other religions as majority of the converts are mostly from the lower castes who intend to escape the centuries old caste persecution. The Supreme Court in the *Rev. Stainislaus v. State of Madhya Pradesh* held that public order or tranquillity has to be provided preference over one's fundamental right to profess and propagate a religion. Dr. Ambedakar observed" *it is the caste which has prevented the Hindus from expanding and from absorbing other religious communities. So long as caste remain, Hindu religion cannot be made a missionary religion and Shudhi will be both a folly and a futility.* " The only option for the lower caste Hindu is to convert to reclaim his dignity in the society. The ruling of the Supreme Court in *Rev. Stainislaus* is erroneous and has an adverse impact on one's fundamental right to religion it has not examined the legislative intent of constitutional makers with regard to article 25 of the Indian Constitution.

India is a signatory to Universal Declaration of Human Rights,1948. Article 18 declares freedom of religion which includes freedom to change his religion,or manifest his religion in teaching,practise and worship[80], Article 25 of the Indian constitution which provides right to freedom of religion. In light of the international treaty obligation and the fundamental rights enshrined in the constitution, the Supreme Court must therefore form a larger bench and decide on this constitutional question which is affecting millions of people.

---

80. UDHR Article 18 :Everyone has the right to freedom of thought, conscience and religion; this right includes freedom to change his religion or belief, and freedom, either alone or in community with others and in public or private, to manifest his religion or belief in teaching, practice, worship and observance

It is also important to highlight that judicial decisions vary from one court to another,one judge to another and a larger bench can always overrule a judgement delivered by a smaller bench. As uniformity is absent in judicial decisions, Judiciary must consider the values present in the constitution of India to achieve social revolution,as discussed in the *SP Gupta case* and *Minerva Mills case*, the court said that justice must not be mere legality or satisfaction of the legal rules or following the due process, the court must deliver the enshrined values in the constitution, consonance with the principles laid down in the part III and Part IV,as the constitution is a document of social reform. The fundamental rights are not an end in themselves but are the means to an end. The end is specified in Part IV, therefore there has to be harmonious construction.

9

Babasaheb Ambedkar: A Dalit Icon and Beyond Reclaiming the Marginalisation and Misappropriation of his works

- Mohammad Asadulla Shareef&Anjali Rawat ***

9.1 Introduction

As we are entering the 123rd year of Ambedkar's birth anniversary, the question still looms large as to why Ambedkar's legacy continues to be marginalised and why is he humiliated and cast as a community leader? Ambedkar continues to face the "curse of untouchability" even after five decades have passed since his death.[1] Instances of desecration of Ambedkar's images and statues point to the continued discrimination of Dalits and a blatant neglect of their interests in spite of untouchability and caste-based discrimination becoming unconstitutional with the adoption of Indian Constitution in 1949. There have been many incidents of vandalisation of Ambedkar's statues in the State of Tamil Nadu and the response to it has one, failed to bring the miscreants to book, and, two, Ambedkar's statues have been put in protective cages to prevent further desecration.[2]

---

*Mohammad AsadullaShareef, Fifth Year B.A.LLB (Hons) NALSAR University of Law, Hyderabad.

**Anjali Rawat ,Fifth Year B.A.LLB (Hons) NALSAR University of Law,Hyderabad.

1. A K Biswas, Untouchable Ambedkar- the Saga of his Discrimination in America, XLVIII(17) Mainstream, (April 17, 2010). The institution of the 'Ambedkar Chair for Studies, Research and Analysis of Indian Political Economics' at his Alma Mater- Columbia University fell prey to caste hatred at the hands of upper-caste Indians on an academic committee. Also see Joseph Berger, Family Ties and Entanglements of Caste, (October 25, 2004, available: http://www.nytimes.com/2004/10/25/nyregion/25caste. html? pagewanted=print & position=&_r=0.
2. D. Karthikeyan and H. Gorringe, Rescuing Ambedkar, 29(19) FRONTLINE available at: http://www.frontline.in/static/html/fl2919/stories/20121005291913600.htm

9.2 Ambedkar Caged in a Niche: Beyond a 'Dalit icon'

Ambedkar's contribution to the scholarship in the non-Dalit arena has largely been ignored. As Stalin Rajangam notes, the nationalist parties and Dravidian parties in Tamil Nadu have only used Ambedkar to augment their electoral political base by using him as a symbol showing their concern for social justice and he has never been given his due.[3] He further mentions that the struggle for liberation advocated by Ambedkar was not aimed towards Dalits alone and targeted all the marginalised sections and in fact Ambedkar envisaged the non-Dalits as also fighting for Dalit liberation.[4] Anand Teltumbde also notes that ghettoising Ambedkar to Dalits alone would do disservice to him and severely harm the cause of Dalits as well.[5] Ambedkar's image is reduced to that of a 'Dalit icon' and his statues become synonymous to Dalit identity and assertion.[6] Ambedkar's grandson, Prakash Ambedkar, makes a similar point when he says that Ambedkar has been imprisoned by caste politics and his economic vision and thought has been largely ignored.[7] Narendra Jadhav similarly laments the fact of Ambedkar being reduced to a liberator of

---

3. StalinRajangam, "Rise of Dalit Movements and the Reaction of Dravidian Parties" in K Satyanarayana and S Tharu (ed.), No Alphabet in Sight: New Dalit Writing from South India (New Delhi: Penguin, 2011).

4. Gandhi shedding clothes not revolutionary, but Ambedkar wearing three-piece suit is, (April 25, 2012), available at: http://www.thehindu.com/news/cities/Madurai/gandhi-shedding-clothes-not-revolutionarybut-ambedkar-wearing-threepiece-suit-is/article3350308.ece

5. Anand Teltumbde, An Ambedkar for our times, THE HINDU,Apil 2, 2014, available at: http://www.thehindu.com/opinion/lead/an-ambedkar-for-our-times/article5859610.ece

6. ConflatingAmbedkar's thinking and appropriating it to only built an account for Dalits is problematic and was recently observed when Arundhati Roy wrote an introduction to Ambedkar'sThe Annihilation of Caste and this created a controversy in Dalit circles about the fact of a non-Dalit writing or producing Dalit literature. This controversy is nothing but an "identitarian obsession" similar to what arose in the 1970s that one has to be a Dalit to introduce either Ambedkar or his text. [Id.]

7. Transcribed by StutiShukla, "'BabasahebAmbedkar a Prisoner of Caste Politics, his relevance will grow': BharipBahujanMahasangh president Prakash Ambedkar", Indian Express, (January 7, 2014), available at: http://archive.indianexpress.com/news/-babasaheb-ambedkar-a-prisoner-of-caste-politics-his-relevance-will-grow--bharip-bahujan-mahasangh-president-prakash-ambedkar/1055407/0

untouchables and depressed classes and describes Ambedkar as the "social conscience of modern India".[8] The invisibilisation of Ambedkar's work is so entrenched that the liberal and educated elite of India are also ignorant of Ambedkar's life and the impact he created on society.[9]

The larger ideals which Ambedkar espoused on "institutionalising legal and political measures to even out the social distinctions, inequalities and injustices of a caste-ridden society, which ultimately resulted in the provision of benefits to all deprived sections of society, including the Backward Classes"[10] are lost in the process of his glorification as only a Dalit leader. N. Ram observes that Ambedkar was reduced by the press to a "sub-national leader, a sectional leader of the Scheduled Castes rather than the towering and challenging national figure that he was in every objective sense."[11]

9.3 The Cartoon Controversy and Vote bank Politics

The political importance granted to Ambedkar as a Dalit leader and icon was a political move to win over the Dalit vote bank. In this course, "the real Ambedkar was forgotten" and Ambedkar was portrayed as "the iconoclast, the painstaking truth seeker, the fearless ?ghter for the cause of the oppressed, and the universalist dreaming of the world sans exploitation and humbug."[12] In the tussle over Dalit votes arose a huge row over a cartoon in the NCERT textbook by Shankar Pillai which shows Ambedkar

8. Manish Chand, DrAmbedkar is Conscience of Modern India, Let's Move Beyond Token Social Justice: NarendraJadhav, available at: http://www.indiawrites.org/india-and-the-world/dr-ambedkar-conscience-modern-india-lets-move-token-social-justice-narendra-jadhav/.

9. NamitArora, Caste Iron Upper-caste India's debt to Ambedkar, Perspectives, (November 1, 2013), available at: http://caravanmagazine.in/perspectives/caste-iron.

10. D. Karthikeyan and H. Gorringe, "Rescuing Ambedkar", 29(19) FRONTLINE, available at: http://www.frontline.in/static/html/fl2919/stories/20121005291913600.htm

11. N. Ram, Relevance of Ambedkar, available at: http://www.frontline.in/static/html/fl2701/stories/19910427014.htm

12. AnandTeltumbde, BathaniTola And The Cartoon Controversy, available at: http://www.countercurrents.org/teltumbde020612.htm

riding a snail with 'Constitution' written on it while Jawaharlal Nehru is hitting the snail with a whip signifying the slow drafting process of the Constitution.[13] The issue escalated largely because of the emotive and symbolic value of Ambedkar to the Dalit identity. The issue was mainly political in nature and was used by opportunistic politicians to stir up a controversy. A negative interpretation of the cartoon as being casteist cannot be denied but it was more in the nature of a satire depicting the upper class/ upper caste power dynamics.[14] The furore, therefore, was an identity- based rhetoric that was figurative to the political trajectory of some.[15]

9.4 Paradox of Ambedkar's Popularity

Teltumbde points to the paradoxical phenomenon of growing public acceptance of Ambedkar in terms of statues, pictures, congregations, books, research, organisations, songs, etc. with a corresponding presence of prevalence of caste discrimination, atrocities, caste discourses and lack of "the spread of an anti-caste ethos" as one would expect to come with mainstreaming of Ambedkar.[16] He explains it by distinguishing the idea of the real

13. The cartoon remained largely unnoticed until Thirumavalavan, leader of ViduthalaiChiruthaigalKatchi (a small petty bourgeois party from Tamil Nadu) and RamdasAthavale of the Republican Party of India (Athavale), demanded banning of the cartoon.
14. Anand Kumar, The Cartoon Controversy, (July 8, 2012), available at: http://socialism.in/index.php/the-cartoon-controversy/; Also note that humour for one section of a society might not be humorous for another especially when the sense of humour is "always embedded in caste, racial, gender, class and religious norms." The social and cultural disabilities define the standing of an individual and a community in society. Therefore, one must be careful in dismissing the row which arose over Babasaheb's caricature entirely. SeeUmakant, BabasahebAmbedkar Cartoon: On Sensibilities, Lies And Half Truths, (June 6, 2012), available at: http://www.countercurrents.org/umakant 060612.htm.
15. StalinRajangam, Hugo Gorringe, and D Karthikeyan, Dalit Political Imagination and Replication in Contemporary Tamil Nadu, XLVII(36) (September 8, 2012), available at: http://www.epw.in/perspectives/Dalit-political-imagination-and-replication-contemporary-tamil-nadu.html
16. AnilTeltumbde, An Ambedkar for our times, THE HINDU, (Apil 2, 2014) available at: http://www.thehindu.com/opinion/lead/an-ambedkar-for-our-times/article5859610.ece

Ambedkar from the unreal, enigmatic and venerated version- and in packaging Ambedkar as "an architect of the Constitution, a great nationalist, the father of reservations, a staunch anti-communist, a liberal democrat, a great parliamentarian, a saviour of Dalits, a bodhisattva, etc. These icons of the harmless, status quo-ist Ambedkar have been proliferated all over and overshadow a possible, radical view of the real Ambedkar."[17]

9.5 Falsifying facts

Arun Shourie in *Worshipping False Gods*[18] vainly and biasedly contended that Ambedkar is wrongly considered the father of the Constitution and is credited as its author because of "verbal terrorism and casteist politics".[19] His other allegations are that Ambedkar opposed the freedom struggle, joined forces with the British for material gains, and converted to Buddhism for mere opportunism.[20] All his allegations have been sufficiently countered by critics and Shourie's work failed to have any significant impact in smearing Ambedkar's legacy. Gadgil rebuts all the four claims of Shourie and shows the shallowness of Shourie's claims.[21] Athavale's remark further shows the prejudice in Shourie's writing for he who blamed intellectuals for not reading the Constituent Assembly Debates seems to have himself skipped reading it for he missed how several speakers showered Ambedkar with a glowing tribute in the Assembly for his remarkable contribution to the drafting of the Indian Constitution.[22]

9.6 Constitutional Morality, Social Justice & Rule of Law

The speech that Dr. Babasaheb Ambedkar delivered in the Constituent Assembly Debate on the 4th of November, 1948 is

17.Id.

18.ArunShourie, Worshipping False Gods: Ambedkar, and the Facts Which Have Been Erased, (New Delhi: ASA Publications, 1997).

19.DevAthawale, Ambedkar and the Indian Constitution, 32(15) Economic and Political Weekly 734, (Apr. 12-18, 1997).

20.V. N. Gadgil, Falsifying The Truth, OUTLOOK, July 30, 1997, available at: http://www.outlookindia.com/article.aspx?203929.

21.Id.

22.Supra note 17.

of prime importance. It was here that the idea of 'Constitutional Morality' was invoked.[23] Quoting a famous historian, Grote, Dr. Ambedkar was of the view that the Constitutional Morality denotes supreme reverence to the ideas adopted in the Constitution.[24] This, of course, will not be a natural sentiment considering that the country has not seen such governance mechanism else before.[25] The idea behind Constitutional Morality is to establish a morality of State Practice while staying within the forms and boundaries established by the Constitution even when such practice means going against what is perceived by the society to be public morality.[26] In another speech on the 25th of November, 1949, Dr. Ambedkar clarified that Constitution is not supposed to be a mere noun, but, in fact, a verb. It may not happen all of a sudden and the Constitutional Morality will need sufficient amount of cultivation amongst the populace.[27] But the fact of the matter remains that the ideas enshrined in the Constitution are those cannot be faulted mere because of public morality.

As put forward by Dr. Ambedkar, the aim of the Constitution and the State Practice based on it should be to ensure both economic and social democracy.[28] Social justice necessarily forms part of such democracy. When there were arguments made with regards to the apprehensions of even having the Directive Principles of State Policy in the Constitution without making them enforceable, Dr. Ambedkar's refutation was based on the principle that they are necessary for attaining the essential goal of the Constitution-an economic and social democracy.[29] Both these principles, coupled

23. EleanorNewbigin, The Hindu Code Bill and the making of the modern Indian state, (January 6, 2008), available at: https://www.repository.cam.ac.uk/handle/1810/225258.

24. GEORGE GROTE, A HISTORY OF GREECE 93 (2000).

25. D. Karthikeyan, He dreamt of creating an ideal society, (April 15, 2011), available at: http://www.thehindu.com/news/national/tamil-nadu/he-dreamt-of-creating-an-ideal-society/article1696900.ece.

26. PratapBhanu Mehta, What is Constitutional Morality?, available at: http://www.india-seminar.com/2010/615/615_pratap_bhanu_mehta.htm

27. Dr. M.R.Singariya, Dr B R Ambedkar and Women Empowerment in India, (December 20, 2013). available at: http://www.questjournals.org/jrhss/papers/vol2-issue1/A210104.pdf.

28. CONSTITUENT ASSEMBLY DEBATES.

29. CONSTITUENT ASSEMBLY DEBATES (quoting Dr. Ambedkar on 25th November, 1949).

with the idea of Constitutional Morality, make the Rule of Law. At this juncture, it is important to note that the Rule of Law is not the same as the Rule of Majority. While few believe that Rule of Law puts the law, pre-given by the stakeholders, at a pedestal so high and unshakable that no one, including those who govern, can violate it, there are, simultaneously, those who believe that it encompasses the "social, economic, educational, and cultural conditions under which man's legitimate aspirations and dignity may be realized."[30] The idea behind adopting Rule of Law is to avoid any decision that may violate the Constitutional Morality in such a way that the minority faces oppression in the hands of the law merely because the majority or the public morality deems it correct. It is in in this context that the present discussion moves on to Dr. Ambedkar's efforts towards realization of the Hindu Code Bill, an illustration by way of which he articulated his ideas of women empowerment.[31]

9.7 The Hindu Code Bill

Empowerment of women is essential in order to achieve sustainable human development, for women are as important stakeholders as anyone else. Ambedkar was as staunch an opponent of patriarchy as of its twin, Brahmanism and the caste system. As early as 1916, the young Ambedkar had put forth the links between oppression of women and caste system which according to Ambedkar thrived on control of women and sustained endogamy.[32] Rege builds an account of Ambedkar's contribution to feminism and credits him with starting a feminist take on caste.[33]

---

30. International Commission of Jurists, The Rule of Law in a Free Society, VII (Geneva, 1959).
31. DevAthawale, Ambedkar and the Indian Constitution, 32(15) Economic and Political Weekly 734., 15 (Apr. 12-18, 1997).
32. B. R. Ambedkar, Castes in India : Their Mechanism, Genesis and Development, Paper presented at an Anthropology Seminar taught by Dr. A. A. Goldenweizer Columbia University, 9 May, 1916, Indian Antiquary Vol. XLI, May, 1917, available at: http://www.columbia.edu/itc/mealac/pritchett/00ambedkar/txt_ambedkar_castes.html.
33. SharmilaRege, Against the Madness of Manu B.R Ambedkar's Writings on Brahmanical Patriarchy, available at: http://navayana.org/against-the-madness-of-manu/.

Laying down the foundations of social justice, Dr. Ambedkar thought it was so important to have gender equality that there has been a mention of it in not just Articles 14, 15 & 16, which happen to be the most important of the fundamental rights, but also in the Preamble of the Constitution.[34] In fact, it was in 1942, during the Mahad Tank Struggle that Dr. Ambedkar called upon women to march along with the men. The same ideas went on to be a part of the Constituent Assembly Debates and the Parliament. In 1948, Dr. Ambedkar introduced the Hindu Code Bill which guarantees various rights such as divorce, property holdings etc. Section 14 of the same provides that any property possessed by a female Hindu shall be held by her as full owner and not a limited owner.[35] When this bill did not clear the muster of the Parliament, Dr. Ambedkar resigned. His resignation was not only from the Parliament, but also from the Indian National Congress, the chief of which, Mr. Jawaharlal Nehru, did not seem to have delivered on the support that his Law Minister required in the passage of the Hindu Code Bill. This further led him to contest against Mr. Nehru for the election to the Parliament. All this stands testament to the fact that Dr. Ambedkar saw the Hindu Code Bill has so enormously important to further the cause of social justice and constitutional morality that he would not stay in a party or with any designation after having been disappointed with the support that has been offered to him.[36]

9.8 Conclusion

Ambedkar was an emancipative thinker and his socio-political thought transcends conception of a society where lower castes are free from caste discrimination and oppression. Partha Chatterjee describes Ambedkar as, "the principle architect of the Indian Constitution, a staunch advocate of the interventionist modernising state and of the legal protection of the modern virtues of equal

35. Dr. VishnurGunjal, Dr. BabasahebAmbedkar and Women Empowerment, (March, 2012), available at: http://researchlink.in/FullIssue/Research%20Link%2096/11%20Social%20Work.pdf.

36. Arundhati Roy, The Doctor and the Saint, (March 1, 2014), available at: http://caravanmagazine.in/reportage/doctor-and-saint.

citizenship and secularism."[37] Ambedkar's worldview was that of a world of inclusion with liberal quality as its foundation and in his own words on an All India Radio broadcast on 3rd October, 1954, he said: *"My social philosophy may be said to be enshrined in three words: liberty, equality and fraternity. My philosophy has roots in religion and not in political science. I have derived them from the teachings of my master, the Buddha".*[38] His thoughts developed out of his practical experience of oppression, discrimination and marginalisation due to his Mahar caste and he fought against these prejudices to become a man of great wisdom and learning possessing a plethora of "intellectual, political and moral gifts and as a towering national figure representing large forces of historical change in a process that is painfully incomplete".[39] Ambedkar was a believer of liberty of thought and an advocate of the justice a social democracy[40] can promise with its ideals of liberty, equality and fraternity. The ogre of caste devoured Ambedkar's legacy and subjected him to "curious apathy"[41] and even humiliation at the hand of the caste Hindus. As surveyed

37. PARTHACHATTERJEE,THE POLITICS OF THE GOVERNED: REFLECTIONS ON POPULAR POLITICS IN MOST OF THE WORLD,8.
38. K. N. KADAM, THE MEANING OF THE AMBEDKARITE CONVERSION TO BUDDHISM AND OTHER ESSAYS, 26.
39. Supranote 11.
40. CONSTITUENT ASSEMBLY DEBATES, Vol. XI, (quoting Dr. Ambedkar on 25th November, 1949). available at: http://parliamentofindia.nic.in/ls/debates/vol11p11.htm.

    Political democracy cannot last unless there lies at the base of it social democracy. What does social democracy mean? It means a way of life which recognizes liberty, equality and fraternity as the principles of life. These principles of liberty, equality and fraternity as the principles of life. These principles of liberty, equality and fraternity are not to be treated as separate items in a trinity. They form a union of trinity in the sense that to divorce one from the other is to defeat the very purpose of democracy. Liberty cannot be divorced from equality, equality cannot be divorced from liberty. Nor can liberty and equality be divorced from fraternity. Without equality, liberty would produce the supremacy of the few over the many. Equality without liberty would kill individual initiative. Without fraternity, liberty would produce the supremacy of the few over the many. Equality without liberty would kill individual initiative. Without fraternity, liberty and equality could not become a natural course of things. It would require a constable to enforce them.
41. Supranote 9.

throughout the essay, Ambedkar's revolutionary thinking was sidelined and his account of social oppression and discrimination was seen only through the lens of caste identity and was relegated to just being a leader of Dalits and a legal scholar.

Ambedkar's story is awe-inspiring and tells us about a man who overcame an enormous individual struggle and battled against the oppression to pioneer a libertarian account of equality and fraternity rooted in the values of Buddhist philosophy. Ambedkar's contribution to the field of economics has also been ignored and his secular and radical egalitarianism and his theorisation of a conception of social justice and dignity has not received its due share in the mainstream.

If not Ambedkar, Which other leader of the 20th century is as relevant to every dream of a just, modern, liberal, secular, humane, and democratic society in India?[42]

---

42. Id.

10

Constitution of India and Social Justice

*- Kush Kalra * & Lalit Ajmani***

10.1 Introduction

The Constitution of India, a dynamic document and a living organism, represents the aims and aspirations of the people and on which our dominant institutions of governance such as constitutional democracy are based. Social Justice is one of the main objectives of the Indian Constitution. Laws cannot be interpreted without reference to social justice, to the achievement of which our country pledged on gaining independence. In the words of Justice Krishna Iyer, "Social justice or distributive justice is a quest for justice. It is a challenge of equality, liberty , and justice".[1] In the words of Justice Y.V. Chandrachud, "it is pursuit of making law an instrument of social change and for reminding lawyers and judges that they are social engineers".[2] Simply put, Social Justice is the comprehensive form to remove social imbalance by law harmonizing the rival claims or the interest of different groups and/or section in the social structure or individuals by means of which alone it would be possible to build up a welfare State.[3] Understanding of social justice accordingly demands having interaction with social purpose, which further requires interpretation of the eternal principles of human freedom to meet the challenges of changing times.

---

*Kush Kalra ,Advocate ,Delhi High Court ,Law Graduate Rajiv Gandhi University of Law,Punjab,India

** LalitAjmani,B.A.LLB Rajiv Gandhi University of Law,Punjab,India

1. Justice V.R. Krishna Iyer, Social Justice- Sunset or Dawn, Eastern Book Company, 1993.
2. Justice Y.V. Chandrachud, The Challenge of Social Justice, Supreme Court of India Publication, Third International Conference of Appellate Judges, 1985, pp.2-3
3. Dalmia Cement(Bharat) Ltd. v. Union of India, (1996) 10 S.C.C 104

Conscientiously, our Constitution is the culmination of social justice through the Fundamental Rights and the Directive Principles of the State Policy, which are directed to achieve means as well as ends of social Justice.[4] Part III and Part IV of the Indian Constitution dealing with the Fundamental Rights and the Directive Principles of the State Policy have been described by Granville Austin as "the Conscience of the Constitution".[5] He also describes the Indian Constitution as "the first and foremost a social document". Part III and Part IV enumerate the basic rights to be ensured by the Government which reflect the commitment of the framers of the Constitution towards the cause of socio-economic justice to the common man.

Thus, justice devoid of social justice is purposeless and is meaningless if confined to the few fortunate and does not take within its sweep large masses of disadvantaged and underprivileged segments of society. When the British came to India, they brought with them their system of administration of justice, especially to serve the ruling class. They set up a hierarchy of courts throughout the country. When India attained independence, the system remained in place with hardly any changes and formed a judicial framework for modern India. However, the value inputs into this modern legal and judicial system have come from India's post-independence Constitution. In the past few decades, a new jurisprudence called the social justice jurisprudence has emerged from the foundations of the Indian Constitution and its judicial cognizance has been well taken by progressive jurists.[6]

10.2 Dimensions of International Justice and Social Justice

"Social justice" first appeared in United Nations texts during the second half of the 1960s. At the initiative of the Soviet Union, and with the support of developing countries, the term was used

4. Dr. Paramjit S. Jaswal, Directive Principles Jurisprudence and Socio-Economic Justice in India, APH Publishing Company 1996.
5. Granvile Austin, The Indian Constitution, Oxford University Press, 1967.
6. Justice Krishna Iyer, 1995 Human Rights- A Judge's Miscellany, BR Publishing Company.

in the Declaration on Social Progress and Development, adopted in 1969.The Charter of the United Nations makes no explicit distinction between international justice, or justice among nations, and social justice, or justice among people. In the Preamble and Article 1 of the Charter, justice is associated with respect for international law. In Article 2, justice is linked to the sovereign equality of all Members and to the maintenance of peace and security. The concept of social justice and its relevance and application within the present context require a more detailed explanation. As mentioned previously, the notion of social justice is relatively new.

The concept first surfaced in Western thought and political language in the wake of the industrial revolution and the parallel development of the socialist doctrine. It was born as a revolutionary slogan embodying the ideals of progress and fraternity. Social justice represented the essence and the raison d'être of the social democrat doctrine and left its mark in the decades following the Second World War. Of particular importance in the present context is the link between the growing legitimization of the concept of social justice, on the one hand, and the emergence of the social sciences as distinct areas of activity and the creation of economics and sociology as disciplines separate from philosophy (notably moral philosophy), on the other hand. Social justice became more clearly defined when a distinction was drawn between the social sphere and the economic sphere, and grew into a mainstream preoccupation when a number of economists became convinced that it was their duty not only to describe phenomena but also to propose criteria for the distribution of the fruits of human activity.

Social justice is treated as synonymous with distributive justice, which again is often identified with unqualified references to justice, in the specific context of the activities of the United Nations, the precise reasons for which may only be conjectured. Social justice, equality and equity were sometimes defined as distinct concepts but were more often used loosely and interchangeably. One of the basic touchstones of social justice is equity. The Universal Declaration of Human Rights, and the International Covenants on Human Rights, and in subsequent texts adopted by the General Assembly, notably the Copenhagen Declaration and Programme of Action and the United Nations Millennium Declaration is never forget about that. They include Equality of rights, primarily implying the elimination of all forms of discrimination and respect for the fundamental freedoms and civil and political rights of all individuals. Equality of opportunities, which requires stable social, economic, cultural and political conditions that enable all individuals to fulfill their potential and contribute to the economy and to society. In the present context, the telling of the "story" of social justice in the United Nations, distinct from an evocation of the avatars of international justice in the same organization, is justified by the need to explain the divorce between human rights and development. Chapter 1 of this Charter includes a list of 15 principles that should govern relations between States, and a few of these are particularly relevant in the present context; the thirteenth principle is the "promotion of international social justice", the first is "sovereignty, territorial integrity and political independence of States", and the eleventh is "respect for human rights and fundamental freedoms".

The notion of equal rights, a foundation of social justice, is an important part of the international discourse and is probably gaining ground overall, at least in the global consciousness. By the time the latter text came out, social justice was a familiar concept in those parts of the Secretariat involved in social affairs. Human rights efforts focused on the individual, while the work on development and social justice concentrated on society and international cooperation for development. Sometime Social justice seen as a substitute for the protection of human rights. Finally, in the new doctrinal orientation of the United Nations with regard to development and social justice, recognition is given to the vital role of non-State and non-public actors in the economic and social evolution of societies and of the world as a whole.

10.3 Constitutional Emphasis on Social Justice

The framers of the Indian Constitution while drafting the document took great care to ensure that independent India gave to its people meaningful social and economic rights and so incorporated safeguards to see that the people of India were not deprived of their basic rights.[7] The Supreme Court in its judgement in Consumer Education and Research Centre v. Union of India[8] as under:

"The Preamble and Article 38 of the Constitution of India the Supreme Law, envisions social justice as its arch to ensure life to be meaningful and livable with human dignity. The Constitution commands justice, liberty, equality, and fraternity as supreme values to usher egalitarian social, economic and political democracy. Social Justice, equality, and dignity of person are corner stones of social democracy. The concept of social Justice, which the Constitution of India engrafted, consists of diverse principles essential for the orderly growth and development of personality of every citizen. Social Justice is thus an integral part of justice in generic sense. Justice is the genus of which social justice is species. Social Justice is a dynamic device to mitigate the sufferings of the power, weak, dalits, tribals and deprived sections of the society and to elevate them to the level of equality to live in a life with dignity of person. Social Justice is not a simple or single idea of a society but is an essential part of complex of social change to relieve the poor etc., from handicaps, penury to ward off distress, and to make their life livable, for greater good of the society at large. In other words, the aim of social justice is to attain substantial degree of social , economic and political equality, which is the legitimate expectation. Social security just and humane conditions of work and leisure to workman are part of this meaningful right to life and to achieve, self-expression of his personality and to enjoy the life with dignity, the State should provide facilities and opportunities to them to reach at least minimum standard of heath, economic security and civilized living while sharing according to the capacity, social and cultural heritage."

7.See Constituent Assembly Debates.

8.AIR 1995 SC 938.

The Law on social justice cannot be discussed without a reference to the Indian Judiciary. The importance of social Justice gained momentum during the early period of independence. Thereafter there was continuous progress and the concept acquired wider meaning during the later period. The intention of the law-makers during the imperial days may have been to strengthen the British Empire. But post-independence the laws needed interpretation vis-à-vis the Indian people of the Indian Republic. To focus on the object of law sometimes introduces a regressive movement. Slowly, the view gained ground that the laws must be interpreted in such manner as to advance the constitutional goals.[9] The Supreme Court in one of its judgment has observed that "A constitutional provision must be construed, not in a narrow and constricted sense, but in a wide and liberal manner so as to anticipate and take account of changing conditions and purposes so that the constitutional provision does not get atrophied or fossilized but remains flexible enough to meet the newly emerging problems and challenges".[10]

The advent of the doctrine of a Welfare State based on notions of progressive social philosophy has rendered the old doctrine of laissez-faire obsolete. The theories of "hire and fire" as well as the theory of "supply and demand", which were allowed free scope under this doctrine no longer hold the filed. It was the social philosophy of the age that initiated the change in labour jurisprudence in the early years after independence. Several rulings of the Supreme Court during that period reflect this change.[11] The greatest asset that the Indian Judiciary possesses is the confidence it commands and the faith it inspires in the minds of the people in its capacity to do evenhanded justice and keep the scales in balance in any dispute. This is largely because of the legal authority and the moral authority of the courts. Those occupying seats of justice have created in the eyes of the people an image of being imbibed with high sense of justice and fairplay.[12]

9. SOCIAL JUSTICE- A Dialogue by Justice D.A. Desai at pg 32.

10. FrancisCoralie v. Union Territory of Delhi, AIR 1981 SC 746.

11. StandardVaccum Refining Co. of India v. Its Workman, (1961) 3 SCR 542, RaiBahadurDiwanBadri Das v. Industrial Tribunal, Punjab, (1963) 3 SCR 936.

12. Judiciary in India and Judicial Process, Justice H.R. Khanna- Tagore Law Lectures delivered in March 1984.

The concept of social justice has its origin in the rights and the writs are the means to enforce these rights. Under the Constitution, it is the duty of the Supreme Court to enforce fundamental rights, the right to approach the Supreme Court being itself a fundamental right. The writs themselves are the rights under the Indian Constitution model. Articles 32 and 226 provide for their direct enforcement.[13] Under this social philosophy of the Constitution, the Fundamental Rights and the Directive Principles, numerous pieces of legislation have been enacted, which cover the entire array of human rights.[14]

The human rights jurisprudence in India is significantly influenced, through constitutional interpretation and by the international human rights norms set out by the Universal Declaration of Human Rights in 1948. The adoption of this document by the General Assembly heralded the beginning of a new legal order and it embraced within its ambit both the right to personnel liberty such as freedom from arbitrary arrest, a fair criminal trial, etc. as well as wider concepts of social Justice such as equality, equal pay for equal work, the right to an adequate livelihood and the right to education.[15] These concepts of human rights and social justice as seen from their inherent characteristics illustrate that they overlap quite considerably. Progress of social justice over the past years shows that there has been a steady transformation of moral clauses into positive rights and greater assertion of protection of human rights.[16]

10.4 Indian Judiciary's Interpretation of Social Justice

After our independence a significant change has occurred in the role of judicial process in our society. Judicial activism figures prominently in the contemporary India with active assistance of social activists and public interest litigators for vindication of

---

13. D. Basu, Shorter Constitution of India, Prentice Hall.
14. SeeMangariRajender, Human Rights Act and Relating Laws, Law Book Agency, 1999.
15. Dr. S. Subramanian, Human Rights: Interanational Challenges, Manas Publication, 1997 at pg 5-55.
16. Dr. S.K. Awasthi and R.P. Kataria, 2001. Law Relating to Protection of Human Rights, Orient Publishing Company.

the governmental commitment towelfare and social justice. One of the meanings of judicial activism is that the function of the court is not merely to interpret the law but to make it imaginatively sharing the passion of the Constitution for social justice.

This judicial activism sharing the passion of our Constitution for social justice and it was started since the Maneka Gandhi case in which fundamental right of personal liberty has been converted into a regime of positive human rights unknown in previous constitutional diction. Thereafter, gradually the Supreme Court, particularly few socialist justices tried to explore social justice in our Fundamental Rights and Directive Principles of State Policy and thus we get an explosion of rights. In this way the courts try to force the government to realize the new concept of social justice in the cases of *Sunil Batra V. Delhi Administration*[17] *(right against torture); Bandhua Mukti Morcha V. Union of India*[18] *(right against bondage); People's Union for Democratic rights V. Union of India*[19] *(right against bondage); Olga Tellis V. Bombay Municipal Corporation*[20] *(right to livelihood); R.L. &. E. Kendra Dehradun V. State of Uttar Pradesh orM.C. Mehta V. Union of India*[21] *(right against environmental pollution), Upendra Baxi V. State of Uttar Pradesh*[22] *(right to human dignity), Sheela Barse V. Union of India*[23] *(right to legal aid); M.K. Sharma V. Bharat Electronics Ltd.*[24] *(right to have safety and protection to the workers); Sankar V. Durgapur Projects Limited*[25] *relying on Olga Tellis the court held that compelling a person to live in subhuman conditions amounts to the taking away of his life; Poola Bhaskara Vijay Kumar V. State of Andhra Pradesh Court held that right to prisoner to get wages (Art 21); Krishen Pattanyak V. State of Orissa*[26] *(victims of starvation deaths in the district of*

---

17. AIR 1980 SCR (2) 557
18. 1984 3 SCC 161
19. (1982) 3 SCC 235; AIR 1982 SC 1473
20. AIR1986 SC180
21. 985 SC 652
22. (1983) 2 SCC 308
23. (1986) 3 SCC 596
24. AIR 1987 SC 1792
25. AIR 1988 Cal 136
26. (1989) AIR 677

Kalahandi, Orissa); Vishal Jeet V. Union of India[27] *(child abuse and forced prostitution); M.C. Mehta V. State of Tamil Nadu*[28] *(right of children against exploitative employment in hazardous industries); Delhi Judicial Service Association, Tis Hazari courts Delhi V. State of Gujarat*[29] *(also known as Nadiad case) (police brutality to C.J.M., Nadiad); Banwasi Sewa Ashram v State of U.P.*[30] where adivasis and other back-ward class people used forest as their habitat and means of livelihood and parts of such forests were declared as reserved. In these cases the judges maintain that in a developing society judicial activism is essential for participative justice and the bureaucrats as well as the elected representative will have to face the judicial admonition and pay the penalty if the people in misery cry for justice.

Art. 23 and Art. 24 mandates that no child below the age of 14 may be employed in any factory

or mine or engaged in any other hazardous employment. These two Articles recently came up for

construction before this Court in *People's Union for Democratic Rights v. Union of India.*[31] Article 38 imposes obligation on the State, albeit unenforceable in a Court of law, to "strive to promote the welfare of the People by securing and protecting as effectively as it may a social order in which social justice shall inform all the institutions of the national life".

In the year of 2001 *Oriental Insurance Co. Ltd. v Hansrajbai V. Kodala*[32] the Apex Court held that "The object is to expeditiously extend social justice to the needy victims of accidents curtailing delay - If still the question of determining compensation of fault liability is kept alive, it would result in additional litigation and complications in case claimants fail to establish liability of

---

27.AIR 1990, SCR (2) 861

28. (1996) 6 S.C.C. 756

29. AIR 1991 SC 2176

30. 1992 SCC (2) 202

31. AIR 1982 SC 1473

32. The Oriental Insurance Co. Ltd vsHansrajbhai V. Kodala&Ors on 4 April, 2001 http://indiankanoon.org/doc/190580/ last visited on 1.11.2011

defendants - Wherever the Legislature wanted to provide additional compensation, it has done so specifically."

The Apex Court in *Ashok Kumar Gupta v State of U.P.,*[33] held that the term Social Justice is a Fundamental Right. In Ajaib Singh v Sirhind Cooperative Marketing-cum-Processing Service Society Ltd.,[34] Court observed that in dealing with industrial dispute the Courts should keep in mind the Doctrine of Social Justice.

Supreme Court in *Municipal Corporation of Delhi v Female Workers (Muster Roll),*[35] the provision entitling maternity leave under the Maternity Benefit Act, 1961, even to women engaged on casual basis or on muster roll basis on daily wages and not only to those in regular employment are in consonance with the doctrine of social justice and any contention against it is contrary. The Supreme Court has firmly ruled in *Balbir Kaur v Steel Authority of India*[36] that "the concept of social justice is the yardstick to the justice administration system or the legal justice and it would be an obligation for the law Courts to apply the law depending upon the situation in a manner whichever is beneficial for the society" as the respondent Steel Authority of India was directed to provide compassionate employment to the appellant.

10.5 Conclusion

In Conclusion, it must not be forgotten that social justice as a goal cannot be worked in isolation. Every day, the various organs of the state are faced with challenges in working the principles of social justice within the framework of the Constitution and the ground realities of our nation and its populace. This balancing act is a delicate one. In this regard Granville Austin's remarks in his book titled 'Working a Democratic Constitution' are relevant. He envisages the Indian Constitution as having three strands;

33. (1997)5 SCC 201 (Para 26)
34. (1999) 6 SCC 82 (Para 5).
35.(2000) 3 SCC 224 (paras 32 and 33) : AIR 2000 SC 1274
36. (2000) 6 SCC 493

protecting and enhancing national unity and integrity; establishing the institutions and spirit of democracy; and fostering a social revolution to better the lot of the mass of the Indians. The framers believe and Indians today agree, that the three strands are mutually dependent and inextricably intertwined." Neither can be gained at the expense of the other and with these three strands the framers have spun a 'seamless web'. "Undue strain on ,or slackness in, any one strand would distort the web and risk its destruction and, with it, the destruction of the nation." While the Constitution squarely charges the Legislature, the Executive and the Judiciary with the duty of guaranteeing the citizen's their human rights and fostering and maintaining an environment of social justice, in truth the power and the ability to strive towards and attain that goal lies with 'We, the people' who gave ourselves this Constitution, and it is only with the awareness and efforts of the people that the objective of complete social justice can be achieved for as has been rightly observed 'constitutions, however 'living', are inert. They do not work, they are worked.'[37]

37. Granville Austin, Working a Democratic Constitution, (OUP, New York, 2006)

11

The Lost Legacy of the Doctor

- *Subhaprada Mohanty* &Divya Suwasini ***

The diffusion of 'constitutional morality', not merely among the majority of any community, but throughout the whole is the indispensable condition of a government at once free and peaceable; since even any powerful and obstinate minority may render the working of a free institution impracticable, without being strong enough to conquer ascendance for themselves.[1]

- Dr. B.R Ambedkar in his speech 'The Draft Constitution', delivered on 4 November 1948

11.1 Introduction

Dr. B.R Ambedkar was an erudite scholar and had impeccable credentials as a humanist. No doubt hailing from a low caste family he went through the usual path of discrimination and abuse from the upper caste members but these ritual injustices shaped his outlook and transmogrified him into a crusader of civil liberties. This above quotation is a testimony to the fact that he was a vociferous champion of minority rights. Caste discrimination which owes its allegiance to a deep-seated religious morality that gave a free ride to upper caste members of Hindu religion to enjoy the exalted status of privilege and deny the same to others from the lower bracket of caste hierarchy. Ambedkar a vocal critic of such social malaise shares his misgivings regarding any imposition of religious morality on the State subjects. The

*SubhapradaMohanty,LL.M Candidate(2015-16) National University of Juridical Sciences, Kolkata,India.

**DivyaSuwasini ,Graduate student of NALSARUniversity of Law, Hyderabad, India.

1. BhanuPratap Mehta, What is Constitutional Morality? 56 India- Seminar (Nov, 2010). available at: http://www.india-seminar.com/2010/615/615_pratap_bhanu_mehta.html.

doctor invoked Grote's principle of Constitutional Morality as a tool of adhesion that will glue people of all caste and creed. Naturally he stressed the importance of minority rights and used the principles of constitutional morality as a bulwark to any kind of violation of their rights.

The phrase 'Constitutional Morality' is rarely used during the Constituent Assembly debates. The term traces its origin to Grote's History of Greece where Grote discussed the aspects of Athenian democracy which, for a brief period, perfectly blended the elements of constitutional morality. Ambedkar raised the topic of constitutional morality during the debates. Since then the phrase has lost much of its significance. Even the Supreme Court of India in its judgments has rarely delved on this topic. Till date there are only six judgments of Supreme Court where the phrase 'constitutional morality' is mentioned. But it will be unfair to apportion the blame solely to the court when our legislators have hardly shown any deference to values that our Constitution espouses. Ramchandra Guha, noted historian, states that how elected legislators who take oath to the elected office haven't seen the constitution before in their entire lifetime till they place their hands on it. Apart from such ceremonial gestures hardly our legislators strive hard to uphold the principles of constitutional morality.

The overarching theme of this essay tries to provide an insight into how this jurisprudence of constitutional morality has progressed since the Constitution of India was adopted. Before delving deeper it's important to discuss what's the exact meaning of the term constitutional morality?

11.2 Decoding Constitutional Morality

For Grote,[2] the central elements of constitutional morality were freedom and self-restraint. Ambedkar's account of

2. Ambedkar quotes Grote:" By constitutional morality, Grote meant... a paramount reverence for the forms of the constitution, enforcing obedience to authorityandacting under and within theseforms, yet combined with the habit of open speech, of action subject only to definite legal control, and unrestrained censure of those very authorities as to all their public acts combined, too with a perfect confidence in the bosom of every citizen amidst the bitterness of party contest that the forms of constitutionwillnotbelesssacred in the eyes of his opponents than his own." from his "Speech Delivered on 25 November 1949' in The Constitution and Constituent Assembly Debates, p. 174.

constitutional morality may seem to put forth the additional elements: *respect for plurality, deference to processes, scepticism about authoritative claims to popular sovereignty, and the concern for an open culture of criticism that remains at the helm of constitutional forms.*[3] The British legal scholar A.V. Dicey emphasized that "constitutional morality" supplemented legal rules in regulating the exercise of political power and limiting the discretion of government officials.[4] He further went on to add:

Constitutional law, as the term is used in England, appears to include all rules which directly or indirectly affect the distribution or the exercise of the sovereign power in the state. The one set of rules are in the strictest sense "laws, "since they are rules which are enforced by the Courts. The other set of rules consist of conventions, understandings, habits, or practices which, though they may regulate the conduct of the several members of the sovereign power are not in reality laws at all since they are not enforced by the Courts. This portion of constitutional law may, for the sake of distinction, be termed the "conventions of the constitution,"

Constitutional Morality.

In a seminal paper titled, "Constitutional Morality & the Rule of Law" the authors stated that Constitutional moralities (there are many possible such) can be understood as anticipated norms of behaviour or even duties primarily on the part of individuals within our constitutional institutions. The term morality has been used and referred to constitutional morality with regard to these norms or duties principally because of the purpose they serve; they can be viewed as imposing an obligation on individuals and institutions to ensure that the constitutional system operates in a coherent way, consistent with its basic principles and objectives.[5]

---

3. Id. at 2.
4. Keith E. Whittington, The Status of Unwritten Constitutional Conventions in the United States

U. Ill. L. Rev. 1847 (2013).

5. Id. at 2.

The aforementioned paper encapsulated constitutional morality to a set of principles that should be adhered within the framework of the Constitution.[6]

Ambedkar, a great visionary as he was, took a liberal view in construing the phrase. He tried to contextualize the term in view of prevailing tensions in the Indian society marked by fissures and cracks. He had apprehensions about Indian democracy[7] which he had described akin to 'top dressing on Indian soil, which is essentially undemocratic'. He genuinely believed in the power of constitution and the morals flowing from it. Any sort of morality be it religious or public guided by caste or creed are not enough unite the otherwise divisive country. Ambedkar genuinely believed that the morals emanating from the constitution are needed to be imbibed in the consciousness of every Indians. Only this school of thought can unite the country already divided on sectarian lines.

11.3 Diffusion of Constitutional Morality

Dr. Ambedkar pointed the importance of "diffusion of constitutional morality' for successful working of a constitution. The question now is to what extent has this diffusion taken place. The stakeholders of Indian Democracy - State along with its organs (Legislature, Executive & Judiciary) and the Citizens (includes Civil Society) have failed to adhere to constitutional morals. Following examples will shed light over their abject failure.

Misuse of Ordinance Power:

The Doctrine of Colourable Legislation elucidates the principle that "what cannot be done directly cannot be done indirectly". Legislators now routinely subvert this principle by taking the ordinance route. Article 123 of Indian Constitution bestows legislative power to the executive to promulgate ordinances when the Parliament is not in session. It was argued in DC Wadhwa v. State of Bihar that the legislative power of the executive to

---

6. Id. at 2.
7. Id. at2.

promulgate Ordinances is to be used in exceptional circumstances and not as a substitute for the law making power of the legislature.[8] However, this provision has been blatantly misused by the legislature for immediate political gains. Last year the Supreme Court delivered a landmark judgment where it had ruled that a Member of Parliament or Member of Legislative Assembly would be immediately disqualified if convicted by a court in a criminal offence with a jail sentence of two years or more.[9] The Government of India, subject to pull and pressure of coalition politics, came up with an ordinance to dilute this very judgment. Subsequently it drew sharp criticism from intelligentsia and all quarters of the society that finally led the Government to withdraw the ordinance. But as this leeway persists, in future too the State can take such steps to usurp the authority of courts and encroach upon their judicial powers. There is a clear indication of how the spirit of law can be violated even though strictly following the letter of law. Another example is the frequent use of legislative amendments as colourable legislations to bypass laws declared by the Supreme Court. The various retroactive legislations in taxation statutes clearly laid bare how the legislature utterly failed to follow the morals of Constitution.

11.4 Public Morality Conundrum

In 2009 the Delhi High Court pronounced a watershed judgment regarding the civil liberties of sexual minorities where it held Section377 of Indian Penal Code unconstitutional and thus decriminalised homosexuality.[10] Section 377 of IPC is a Victorian legislation and completely anachronistic. United Kingdom which has bequeathed this colonial legacy to us has itself abolished this law.

One of the contentious during the proceedings of the case was the apparent conflict between constitutional morality and public morality. The Naz foundation case discussed the "compelling

8. DCWadhwa v. State of Bihar, AIR 1987 SC 579.
9. Lily Thomas v. Union of India, AIR 2013 SC 2662.
10. Naz Foundation v. Government of NCT and Ors., 160(2009)DLT277

state interest" test evolved in Gobind case and how this test was used in the present context to justify keeping the elements of public morality intact by the state.[11] The Court held that

Popular morality or public disapproval of certain acts is not a valid justification for restriction of the fundamental rights under Article 21. Popular morality, as distinct from a constitutional morality derived from constitutional values, is based on shifting and subjective notions of right and wrong. If there is any type of 'morality' that can pass the test of compelling state interest, it must be 'constitutional' morality and not public morality."[12]

This paradigm shift in the reasoning of the line of public morality and instead comparing it with constitutional morality is the most significant feature of the judgment. Public morality and constitutional morality might overlap in some areas of law but not necessarily in every aspect. There can be divergence of views such as around the homosexuality debate but ultimately it's the constitutional morality that prevails. The clear and concise difference between the above two is put forth below:

The essence of the distinction between public and constitutional morality is that public morality is merely a reflection of the moral and normative values of the majority of the population (as expressed by the legislature), while Constitutional morality not only reflects the majority's values, but also shapes and changes them as part of the social engineering aspect of our Constitution.[13]

A constitution is itself a relationship between abstract personae bound together by abstract rules. As constitution is a living organic document susceptible to changes in society, the same can be attributed to constitutional morality that is also perceptible to changes around. The expansive nature of constitution is therefore indispensable to tide over the tumultuous waves of changes in the coming generations.

---

11. Gobind v. State of Madhya Pradesh and Anr., AIR 1975 SC 1378
12. Naz Foundation, supra note 1, at 7.
13. Rohit Sharma, The Public And Constitutional Morality Conundrum: A Case-Note On The Naz Foundation Judgment, 2(3) NUJS L. Rev. 445 (2009).

Notwithstanding such brilliant application of legal minds that went in to put the principles of constitutional morality in a higher pedestal, the celebrations were short lived. In December last year a division bench of Supreme Court set aside the judgment and turned the clock back especially for sexual minorities.[14] The most scathing part of the judgment was that the Court refused to recognise the rights of sexual minorities and termed them as miniscule for whom hardly any fundamental rights can be warranted. Such blatant disregard for constitutional morality hit a new low as the violator here was the highest court of the land which is considered as last bastion of fundamental rights of citizens. The quote by Ambedkar in the beginning of the essay clearly enunciates how the rights of the minority are needed to be protected at any cost for the diffusion of constitutional morality. Moreover the Supreme Court opined that it is for the legislature to change the law as the law-making power is not vested with the courts. Clearly the court missed the whole point of Article 141 of the Constitution of India.[15] This escapist attitude of the judges delivering the judgment raised the question where judges are dictated by public morality rather than constitutional morality. As personal opinion we believe that judges should preach only constitutional morality, so judges can moralize as long as their source is Indian Constitution.

Grammar of Anarchy

Ambedkar theorized an open culture of criticism that will be a check on various organs of the government. Ambedkar further stressed the importance of constitutional methods to achieve the objectives - critiquing the State or redressal of any kind of grievances. The doctor even showed his disdain for both violent methods and passive resistance like civil disobedience movement when it comes to censuring the State. The presence of constitutional methods justifies no other kind of methods. But an exception

14. Suresh Kumar Koushal and Anr. v. State of Madhya Pradesh and Anr. AIR 2014 SC 563

15. Law declared by Supreme Court to be binding on all courts.INDIAN CONST. art. 141.

can be carved out here in the wake of Delhi gangrape case. The heinous crime not only shocked the conscience of the country but exposed the failure of the entire society regarding gender rights. The subsequent conviction and passage of new laws following strong protest all over the country to some extent assuaged a few. But this exception shouldn't become the norm.

Sadly, the revered statesman must be turning in his grave if he has witnessed the present scenario. The tools of protest have undergone several modifications. A Chief Minister of State along with his party followers sits on a Dharna[16] and brings the entire city to a halt. Creative artists face threats from religious hooligans over the latter's violation of religious sentiments.[17] Vandalism and destruction of public property have now become order of the day and no more elicit any sharp reactions.

But the pertinent point here is how the State has responded to it. The State has shown half-hearted measures to curb any such lawlessness. Moreover these law-breakers enjoy considerable patronage from legislators and are out of bounds from the reach of law.

Ironically the principle architect of the Constitution, Ambedkar similarly drew ire from the radical right wing organizations when he authored his most 'The Annihilation of Caste ' and nobody came forward to publish it. As a result he self published the book and it went on to become his immediate classic. Therefore, Ambedkar knew that an open culture of criticism is vital for smooth functioning of Indian Democracy.

Cult of Personality Worship

Ambedkar quoting John Stuart Mill "to lay their liberties at the feet of even a great man, or to trust him with power which enable him to subvert their institutions" cautioned on any form of cult of personality worship. He regarded this as an essential feature of constitutional morality. In the Indian context this

---

16. AtulDev, The politics of populism or misplaced notions of polity, The Sunday Guardian, February 1, 2014

17. AnanyaVajpeyi, The Triumph of the Hindu Right: Freedom of Speech and Religious Repression in Modi's India, 93(5) Foreign Affairs J. 150-156 (2014).

forewarning assumes much significance. Indian masses being plagued by illiteracy and superstition (during that period of time) are prone to get trapped in this form of worship which may eventually lead to degradation of democracy. He was a sceptic about any power being wrested on a sole individual.

In the present scenario Ambedkar's ominous remarks holds true. Ironically, the same Ambedkar who was against any form of cult worship had been turned to a demigod by political parties. His ideology and thoughts are being twisted to subserve their political interest. The country averted a tide of crises when this same practice of personality worship led to emergency. The emergence of dynastic politics *ad nauseam* is just an offshoot of such practices.

11.5 Conclusion

" I feel, however good a Constitution may be, it is sure to turn out bad because those who are called to work it happen to be a bad lot. However bad a Constitution may be, it may turn out to be good if those who are called to work it, happen to be a good lot".

Ambedkar prophetic words rang true during the period of emergency in 1970s. The attempted subversion of entire constitution and the gridlock in different organs of the State was a dark phase in Indian Democracy. Truly, how good the constitution maybe it can be violated by machiavellian forces of state. So there should be an underlying deeper philosophy stemming from the Constitution itself that can be the moral fabric guiding the country. In the celebrated Keshavnanda Bharti case the theory of basic structure was propounded to save some parts of the constitution from any transgression. While the basic theory coalesced important constitutional provisions in a protective cage, the rest remains in perennial danger.

There is absolutely no doubt that Indian Democracy has faced several challenges in the past but its ability to hold forth and evolve proved naysayers wrong. But the question here is on what kind of democracy are we living? Is it just a political democracy? The doctor singled out the importance of social democracy incorporating the values of liberty, equality and fraternity as beacon of true democracy. Sadly, on the social democracy front we have achieved moderate success.

Is the time now ripe to take forward the basic structure theory? Is there a need to revisit the principles of constitutional morality, finely attune them to remove the societal ills? Now that's for the court to ponder upon as the court has proved to be ultimate harbinger of change. But surely it will be a fitting tribute to the man whose immense contribution to safeguard the fundamental rights of the countrymen can never be forgotten.

12

Ambedkar's Idea of Equality

- Jadumani Mahanand *

12.1 Introduction

One must ask why the question of equality needs to be understood in the contemporary times, this being a primary question that is necessary to be explored in the context of society and state. As equality has been a central question to the modern political thought, and the concept of equality has been long debated in state and society at large. Ambedkar thought shows the gap between society and state as a central point, calling it 'contradictions'. This is the paradox, that is not only visible in modern society, but also exists in the nature of Indian society and politics. The study of human nature, in Indian society, from Ambedkar's point of view is important to know. In this context, the first section tries to explore Ambedkar's engagement of equality in a philosophical sense, and how the concept of equality has an ontological outlook in Ambedkar thought. The second section deals with the modern notion of equality and links it with the state in the form of citizenship, participation and recognition, here, I will argue, how the question of equal recognition is embedded with distribution of resources. All I will do by engaging Ambedkar thought.

12.2 Ambedkar's Understanding of Human Nature and the Concept of Equality

The job of philosophy is to understand the nature of society in order to know the attitude, thinking, belief, practice and social structure of the people. The nature of society has to be

*JadumaniMahanandM.philScholar ,Jawaharlal Nehru University , New Delhi, India.

contextualized, in reading Ambedkar's texts and his engagement with Indian society should be looked ontologically. Ambedkar believes that human beings are born naturally, hence human beings are equal and free, which is natural to all human beings. In contrast, he accepts that human beings are 'born unequal' in terms of their differences as some are 'robust, weakling and intelligence'[1] and he accepts that 'inequalities exist in physical strength, in artistic skill, in material wealth, or mental capacity'[2] also 'physical heredity, social inheritance or endowment in the form of parental care, education, accumulation of scientific knowledge and finally in his own efforts'[3] In all these three aspects human beings are undoubtedly unequal. But these criteria do not satisfy humans as equal beings, rather it recognizes the inequality which supports the capable individual and ceases the incapable. Similarly, he understands that,

Every human being, without choice on his own part, but simply in virtue of his birth and upbringing, becomes a member of what we call a natural society. He belongs that is to a certain family and a certain nation. This membership lays upon him definite obligations and duties which he is called upon to fulfil as a matter of course and on pain of social penalties and disabilities while at the same time it confers upon him certain social rights and advantages.[4]

This is a close understanding of human nature, where society is enclosed with restrictions which do not provide a scope to treat individuals as equal. Another instance, if we accept that

---

1. Valerian Rodrigues. Good society: Right Democracy and Socialism, In Ambedkar in Retrospect: Essay on Economics, Politics and Society 145 (ed. SukhadeoThorat and Aryama, Rawat Publication 2007)
2. BabasahebAmbedkar Writings and Speeches. Vol. No 3. SourceMaterial Department of Education, Mumbai: Government of Maharashtra 96. (2d 2008).
3. BabasahebAmbedkar Writings and Speeches. Vol. No 1. SourceMaterial Department of Education, Mumbai: Government of Maharashtra 58. (2d 2010).
4. BabasahebAmbedkar Writings and Speeches. Vol. No 3. SourceMaterial Department of Education, Mumbai: Government of Maharashtra 13. (2d 2008).

humans are unequal in terms of their differences and the difference has to be there, because they are unequal; this study definitely provides a scope to understand differentness that may be helpful to study different cultures, aesthetic and belief practice etc. Which is primarily determined by their location and context? But this is a problematic path which justifies the limitation of the individual but will not encourage being a full human being. The individual becomes close, but not open. And the difference may create inequality further. As a matter of fact, human nature changes according to time and situation. If differences are to be respected then the question of equality can be enjoyed. In this context, Ambedkar raises a serious question 'if human were treated unequally' then they would glorify and exercise their status and human power, the society is evidence to the fact that difference in term of inequality creates domination and discrimination.

Ambedkar would say that inequality cannot be entertained just because they are unequal. Indian society verifies this calamity. Ambedkar goes beyond, he says 'at the end equality remains a fact that fundamental characteristic appear in all human beings'[5] also he says 'individual is an end in himself'[6] to make it clear that this is not merely modern political ideas or human rights perspective, that he endorses, but also that this idea is essentially present in Buddhist thought, which says that each individual has potential to become full capable human being, in other words, one can achieve enlightenment. Because human beings cannot live with difference, but live with human relationship, to Ambedkar, human needs right relationships, that relationships are essentially equal relationship between both entities. Hence, equality is a 'moral principle' of human life, to quote him, ''moral equality' assert in ethical value, a belief to be sustained, and recognition of rights to be respected.'[7]

5. Id. at 96-97
6. BabasahebAmbedkar Writings and Speeches. Vol. No 1. SourceMaterial Department of Education, Mumbai: Government of Maharashtra 409. (2d 2010).
7. BabasahebAmbedkar Writings and Speeches. Vol. No 3. SourceMaterial Department of Education, Mumbai: Government of Maharashtra 97. (2d 2008).

Ambedkar's critique of Plato's understanding of human nature and his classification of three classes is equally applied to *Chaturvarna* system, the *Chaturvarna* is based on four divisions of society. 'To Plato, men fell by nature into three classes'[8] such as appetites, courageous and guardians as it is Brahman, Kshatriya, Vaishya and Shudra in *Chaturvarna* system, but one class is added called as *Panchamas* or Untouchables or *Ati-Shudra.* Ambedkar says,

Plato is that his idea of lumping of individuals into a few sharply marked-off classes is a superficial view of man and his powers. Plato had no perception of the uniqueness of every individual, of his incommensurability with others, of each individual forming a class of his own. He had no recognition of the infinite diversity of active tendencies and combination of tendencies of which an individual is capable.[9]

Further, Ambedkar says that, 'modern science has shown that the qualities of individuals is incompatible with their stratification of classes, since the qualities of individuals are so variable',[10] this critic applies to *Chaturvarna* system. Moreover, the *'Chaturvarna* system is the maintenance of the penal system which could maintain it by its sanction.'[11] This system is also 'contrary to human nature.'[12] According to Hindus, the *Chaturvarna* is not based on birth, but worth, but Ambedkar raises serious questions, to him *'Chaturvarna* is impracticable, harmful and has turned miserable failure in practical point of view.'[13]

The names Brahmin, Kshatriya, Vaishya and Shudra, are names associated with a definite and fixed notion in the mind of every Hindu. The notion of hierarchy based on birth. So long as these names continue, Hindus will continue to think of the Brahmin, Kshatriya, Vaisha

8. BabasahebAmbedkar Writings and Speeches. Vol. No 1. SourceMaterial Department of Education, Mumbai: Government of Maharashtra 60. (2d 2010).
9. Id.
10. Id.
11. Id.at 60
12. Id.

and Shudra as hierarchical divisions of high and low, based on birth, and act accordingly.[14]

This is a fundamental problem that is associated with the system; Ambedkar raises serious question that,

How are going to compel people who have acquired a higher status based on birth without reference to their worth to vacate that status? How are going to compel people to recognize the status due to a man in accordance with his own worth, who is occupying a lower status based on his birth?[15]

One must not. doubt that the *Chaturvarna* system is a Hindu Social order, Ambedkar says 'men are born equal is a doctrine which is repugnant to the Hindu social order.'[16] His analysis of the nature of Hindu society is a 'principle of graded inequality.'[17] He further explains that,

In the Hindu social order, there is no room for individual merit and no consideration of individual justice. If the individual has a privilege it is not because it is due personally. The privilege goes with the class, and if he is found to enjoy it, it is because he belongs to that class. Contrawise, if an individual is suffering from a wrong, it is not because he by his conduct deserves it. The disability is the disability imposed upon the class and if he is found to be labouring under it, it is because he belongs to that class.[18]

The system is not only based on division of status, positions, purity and pollution according to the *Chaturvarna* system, but occupation is also attached to it, which determines the material life. That is to say, the Hindu social system recognizes the status, positions and occupation based on their birth which is caste and Varna. In other words, 'the principle of graded inequality has

13. Id.at 59
14. Id.
15. Id.
16. BabasahebAmbedkar Writings and Speeches. Vol. No 3. SourceMaterial Department of Education, Mumbai: Government of Maharashtra 106. (2d 2008).
17. Id. at 111
18. Id. at 100

been carried into the economic field.'[19] Ambedkar further emphasizes that 'caste system is not merely the division of labour. It is also a division of labourers.' 'This division is unnatural division of labourers[20] into water-tight compartments. It is a hierarchy in which the divisions of labourers are graded one above the other. It is not based on natural aptitudes.'[21]

The Hindu social order does not recognize equal need, equal work or equal ability as the basis of reward for labour. Its motto is that in regard to the distribution of the good things of life those who are of life those who are reckoned as the highest must get the most and the best and those who are classed as the lowest must accept the least and the worst.[22]

Therefore, the *Chaturvarna* or caste system is against the human nature, because it does not endorse what human beings want to do, but it is being imposed by the system. Furthermore, if '*Chaturvarna* is an ideal, that must be practiced and therefore it is real, as Nietszche said 'realize the ideal and idealize the real. The value must be tested by its result.'[23] Hence, the theory and practice both are very dangerous projects, which establish inequality.

These are Ambedkar's engagement with Hindu text in understanding the nature of equality. The other aspect is his engagement of socio-political activism which also plays an important role to shape his ideas on equality; this is basically known as democratic aspiration in order to have equality both in the public sphere and the state apparatus. In this context, the experience of caste and untouchability in Ambedkar life is a vantage point, which is not merely his personal experience, but empirical experience of the whole of Untouchable communities in particular, and the caste experience in general. The practice of untouchability denies that the being is human, treated less than a human, in other

19.Id. at 111

20.Id. at 67

21.Id.

22.Id. at 111

23. Id. at 67

words it is a denial of human recognition. That is to say, the experience is based on 'humiliation, cancelation rejection, reduction, annihilation'[24] and discrimination. It happens because of caste impulses, which operate in all spheres of Indian life.

To Ambedkar experience, untouchability, segregation, humiliation and exploitation was to be faced, because the caste system does not recognize individual as equal human being. There are so many instances where Ambedkar fought for equality, which were basic and essential to any human being. For example, temple entry movement, fight for water, fight for public usage, fight for walking in the public street, etc. these are not just human rights of a community but this is struggle for existence to claim that all are equal. In other words, it is a struggle for self-respect and dignity that is deeply enmeshed in the caste system. As mentioned earlier, the caste system also determines the materiality of society. Therefore, self-respect and dignity is deeply attached to the system, which does not allow these to those whose status is low and impure. To make it clear that, epistemologically the concept of equality has been denied in Hindu philosophy. To put it differently, Brahminism neither acknowledges the idea of difference nor the equality. It's philosophy is to maintain the doctrine of inequality as a moral principles. I argue that epistemology of Brahminism is based on false premise, which negates and rejects the ontological nature of human beings as equal entity.

12.3 Ambedkar's Concept of Equality in the Framework of State

This is a serious question, how Ambedkar would believe in a state which is built on the foundation of unequal society. In this context, Ambedkar's engagement with the state needs to be clarified. There are various interpretations on his idea of state. To make it clear he is not a Marxist, Liberal or Communitarian, he claims himself as 'progressive radical'[25] but in his imagination of

24. Gopal Guru. "Rejection of Rejection" in Humiliation: Claim and Context 210. Oxford University Press, New Delhi (Gopal Guru ed. 2008).

25. Valerian Rodrigues. Essential Writings of B. R. Ambedkar 21. Oxford University Press (2d 2011)

state, there are components from these schools of thoughts. In his book State and Minorities, he urges for 'state socialism' by adopting parliamentary democracy. Again the question arises as to why he was in favour of parliamentary democracy which seems to be liberal framework of democracy as has been understood by many scholars. To him parliamentary democracy is a method of government which firstly says 'free and fair elections are necessary for the transfer of power from one section of the community to the other in a peaceful manner and without any bloodshed.'[26] Secondly, 'democracy is a form and a method of government whereby revolutionary changes in the economic and social life of the people are brought about without bloodshed.'[27] His notion of parliamentary democracy has deeper meaning to translate. It is power of the people, who can change the government if government goes against them. 'Parliamentary government means negations of hereditary rule; no one can claim to be hereditary ruler.'[28] In contrary, the Indian society does not prescribe the right to equality; but in parliamentary democracy anyone can take part by the support of majority of the people. In other words, anyone can come to power in the system. The question of equality is deeply ingrained here, though there is some problem in parliamentary democracy as well.

In this context, I would try to look at the idea of equality as to be of prime importance to his idea of state. That is necessarily addressed to the question of social and economic inequality of the society. The sole aim of the state is to redress the gap and contradiction through the state policies and interventions. That the social and economic inequalities are based on the structure of the society has been explained in first section of this paper. For instance, the impact of pragmatism shapes Ambedkar's thought, that's why he was an action oriented man, in other words theory

---

26. BabasahebAmbedkar Writings and Speeches. Vol. No 17 Part Three. SourceMaterial Department of Education, Mumbai: Government of Maharashtra 427. (2003).
27. Id. at 475
28. Id. at 425

has to be practiced. Another view is that, the experience of caste and untouchability ruined the society, particularly the untouchables were crying and dying for equality. Both these views are to be seen in terms of the practice of inequality, and this may be one of the reasons why he adopted Buddhism. Moreover, Ambedkar's firm faith on the state to achieve equality, that the state will adopt all the majors policies which will work against discrimination and domination etc. and it would be based on egalitarian welfare policies, that can also redress the economic inequality of the depressed and oppressed communities.

However, he endorses the democratic state, but his normative questions are to be discussed in order to understand the state and equality. The aim of society and state is to have a good life, that he endorses 'every human being will have the right to liberty, property and pursuit of happiness.'[29] This can be achieved when equality becomes the foundation of society, because inequality is a major impediment, which is exclusionary by its nature. Hence, he had full faith in democracy which is to exercise equality, to him, 'equality is the governing principle'[30] and 'democracy is more than a form of government. It is primarily a mode of associated living. The roots of democracy are to be researched in the social relationship, in terms of associated life between the people who form a society.'[31] To further quotes Ambedkar:

Social and economic democracy are tissue and fibre of a political democracy.' The tougher the tissue and the fibre, the greater the strength of the body. Democracy is another name of equality. Parliamentary democracy developed a passion for liberty. It never made even a nodding acquaintance with equality. It failed to realize the significance of equality and did not even endeavour to strike a balance between

---

29. Valerian Rodrigues. Essential Writings of B. R. Ambedkar 60. Oxford University Press (2d 2011)

30. BabasahebAmbedkar Writings and Speeches. Vol. No 1. SourceMaterial Department of Education, Mumbai: Government of Maharashtra 60. (2d 2010).

31. BabasahebAmbedkar Writings and Speeches. Vol. No 17 Part Three. SourceMaterial Department of Education, Mumbai: Government of Maharashtra 519. (2003).

liberty and equality, with the result that liberty swallowed equality and has made democracy a name and a farce.[32]

In his context, equality has to be practiced not merely in politics but also in social and economic life. That is to say, equal participation in state activities, where he draws the relevance of equal citizenship, representation and reservation are to be seen in terms of equality. This is the distribution of resources in a democracy, where state has a greater role to play. Each community has to get an equal share according to their proportion of population. His idea of representation in democratic institutions is a deeper reflection of equality. The idea of state is a composition of representative of respective regions, communities etc. on the basis of equality.

The reason behind believing in the state has substantial points to support. First, it is a democratic state represented by the people. The second important point is the constitution which binds all its citizens regions, and heterogeneity, the constitution provides equality, liberty, fraternity and justice, which are the guiding principles of society. It is not only legal equality which can provide perfect notion of equality but Ambedkar reiterated social equality that, he says 'one man and one value',[33] that is yet to be achieved by the society and the state only. That is why he puts the condition of *Constitutional morality, and emphasizes that, constitutional morality is not a natural sentiment. It has to be cultivated. We must realize that our people have yet to learn it. Democracy in India is only a top-dressing on an Indian soil, which is essentially undemocratic.*[34]

32. Valerian Rodrigues. Essential Writings of B. R. Ambedkar 62. Oxford University Press (2d 2011)
33. Constituent Assembly Debates. Speech by B. R. Ambedkar, Volume XII. 26, January 1950
34. Valerian Rodrigues. Essential Writings of B. R. Ambedkar 485. Oxford University Press (2d 2011)

Further, he justifies his stand by stating 'moral equality in democracy.'[35] Why Ambedkar endorsed parliamentary democracy despite of its limitation. It is to believe that the Russian and French Revolutions had their own limitations, Russian lack of liberty and French lack of equality. To him, probably, a complete notion of democracy that is equality, freedom and fraternity can bring social and economic democracy to have equality. It is a principle which challenges the social and religious order of the existing society, through the state and its normative the change is possible which could bring equality.

I would like to raise some theoretical issues on the question of equality that how equality is achieved in Ambedkar's philosophy. Is it sufficient what Ambedkar had proposed to achieve equality? One must think critically or problematize the idea of equality in post-independence India. As Ambedkar warns that if democracy is to be achieved one must adopt the principles of equality, freedom, fraternity and justice. But the question remains to be the same, why Indian democracy has failed to realise the importance of its normative principles. In other words, one could argue that, though Ambedkar's idea of equality is warned to people of India, but they ignore to adopt it. The reason why it was not realised yet, it is because; the social and religious structure did not annihilate the caste and that's what he proposed to do. In the contemporary India, caste becomes a political and electoral tool to use the vote and representation. In a way caste is getting strengthened rather than moving to the point of annihilation. Now, political democracy changes to electoral democracy. Equality is rhetoric in terms of voting but it is not real equality in terms of one human one value with dignity and self-respect.

12.4 Conclusion

To sum up, Ambedkar's notion of equality is embedded in his social and political thoughts. His critique on Chaturvarna system and engagement in state affair has ontological perception. To him, equal recognition of individuals has a deeper meaning.

---

35. BabasahebAmbedkar Writings and Speeches. Vol. No 17 Part Three. SourceMaterial Department of Education, Mumbai: Government of Maharashtra 485. (2003).

Hence, recognition of caste-imposed identity on the basis of its foundational ideas is misappropriation of resources, which determines the materiality of individual life. Though, democracy has its own institutions, which is free and equal to all, even that does not see the traditional value system, but caste-based occupation and discrimination is still working even in post-independence India.

INDEX